Praise for
Mentors, Muses & Monsters

"These inspiring essays are written by some of the most brilliant literary figures today … It is always interesting to read about the influences that make a person go down a particular path, and with these thirty writers, it is a most interesting journey and a great compilation for the literature lover."
— *San Francisco Book Review*

"Highly recommended."
— *Library Journal*

"A mesmerizing book of essays by famous pens who themselves were once helped—or hurt—by established talents as they tried to climb their way up the literary ladder. [*Mentors, Muses & Monsters*] beautifully captures the experience of being a literary aspirant—wide-eyed, enchanted by words, and eager for the tutelage of a mentor —one who's already scaled the temple wall and emerged, shining, in a turret."
— *Christian Science Monitor*

"This anthology is that rare gem, a collection whose whole is greater, even, than the sum of its parts. Where else could you read musings-about-muses, accompanied by juicy tales from deep inside the writing life, by 30 of the best minds of our generation, all between the covers of one book?"
— *San Francisco Chronicle*

"Deliciously rich and illuminating … Each writer shades in the nuances of character and experience that make his subject come to life, and each reads like a short story."
— *Martha's Vineyard Times*

"A unique collection of essays about the infinite varieties of literary mentoring…"
— *The Writer*

"Margot Livesey, Jane Smiley, Denis Johnson, ZZ Packer, and Jonathan Safran Foer are among the stellar cast that weighs in on good, bad, and ugly encounters with, and advice from, their influences."

— *Elle*

"… a treasure trove of a book: every essay is charged with a young person's determination to be a writer, persisting often through hardship, but gaining in assurance as one reads, and before the end confidently displaying real talent. A true satisfaction!"

— Peter Pouncey, author of
Rules for Old Men Waiting: A Novel

"Writers work alone more often than not, but their heads are full of people: imagined, remembered, waiting to be born. The ingenious, grateful, and often moving essays in this book evoke a certain class of these people, the alliterating authorities of the title. Words like 'rescue,' 'permission,' 'save,' 'changed,' 'devastating' appear in these pages, suggesting effects a good deal more immediate than anything called up by 'model' or 'influence.' Do writers really need rescuing and the rest? Read and see. This is a wonderful book about what writers have found necessary, not what they thought they might need."

— Michael Wood, author of
The Road to Delphi and *America in the Movies*

"Whatever justified, or deluded, fascination these writers have toward their teachers, and however much or little reciprocity is granted, they weave riveting tales of their own evolution, sometimes outstripping their mentors."

— Mopsy Strange Kennedy,
The Improper Bostonian

mentors, muses & monsters

Also by Elizabeth Benedict

The Practice of Deceit

Almost

Safe Conduct

The Beginner's Book of Dreams

Slow Dancing

The Joy of Writing Sex: A Guide for Fiction Writers

mentors, muses & monsters

30 WRITERS ON THE PEOPLE WHO CHANGED THEIR LIVES

edited by

ELIZABETH BENEDICT

excelsior editions

AN IMPRINT OF STATE UNIVERSITY OF NEW YORK PRESS

Published by

STATE UNIVERSITY OF NEW YORK PRESS, ALBANY

© 2009 by Elizabeth Benedict
Originally published by Free Press, a Division of Simon & Schuster, Inc.

First Excelsior Editions paperback printing 2012
© 2012 State University of New York

Excelsior Editions is an imprint of State University of New York Press

For information, contact
State University of New York Press, Albany, NY
www.sunypress.edu

Production, Laurie Searl
Marketing, Fran Keneston

Library of Congress Cataloging-in-Publication Data

Mentors, muses & monsters : 30 writers on the people who changed their lives / [edited by] Elizabeth Benedict.
    p. cm.
"Originally published by Free Press"– T.p. verso.
Includes bibliographical references.
ISBN 978-1-4384-4350-8 (pbk. : alk. paper)
   1. Authors, American–20th century–Biography. 2. Authors, American–21st century–Biography. 3. Autobiographies. 4. Influence (Literary, artistic, etc.) 5. Mentoring of authors. 6. Authors, American–Books and reading. I. Benedict, Elizabeth. II. Title: Mentors, muses, and monsters. III. Title: Thirty writers on the people who changed their lives. IV. Title: 30 writers on the people who changed their lives. V. Title: Writers on the people who changed their lives.
   PS129.M475 2012
   810.9'0054–dc23
   [B] 2011042411

10 9 8 7 6 5 4 3 2 1

For these mentors and muses:

James Harold Smith

Emily Daggett Smith

Julia Farrell Smith

Janet Farrell Smith (1941–2009)

Even on those occasions when he had no active hand in something I wrote, the choices I made, the way I approached a subject, the order in which I told what I knew, the attitude I adopted, were determined by his example and his influence.
　　　　　　　—Alec Wilkinson, *My Mentor: A Young Man's Friendship with William Maxwell*

One night a friend lent me a book of short stories by Franz Kafka. I went back to the pension where I was staying and began to read *The Metamorphosis*. The first line almost knocked me off the bed. I was so surprised. The first line reads, "As Gregor Samsa awoke that morning from uneasy dreams, he found himself transformed in his bed into a gigantic insect. . . ." When I read the line I thought to myself that I didn't know anyone was allowed to write things like that. If I had known, I would have started writing a long time ago.
　　　　　　　—Gabriel García Márquez, interview in the *Paris Review*, Issue 82, Winter 1981.

CONTENTS

Contents

PREFACE TO PAPERBACK EDITION

Every book is special to its author or editor, but this anthology has a particular place in my affections for several reasons. When I asked the writers whose work you are about to read to contribute to the collection, I knew what they wrote would be good—but there was no way of knowing just how good each of these essays would be. As they arrived in my e-mail inbox, one after another, and I read them sitting at the screen, I often felt the wind knocked out of me. It was clear from the depth of feeling and the care lavished on each sentence that the writers had devoted themselves to this project, to these tender and complex tributes to the people, books, and events that had altered the course of their lives. Even those few who wrote about "monsters" had something profound to say.

I am honored to have shepherded these essays and this collection into being, and I'm especially moved that the collection itself has changed lives. Shortly before the book came out, about half of the essays were selected for pre-publication attention in a wide variety of magazines, literary journals, and, in one case, an online nonfiction magazine.

Sigrid Nunez's essay, "Sontag's Rules," appeared in *Tin House*—and led to a book contract to write a memoir about her relationship with Susan Sontag, *Sempre Susan*, published to much acclaim in 2011.

Two of the essays—Sigrid's and Cheryl Strayed's piece on the influence of Alice Munro—won Pushcart Prizes, Cheryl's after it appeared in the *Missouri Review*. Her piece was a Notable Essay in *The Best American Essays of 2010*, as was Maud Casey's about the influence of her writer parents, one them John Casey, who also has an essay in this collection.

And the early online publication of Alexander Chee's essay on studying with Annie Dillard at Wesleyan turned his essay into an Internet sensation whose effects are still being felt. It appeared on *The Morning News* Web site, and Alex then posted it on his Facebook page. It went viral within hours. He described what happened in a recent e-mail: "When I googled the search terms 'Alexander Chee Annie Dillard' a week later, hundreds of blog posts appeared, almost all saying 'You must read this.' By now, almost two years later, I think more people have blogged this essay than have read my first novel….What moves me now is when I hear from writing teachers who are using the essay to teach their students. I like the idea that I've been able to democratize what [Annie Dillard] offered, in a way that I think is at the core of her teaching ethics. She really does believe anyone can do this if they just practice the methods she taught."

One last story of a change brought about by the book: Contributor Robert Boyers told me that the essay he wrote here, on Natalia Ginzburg's influence on his writing fiction, was the most personal essay he had written in his distinguished career as a literary critic—and that the experience has sparked in him an appetite for writing more autobiographically in his criticism. As this edition goes to press, he is putting finishing touches on a new collection of memoiristic essays.

I remain hugely indebted to each of the contributors; to the many editors who published the pieces early on; to Robert Boyers and Don Faulkner for their unflagging support; to William Kennedy, founder of the New York State Writers Institute at SUNY Albany; and to the good people at SUNY Press, who have given the anthology a new incarnation and the chance to change a few more lives.

INTRODUCTION

MENTORS, MUSES AND MOZART

The response to my invitation was overwhelming. One after another, in e-mails, on the phone, and in person, in a matter of weeks, two dozen fiction writers said yes, they wanted to contribute to this anthology. Some days I would hear from two or three or four people, saying yes, count me in. Of course, I was delighted—and slightly flabbergasted by the wellspring of enthusiasm. I seemed to have hit a nerve.

Several knew right away whom they wanted to write about—Mary Gordon on Elizabeth Hardwick and Janice Thaddeus, Jay Cantor on Bernard Malamud, Lily Tuck on Gordon Lish, Jim Shepard on John Hawkes. But quite a few said yes, emphatically, without knowing their subject for sure. Early on, Jonathan Safran Foer was deciding from among Joyce Carol Oates, with whom he studied at Princeton, the artist Joseph Cornell, whose famous boxes enchanted him at a young age, and the Israeli poet Yehuda Amichai. At first, Margot Livesey wasn't sure whether to choose her adopted father— an English teacher at a Scottish boarding school—or a long-dead muse.

In saying yes before they had settled on a subject, I picked up in writers' voices and in their e-mails a yearning to acknowledge and to thank the people who had made a landmark difference in their lives—to recognize them the best way a fiction writer can, by telling the story of their association. Because most of these encounters occurred when the writers were young and vulnerable—uncertain about their identities and what they were capable of—some of the pieces have a sweetly aching quality, and nearly all of them express abiding gratitude. But sweetly aching or not, a good many of the writers are looking back at themselves at a tender age when something powerful happened to them, a moment when an authority figure saw talent in them, or when they came to believe they possessed it themselves—and their wobbly lives changed direction and

1

velocity. They knew, in a way they hadn't before, where they were headed; and what is more potent, and more moving, than that? It's like being rescued. No, it *is* being rescued—from uncertainty, indecision, mediocrity.

Life brings us emotional experiences to compete with that one in intensity, but the others invariably involve romance, children, family ties, two-sided associations that inevitably become messy, fraught, downright imperfect. But the feelings of gratitude a student or supplicant usually has for a mentor have an aura of purity about them—uncluttered, unalloyed gratitude—that's absent from most other intense relationships. It's fitting that we idealize our mentors. They are more accomplished than we are; they are in a position to bestow feelings of worth on us that carry more weight in the real world than praise from even the most ardent parents. Their praise counts for something *out there*—and because of that, it also counts *in here*, where we live and work and proceed with nothing but whatever talent we possess, whatever nerve we can summon, and the knowledge that the only way to get to Carnegie Hall, or its literary equivalents, is practice, practice, practice, which is to say, write, rewrite, rewrite.

Mentors are our role models, our own private celebrities, people we emulate, fall in love with, and sometimes stalk—by reading their books compulsively. In her essay on Alice Munro, Cheryl Strayed writes, "*I love Alice Munro*, I took to saying, the way I did about any number of people I didn't know whose writing I admired, meaning, of course, that I loved her books. . . . But I loved *her* too, in a way that felt slightly ridiculous even to me." When things go well, we are the beneficiaries of our mentors' best selves, not just their admirable writing but the prescient insights that divine talent in us before we know it's there ourselves.

Alongside the mentor's noticing us, much of the force of our feelings is revealed in how much energy we invest in noticing the mentor; but what would you expect from writers obsessed with other writers? Obsession is an occupational hazard. Or do I mean an occupational necessity? In his essay on Annie Dillard, Alexander Chee writes, "By the time I was done studying with Annie, I wanted to be her." He wanted her house, her car, and most of all, a boxed set of the books he had not yet written, like the boxed set of her books he admires in a store. When she was in her twenties, Sigrid Nunez lived with her boyfriend and his mother—Susan Sontag. In her essay "Sontag's Rules," in crystalline detail, she remembers Sontag's elaborate rules for living the life of a writer and intellectual—and Nunez names each rule she adopted for herself. In the more complicated case of Maud Casey, whose influences are the writers John Casey and Jane Barnes—who happen to be her parents—she admits that as a child, she imagined that she would grow up to *be* her parents, and that until she went to graduate school, she could not read a novel, any novel, without hearing their voices in her head.

Not all writers have quite such complicated relationships with their mentors or mentor equivalents. John Casey, father of Maud, had an unfraught, collegial relationship with Peter Taylor after they met while Casey was a law student taking a creative writing class on the side. Julia Glass writes a glowing paean to her longtime book editor and muse Deb Garrison, and tells us, along the way, how she herself went from being a painter to a novelist rather late in life. Carolyn See honors an unlikely pair of influences, an English professor whose lectures on poetry she attended for three weeks when she was twenty, and her beloved, eccentric father, who had always yearned to be a serious writer; the closest he came was writing seventy-three books of pornography near the end of his life.

Joyce Carol Oates answered my invitation by telling me that her mentors had been Emily Dickinson and Ernest Hemingway and several contemporary writers she had never known. I replied that it would be fine to write about mentors of that kind—to which Oates replied with an essay far more ambitious and illuminating, "On the Absence of Mentors/Monsters: Notes on Writerly Influences," that includes stories of her friendships with Donald Barthelme and John Gardner—and her childhood passion for *Alice's Adventures in Wonderland* and *Through the Looking-Glass*.

Other writers arrived with more unconventional sources of inspiration. The distinguished critic Robert Boyers, who found his fictional voice at fifty, is indebted to the Italian writer Natalia Ginzburg, because of his poet wife's connection to her. Evelyn Toynton, an American who lives in England, recalls the sorrows of her beloved handicapped mother, who showered Toynton and her sister with books and stories about English kings and queens when they were sorrowful children in New York City, on their twice-monthly visits to their mother's shabby, book-filled apartment. The story of Arnon Grunberg's literary awakening as a high school dropout in Amsterdam is so exotic—and funny and heartbreaking—that I am loath to try to summarize it in a sentence. Edmund White's portrait of the late

Harold Brodkey, set in gay New York in the 1970s, provides the anthology its single full-blown "monster." Monstrous though he was, White acknowledges his writerly debt to Brodkey.

Like Joyce Carol Oates, a number of writers felt they had been mentored not by people but by specific books or a writer's *oeuvre*. Samantha Hunt, Denis Johnson, ZZ Packer, Anita Shreve, and Martha Southgate offer not only their lucid memories of encountering these works but a booklist you're not likely to find anywhere else: *The Stories of Breece D'J Pancake*, *Fat City* by Leonard Gardner, the short stories of James Alan McPherson, *That Night* by Alice McDermott, and *Harriet the Spy*, respectively. Michael Cunningham, who identifies Virginia Woolf as his muse, wrote about the lifelong companionship *Mrs. Dalloway* has given him, "a devastating if one-way friendship" that led him to write *The Hours* when he was in his forties.

Another group of writers had something entirely different in mind in response to my invitation—and I was so eager to read their essays that I happily went beyond the boundaries of the title. Five people wanted to write about institutions or extended periods of their lives that had changed everything—altered their ambitions, rearranged their sense of who they were, what they were capable of, and what they wanted. Jane Smiley dove back into her first year as a graduate student at the Iowa Writers' Workshop, 1974, and the influence of her classmates, including Allan Gurganus. Christopher Castellani examined what nine summers at the Bread Loaf Writers' Conference have meant to him, beginning with two summers as a waiter. Neil Gordon recollected two transformative years as an editorial assistant at *The New York Review of Books*, while he finished his doctoral dissertation and charted his ambivalence about writing fiction. Dinaw Mengestu, born in Ethiopia and raised outside Chicago, ran an after school program in Harlem while he licked his wounds at not being able to sell his novel, and learned anew the power of storytelling in his efforts to entertain and soothe his students. Caryl Phillips, born in St. Kitts, raised in Leeds, England, and now a professor of writing at Yale, takes a long look backwards in "Growing Pains," isolating moments that moved him in the direction of a literary life.

This anthology came into being on the night of March 17, 2008, hours after I submitted an essay to *Tin House* on my mentor, Elizabeth Hardwick, who had died three months before and with whom I had had a senior tutorial at Barnard College in the 1970s. I remember walking through my apartment, feeling especially content, not only at having finished the piece but at having dwelled on that distant time before I knew what I would do with myself. Back then, one event had led to another, and another, and landed me in Miss Hardwick's office every two weeks during my last semester, at the end of which—well, I guess you could say that she liked my work. Liked it well enough to say so, which was well enough to keep me going as an aspiring writer for the next nine years until I finished and sold my first novel. A little praise from the right person can go a very long way.

There must be a collection somewhere of writers on the subject of their mentors, I said to myself in this upbeat mood, and I went to Amazon.com to look for it. But it was not many minutes before I saw that there isn't one. The very next day, armed with my title—*Mentors, Muses & Monsters*—I started making inquiries. The first person I asked, Mary Gordon, said yes right away. You hold in your hands the rest of the story.

Though this may be the only collection of essays by writers about their mentors and muses, the history of literature and of every other art overflows with stories about mentors, muses, and influential monsters, about institutions that have produced extraordinary talents, and about decades (Vienna in the 1890s, Paris in the 1920s) when geniuses collided and changed the course of history. There are stories yet to be told about today's teachers who nurture and direct gifted students, and plenty of stories to be retold about distant writers and artists who inspired acolytes in their immediate orbit, and inspire them now, centuries later, with their work.

In the 1780s, Mozart wrote six string quartets dedicated to Joseph Haydn, who is considered the father of the string quartet, and whose work Mozart had begun studying at the age of six. In 1785, after hearing the six quartets, Haydn made a now famous remark to Mozart's father: "Before God, and as an honest man, I tell you that your son is the greatest composer known to me either in person or by name. He has taste, and, what is more, the most profound knowledge of composition."

Would Mozart have been Mozart without Haydn's influence? Would Shakespeare have been Shakespeare without *Plutarch's Lives* and *Holinshed's Chronicles* to draw on? Would T. S. Eliot's *Waste Land* have become what it is without Ezra Pound's edits? Jonathan Safran Foer claims in his essay "The Snow Globe" that had he not gone to Yehuda Amichai's reading as a high school student visiting Israel, he might never have become a writer. Anita Shreve is certain that had she not read Alice McDermott's novel *That Night* at the moment she did, she "would not be a novelist today." I find it impossible to accept that all this talent might never have flourished had it not been for a chance encounter or a single book. Surely it would have found expression sooner or later, in one form or another — wouldn't it? In any case, the essays in *Mentors, Muses & Monsters* are about what did happen, and in its own way, each is a celebration of that potent elixir made up of influence and serendipity.

Some writers in this collection refer to transformative figures as mentors, some as muses, and some do not have a ready label. But it's worth noting that none of the writers tells the archetypal story of artist and muse: the great man inspired in his great work by a woman destined to play second fiddle, or no fiddle at all. I like to think this absence is not a fluke, that it marks a trend in the arts and in life, and that it's something else to celebrate in these pages.

I knew these essays would be good when I asked this extraordinary group of writers to undertake them, but I could never have imagined just how good they would be, until they began arriving in my computer from around the country and across an ocean or two. Here's what I think happened: Given the chance to thank the people, living and dead, writers, parents, professors, editors, and dance teachers who changed their lives — and to remember times and places when magic happened and influence of all kinds put down roots — these writers made the decision to write their hearts out and let us in on stories they have carried around for years.

Writers can be a grumpy, cantankerous bunch, self-involved, highstrung, hostile to authority, annoyed, sometimes, if they have to leave the house. But it turns out that if you ask them to remember who gave them the idea to write or the permission or the encouragement, ask them to remember the voice that said, "You can do this, and here's how," whether it was a human voice or an author speaking from the page of a book, there's a good chance they'll tell you a story that just might take your breath away.

Part I

PEOPLE WE ENCOUNTERED

"WHY NOT SAY WHAT HAPPENED?"

REMEMBERING MISS HARDWICK

Elizabeth Benedict

Elizabeth Hardwick, novelist, essayist, cofounder of *The New York Review of Books*, and former wife of Robert Lowell, died on December 2, 2007, at ninety-one years of age. In the days and weeks afterward, there were the predictable public reactions—obituaries in *The New York Times* and elsewhere—and an unusually large number of private responses that came my way. For all to see but not seen by many, Wayne Koestenbaum's celebration of her sentences on the PEN Web site reminded us why the biographical details matter:

> I love Elizabeth Hardwick's sentences. They're strange and way-ward. They veer. They avoid the point. Sometimes they are specific, but often they grow soft-focused and evasive at the crucial moment. They fuzz out by adopting a tone at once magisterial and muffled. When I was writing my biography of Andy Warhol, I told myself, "Imitate Elizabeth Hardwick." By that advice, I meant: be authoritative, but also odd.

Because I had penned a sort of eulogy on the *Huffington Post*—having had a senior tutorial with Hardwick at Barnard, in 1976—a good number of people wrote to me from whom I wouldn't otherwise have heard. Two men who had taught with her at Columbia were enchanted; several others who had served with her on literary committees—where she was famously difficult—were not. And there were feverish phone calls and e-mails with a group of women who had also studied with her at Barnard in the 1970s. She had been a towering figure to us when we were very young, the first real writer any of us knew at a time that's hard to imagine now, when "women writers" were an exotic species, and when wanting to grow up and be one put you in far more exclusive company than it does today. It was not as rare as wanting to be president—which no one wanted to do—but for either sex, it was far from the bustling, vocational school industry that it is today. The writer's work was much more understood to be something endured "painfully and all alone," in Virginia Woolf's words, with the help of a few good readers, rather than through an endless series of courses, workshops, conferences, and "terminal degree" programs. In those days, there was no such thing as a PhD in creative writing. When I graduated from college, there were fourteen MFA writing programs. Today, there are ten times as many.

In scanning my memory for sightings of Elizabeth Hardwick, I stumble into an antiquated world, as though I'm walking through one of Joseph Cornell's boxes or the London house of Thomas and Jane Carlyle, monuments to days gone by. The literary culture of the 1970s had more in common with the nineteenth century than with the twenty-first, yet that faraway period intersected at Barnard and Columbia with another culture just being formed. This new one noisily insisted that women were the equals of men, that women's sexuality was more complicated than men's, and that the old ways were not the best ways, which extended even to the novel, which had been declared dead in many quarters. On hand to replace it was "the new fiction," which, in Hardwick's 1977 essay "The Sense of the Present," included Donald Barthelme, Thomas Pynchon, Kurt Vonnegut, and Renata Adler's novel *Speedboat*. Her analysis speaks of honor, and it honors the old and the new, the dead and the just-born:

> What is honorable in "so it goes" and in the mournful brilliance of Barthelme's stories . . . in *Speedboat*, in the conundrums of V. is the intelligence that questions the shape of life at every point. It is important to concede the honor, the nerve, the ambition—important even if it is hard to believe anyone in the world could be happier reading *Gravity's Rainbow* than reading *Dead Souls*.

In looking back over my shoulder, I see the culture in dazzling turmoil, and I see my own naïveté, my wonder, my fledging ambition. But as I write this remembrance, I seem to have more in common with the narrator, a woman of a certain age, on the first page of our favorite of Hardwick's books, the novel *Sleepless Nights*:

> This is what I have decided to do with my life just now. I will do this
> work of transformed and even distorted memory and lead this life,
> the one I am leading today. . . . If only one knew what to remember
> or pretend to remember. Make a decision and what you want from
> the lost things will present itself. You can take it down like a can
> from a shelf. Perhaps. One would be marked Rand Avenue in Kentucky and some would recall the address at least as true.

For me, one would be marked the Columbia professor's apartment on Morningside Drive where I first learned of Hardwick's existence. I was a freshman and a regular babysitter for the professor's children, but because the family had found me through the Barnard Babysitting Service, they complied with its rules about getting me home. After nine o'clock, I had to be given cab fare or escorted to my residence. The father always chose to walk their dog and take me to my apartment building at the end of the night, but they were a social pair and sometimes returned with the people they had spent the evening with, for a nightcap and more conversation. Because the father was not going to take me home when he had guests, I was always invited to sit with them, other professors and their wives. I'm sure they would have listened to anything I had to say, but I was so intimidated that I might as well have been clinically mute. One New Year's Eve, two couples sat discussing the psychologist Piaget, and at one point the father looked at his watch and said matter-of-factly, "It's five after twelve," meaning the New Year had begun, and the conversation returned without a flutter to Piaget. I would not have been more surprised if they had begun removing their clothes.

That was it? They weren't even going to flip on the television for the big moment? No kissing, no champagne? Had my parents got it wrong all these years? To make it in the smart set, would I have to pretend that New Year's Eve was a scratch on the ear?

It wasn't New Year's Eve when the professors and their wives discussed the melodramatic problems of Lizzie and Cal, whose names, I would soon learn, were Elizabeth Hardwick and Robert Lowell. It seems he had run off with an Englishwoman, Lady Caroline Blackwood, whom none of them knew, and there was much rage and grief on Lizzie's part, and agreement that Cal's problems had never made life easy for anyone. They were divorced or about to be. I don't remember the sentences they spoke, but I remember the somber tone, as though they were recounting the course of a friend's terrible illness. Lizzie taught writing at Barnard, but this meant little to me at the time. I did not decide I wanted to be a writer until the following year, when an English professor intuited that I wanted to write a novel, an ambition that seemed as grand, given my background and the dearth of women writers, as wanting to be president.

I began to notice books by the two writers. In the bookstore on 112th Street and Broadway, one night I stood reading Lowell's collection *Dolphin*, many of whose sonnets seemed like language taken from actual letters. Because I knew the story, I assumed the letters were hers to him. Describing what it's like to read one of his letters, the abandoned wife, in the poem "Records," admits: "I thought my heart would break a thousand times . . ." The line made the world crack open for me. I was heartbroken for Professor Hardwick and her daughter, but strangely comforted in my rickety ambitions. These exalted people who might, like the professors and their wives, be blasé about New Year's Eve, were not blasé about abandonment. If I were going to be a writer, which I knew took a very long time, perhaps I could do this too—reach for plain speech, for the deeply felt, not the elaborately obscure, the impossibly blasé.

I tucked away this revelation, thinking the poem was my little secret, not knowing for decades that Lowell's decision to publish this book, to use Hardwick's letters so baldly, was a scandal among their friends and colleagues. Not knowing for decades that it was Hardwick who had said famously to Lowell, "Why not say what happened?"—which ended up in his poem "Epilogue." Not knowing then that Lowell's confessional poetry and his teaching at Harvard were the catalyst for so many writers who moved so bluntly in the direction of saying what happened. And that the direction would lead us, decades later, to complete candor becoming as fashionable as modesty and discretion had once been. Candor itself would become a genre, a currency of its own, morphing from daytime talk show revelations (*I had sex with my Standard Poodle! My mother slept with my math teacher!*) to memoirs about vaginal pain and gambling addictions, leading right up to the way we live now, when all a writer needs is one hundred gigabytes a year and a blog of her own.

For a variety of reasons, I didn't know until I was a senior that I could be a creative writing major, or at least an English major with a creative writing minor. When the news reached me, I went to Hardwick's office and asked if I could be admitted into her fiction workshop. The class was full, but after seeing my work, she offered me a senior tutorial.

On my own with Miss Hardwick, as I called her on the rare occasions when it was necessary, I handed over four or five pages every time we met. I'd watch her read them in her wooden swivel chair, her auburn curls brushing her cheeks, lipstick always freshly applied. She liked but did not love what I wrote. There was not enough there to love, neither enough skill nor life experience. I was working on a small scale, pecking out very short stories whose modest length she remarked on humorously from time to time. She did not say much; I doubt the meetings lasted more than half an hour, but I don't remember feeling tense or rushed. She was very jolly, and had a ready laugh and an easy smile. She talked about her daughter fondly and made cracks now and then about not having enough money. Her languid Kentucky drawl was intoxicating, and her offhand remarks were a kind of performance art.

She was different from other teachers; the idea was to study *her*, not a particular subject. What exactly did I learn when I overheard her say, "Ah *hate* to go to a first-class restaurant and have a lot of *happy* birthdays"? I still don't know, but the world somehow expanded with this remark in it, or maybe all it shows is that I was destined to spend my life listening to what people say, listening for information, the pure poetry of speech, for cultural markers that place us in one social class or another, or maybe in two at once—all essential lessons for a fiction writer.

On the writing front, she disapproved of creating characters who were artists, and I think she disapproved of characters who were writers. She had modest ambitions as a teacher: "The only thing I can do for you is to suggest books to read." This lesson was clear: the only way to learn to write was to read. The book she loved, it seemed, above all others was Rilke's *The Notebook of Malte Laurids Brigge*, which of course I read many times.

13

During one meeting, I reported that a Columbia professor had encouraged me to be a writer, and I shyly asked if she agreed with him.

"I think you can do the work," she said kindly, "but you have to decide if you want such a hard life."

I'm not sure now that she believed I could "do the work," but I was too young and grateful to question her. And I dismissed the caveat entirely, that it was a hard life. With all the dumb confidence of youth, I said to myself, "*She* has a hard life because she's an old lady. *I* will not have a hard life."

There were two categories of private responses to Elizabeth Hardwick that came to me after she died. "She was utterly lovely to me, always," one former colleague from Columbia wrote. "I found her enchanting, filled with goodness, and of course brilliant. So much sadness, though. She knew what it is to ache." The other category was much less kind, and I mention it reluctantly, but because it speaks to the literary culture that shaped her, the male-dominated *Partisan Review* crowd of the 1940s and '50s. A writer who had sat with her on committees said that "you didn't want to make a remark before she did, because of course she would demolish you. It wasn't a matter of gender, it was just being mean for the pure exercise of it, and we knew it, and tried to change seats when she came in. And she was devastating in her remarks about other writers." Another observed her behavior through a wide-angle lens: "I think that she and [Mary] McCarthy and [Barbara] Epstein, and—even in politics—Bella Abzug, must have felt that the only way to make it in a man's world was—because men are so often bullies—to bully. Being mean was a kind of secondary sexual characteristic."

Reports came my way of cutting, hurtful remarks. In the *Times* obituary I learned that she had written a "mischievously effective" article parodying her dear friend Mary McCarthy's bestselling novel *The Group*, called "The Gang," published in *The New York Review of Books* under the pseudonym Xavier Prynne. People wondered privately what sort of gesture this was—to mock a friend's book in public.

For weeks I was haunted by Miss Hardwick's jabs, by the acutely sensitive writer who could be so insensitive to the feelings of others. I wondered about her childhood in Kentucky, her being the eighth of eleven children. There could not have been an abundance of personal attention, of parental devotion to any one child. I wondered about the costs of her difficult marriage, decades of caring for the manic-depressive, oft-hospitalized Lowell, a man whose breakdowns frequently led him into the arms of other women. It's not a secret that people learn from their oppressors or that the powerless need people next to whom they can feel superior. A child bullied by his parents will bully a smaller child, not because he's rotten but because all that negative energy needs somewhere to go. And there was the culture in which Hardwick had come of age, long before the heady days of the women's movement that marked my time at Barnard.

I went looking for a taste of that time and picked up Mary McCarthy's autobiography, *Intellectual Memoirs*, and felt I'd hit the jackpot: Hardwick had written the introduction. And there was my answer, or a piece of it, in her description of being a guest at the home of Philip Rahv, editor of *Partisan Review*: "An evening at the Rahvs' was to enter a ring of bullies, each one bullying the other. In that way it was different from the boarding school accounts of the type, since no one was in ascendance. Instead there was an equality of vehemence that exhausted itself and the wicked bottles of Four Roses whiskey around midnight—until the next time."

She had been there as a young woman in the 1940s, one of the few women learning the tricks of this scalding trade. Add to that the hardships of the marriage, of being the caretaker, the one who cleaned up after disasters. In her obituary it was reported that she felt her relationship with Lowell was "the best thing that ever happened to me," but day to day, year to year, such burdens take their toll. Why bother to be kind to all when life had been so unkind to her? Perhaps. My speculations swirled, and I went back and forth as to whether even to mention this issue in this piece, or whether to mention my armchair psychologist theories. One evening I remembered that I might have a postcard from her, sent in response to a review I'd written of her early, reissued novel *The Ghostly Lover*. In a box of letters, I found instead a typed letter she had written me in 1982. I'd asked her to write a letter of recommendation for graduate school and had sent along three stories. How could I have forgotten this letter, typed on crinkly onion skin, her name, first and last, signed with a fountain pen?

She provides a frank, specific critique of the stories, then a general critique—"What I don't see in these yet is a voice that would let me know they come from the same author, a voice, a particular vision, a way of

15

style or whatever"—and several sentences that kept me going for the year it took me to finish my first novel: "On the other hand, the stories are not awkward, not amateurish and I have the feeling you are on the brink of actually being able to write a lot better suddenly. Anyway, good luck to you and you have reason to persevere in the effort to write fiction. I'm sure you are, as I said, on your way."

I had not been keen on going to graduate school, but it seemed a way to buy some time. When I ended up on the waiting list, I was gleeful: a validation without the obligation to go. I had just been laid off from a full-time job and could collect unemployment insurance for a few months while I worked on my novel. And Elizabeth Hardwick had told me I was going in the right direction. When I thought of that, it sometimes made me stop writing and look up from the typewriter in astonishment and gratitude. Then it made me lower my eyes and get back to work.

Imagining Influence

Robert Boyers

Is it possible to have an exaggerated respect for masterpieces? For many years I believed that to aspire to anything less than *Death in Venice* or *To the Lighthouse* was unworthy of the writer I might hope to become. As a result I wrote no fiction at all after my undergraduate years at Queens College in New York City, where I tried my hand at poems and plays and stories and discovered that my gifts then ran principally to easy symmetries and predictable reversals of commonly accepted ideas. When I sent a few poems to *The Nation* as I entered graduate school in the fall of 1963, I received a letter from Denise Levertov that nicely summarized what I had already come to think of my own "creative" efforts: "You're obviously very bright," she wrote, "but I would recommend that you try something else." Of course an even brighter boy, age twenty-one, would have been moved at that point to send Ms. Levertov a note telling her to go fuck herself, and then gone back to work. But then I could not make myself believe that I would soon turn out the equivalent of "Sunday Morning" or make my latest novella-in-progress a worthy successor to Saul Bellow's *Seize the Day*, which I wished with all my heart that I had written.

I have never suffered from anything remotely resembling writer's block. In graduate school I began turning out reviews and essays for magazines like *Dissent* and *Partisan Review*, and in 1965 I made myself the editor of a new quarterly magazine called *Salmagundi*, in whose pages I would be free to place whatever I liked. But I remained, no doubt for complex reasons I'll never fully understand, reluctant to write the stories I had it in me to tell and soon pretended that I could say all that I needed to say in the literary essays and critical books I produced. My reluctance had nothing to do with "hugging the shore." Often I found myself embroiled

17

in disputes as a result of the essays I published, and I took special pleasure in complaining about aspects of the culture wholeheartedly endorsed by most of my friends and academic colleagues. Of course I don't know what would have happened had I continued to write fiction in my twenties and thirties, but I suspected even then that my fondness for argument and controversy would have infected the work and made it pedagogically earnest and overdetermined in a fatal way.

At any rate, for many years I ceased even to think about writing fiction. In 1990, nearing fifty, I spent a sabbatical year in Florence with my wife Peg and our youngest son. Peg had been reading the work of the Italian writer Natalia Ginzburg, writing her letters and ceaselessly extolling her virtues, and by October Ginzburg had invited Peg to visit her in Rome. Bring your family along, Ginzburg had recommended, but my Italian was poor, and Ginzburg, who had lived for a time in London, thought no better of her own English. I thought it best to stay out of the way, and spent a long afternoon entertaining our son in the sweltering Roman streets around the Piazza Navona, ducking into the nearby air-conditioned McDonald's for snacks and cold drinks and speculating with young Gabriel as to the reception his mother would find around the corner in the company of her idol. In my knapsack I carried a copy of Ginzburg's book *Family Sayings*, from which I read aloud to nine-year-old Gabriel whenever he would listen, and we agreed that "Mom" would get along beautifully with the seventy-four-year-old writer.

By November I had read four of Ginzburg's books, including her World War II novel *All Our Yesterdays* and a more recent epistolary novel called *The City and the House*. Soon we returned to Rome for another long afternoon, when Ginzburg cooked lunch for Peg and sat for a two-hour taped interview slated to appear in a special issue of *Salmagundi* devoted to Ginzburg. Again I entertained our son in the great outdoors and managed not to envy the hours Peg would spend with someone I had never met. Peg was not typically given to infatuations, and this one was so pronounced and infectious that my own satisfaction was considerable.

I never met Ginzburg—she died some months after our visits to Rome—but I became a fan of her work in translation and went on to teach her writing in literature classes and eventually, many years later, wrote an essay on her for *Harper's* magazine. But Peg's involvement was by far the greater. In the late 1990s she began to write poems spoken in the imagined voice of Ginzburg, covering aspects of her life in Fascist Italy, and frequently inventing later experiences for Ginzburg that would seem plausible given her predilections. The poems became the collection *Hard Bread*, published by the University of Chicago Press in 2002.

What had drawn Peg to Ginzburg was an improbable combination of acerbity and sweetness, along with Ginzburg's ability to write in utter disregard of fashion or decorum. Though she had many loyal friends, Ginzburg did not hesitate to publish devastating things about these friends when she thought that they had betrayed their gifts or their responsibilities. Though she believed women should be free to make their own decisions about abortion and other matters, she deplored the culture in which ostensibly enlightened women took their reproductive rights for granted and refused to regard abortion itself as a grave, even terrible choice. Most intellectuals, she felt, were not serious about matters that ought to have seemed troubling, and she routinely criticized what she took to be the spiritual and intellectual deficiencies of a women's movement whose objectives she shared.

Of course, I too was drawn to Ginzburg's prickly independence of spirit and the utter lack of affectation in her voice, though it took me a few years to discover that Ginzburg would somehow inspire my long-delayed return to the writing of fiction. There was something hard and direct in her sentences that bespoke an enviable decisiveness. Even when she confessed to confusion or inadequacy she was definite about it. She didn't have to search out flaws in those she wrote about because she truly saw them as they were and thus could not miss what was weak or vicious or foolish in them. Reading her, you had no sense that she intended to be provocative or to generate unwelcome revelations. She was generous and harsh in more or less equal measure and clearly did not write to cut people down to size or to prove herself superior to ideas she disliked. If seeing clearly entailed contradiction, she embraced contradiction, and she was willing to have one favorite character muse, "it was an idiotic thought, but he himself might happen to have an idiotic thought of that kind."

Was it possible, then, I wondered, to make myself into the sort of writer Natalia Ginzburg might have admired? Perhaps that was one of those idiotic thoughts I allowed myself, more than occasionally, to entertain without supposing that they were anything less than idiotic. In truth, Ginzburg liked many things that left me cold, and was bored by others — like music and painting—which I adored, and obviously I could not reasonably hope to tailor my accent or passions to satisfy or amuse her—even had she been around to encourage me or to ridicule my fledgling efforts.

Still, with some misgiving, I found myself more and more drawn to Ginzburg's voice and posture, feeling in some incomprehensible way that my growing need to write fiction had much to do with her. Why with misgiving? In part because Ginzburg's authority had much to do with what she herself had lived through, with experiences entirely remote from my own. In her fiction, as in her memoiristic work, there is the unmistakable accent of bereavement and bewilderment. To be sure, she does not often allow herself direct reference to the death of her first husband, Leone Ginzburg, an anti-Fascist resistance fighter who was tortured and killed in Regina Coeli prison in 1944, though she writes poignantly about the experience of living under house arrest in the Abruzzi during the Fascist years, of painful separation from her children, of the failure or suicide of friends like the writer Cesare Pavese. When she writes that people of the World War II generation will never feel secure in their lives, that there is something in them that can "never be cured no matter how many years go by," we believe her, and if we are honest with ourselves we know that nothing in our own lives can generate so comprehensive a darkness. "A ring at the doorbell in the middle of the night," Ginzburg writes, "can only mean the word 'police' to us . . . [and] it is useless for us to tell ourselves over and over again that behind the word 'police' there are now friendly faces whom we can ask for help and protection." Just so, it is useless for someone like me—who has been spared so horrific and protracted a siege as Ginzburg experienced as a Jew in Fascist Italy—to tell myself that my life too has had its share of suffering and that I too am acquainted with the night. I know that I cannot pretend to anything remotely resembling Ginzburg's sense of life, and that I ought not, ever, to wish it upon myself.

Maybe no one ever quite gets to the bottom of an infatuation or an influence. Often, before I fell under Ginzburg's spell, I had been deeply moved by very different kinds of writers, writers with greater range and grander ambition. But Ginzburg alone awakened in me a desire to try things I had never attempted before. However forthright I had been as a critic, I had always seemed to myself fair-minded and judicious. I had wanted my work to be useful, to contribute to the ongoing, civilized debates taking shape around books, issues, and ideas. Ginzburg too had made contributions to such debates, and she had even written a regular column for the Italian newspaper *La Stampa*. But she was, for me, principally a writer about whom one would never use the words "judicious" or "fair-minded." And that, I suppose, is what fired my imagination and made me understand that I could write compelling stories only if I wrote with the combination of "moral and amoral seriousness" that Susan Sontag once noted in the work of Elias Canetti.

I am speaking here of qualities not easy to describe, though in Ginzburg I knew that I had found them and that I wanted never to do without them: not merely the absence of bullshit or pretense but the weight she seemed to accord to everything, even where she was playful. The weight, no doubt, had to do with Ginzburg's sense that "We cannot lie in any of the things we do" and cannot "allow others to lie to us." She doesn't invariably express contempt for persons susceptible to weakness and complaint, but she is typically withering toward those who are comfortable with illusion and casual about their feelings. In Ginzburg, adults who "fall in love easily" or manage to believe that adultery or the neglect of children are ordinary affairs of potentially little consequence are made to seem fatally disappointing. She knows that equilibrium may be difficult for many of us to achieve, but she mistrusts people who are armored against shock and temptation and at all costs moderate in behavior and inclination. To feel that things have weight, Ginzburg believes, is to accord to them the capacity to move us and disorient us and make us fearful. Fearful of what? For a writer, there is always — there must always be — the fear of "cheating and being dishonest," of saying things we don't mean, of currying favor with readers, or reaching for "words that do not really exist within us." There are, to be sure, other kinds of fear, but for Ginzburg, the fear of "cheating and being dishonest" is always present.

Had I been "dishonest" in the books and essays I had written? I didn't think so, though I had prided myself on a certain gift for equanimity and tolerance that now, increasingly, seemed to me perhaps a form of dishonesty or denial. Of course I knew that clarity, tolerance, and moderation were virtues when it came to certain kinds of intellectual work. But these were not always compatible with other virtues that more and more seemed indispensable to the kind of imaginative work I wished to undertake. I wanted, all of a sudden, to get to the bottom of the sentiments of rage and resentment that had long colored my relations with my own unlovely and unhappy mother. I allowed myself to wonder, for the first time, whether the boundless patience and geniality I displayed when confronted by rude or otherwise offensive students did not betray an alarming fear of certain kinds of intimacy and struggle. Was it possible, I wondered, that the controlled dispassion typically evident in my cultural criticism would prevent me from getting inside characters whose fevers and confusions I wanted very much to penetrate and evoke?

In the first stories I wrote I did not at all think of Ginzburg as a model I would do well to adopt. In fact, I thought of nothing beyond my imagined characters and their situations and the logic I needed to discover to bring them to life. Only now, as I look back, does it seem to me that the courage—or permission—I needed was there for me in Ginzburg's example, though by no means obvious. An aspect of her importance for me will come clear when I say that I do not think of her as the author of works comprehensively ambitious or virtuosic. Her sentences are not sublimely quotable, and her narrative virtues have principally to do with clarity of observation, resistance to frivolous embellishment, taut pacing, and unfailing quotidian specificity. Often, in attempting to account for the spell she casts, one is hard put to speak in essentially literary terms, as one does with writers—Gordimer, Saramago, Kundera, Vargas Llosa—more obviously brilliant, original, and enigmatically suggestive. For someone— like me—terminally hung up on the idea of masterpieces and intoxicated still by the aura of "LITERATURE," Ginzburg was attractive at least in part because she did not much inspire me, a devout admirer, to think of her as an indisputably great writer who had created monuments of unaging intellect.

In fact, I knew that if I was to write fiction, I would have to proceed without worrying about this sort of stuff. Ginzburg herself had derided the notion that, to be taken seriously, she would have to ask how she stacked up against Proust or Joyce or Kafka, and in some way her inveterate unconcern fueled my own and allowed me simply to write without noticing the shadows on the wall. When I was young and fresh out of college I wished to write sentences as intricate and original as Stendhal's. But as I wrote in my fifties I felt free at last to proceed as if the word "masterpiece" had nothing whatever to do with the real, immediate, heart-stopping business of fiction.

Again I note that influence is a slippery subject, and in my case, the influence I think I can identify is not reflected in any explicit way in my short stories. And yet I have no doubt whatever that Ginzburg's voice steeled me to do the hard work I needed to do. Hard in what sense? In the sense that I knew from the first that this writing would deliver to me not consolation but, much of the time, regret. That it would not serve to quiet anxiety but to exacerbate it. There may be writers for whom the writing of fiction is a matter of emotion recollected in tranquility, but no one who reads the fiction of Ginzburg will suppose that emotion has been successfully mastered, that she works from the far side of—far removed from—anguish or disgust. And as I set to work on my own fiction, I knew that I needed to be very much inside the feelings that I wished to explore in the stories I projected.

Of course, this will not seem hard—not in the sense I intend—when the emotions at issue are more or less tame or decorous. In Ginzburg, even where the situations of life seem more or less settled for certain characters, the attendant emotions are rarely tame, and most often they are troubling. A woman who decides to marry acknowledges that her reasons are entirely practical and no less compelling for being exclusively so. A man who has long put up with his wife's serial infidelities entertains the thought that there may yet be for him a better life, though he fears the effect that a decisive marital rupture will have on their children. Another man, generous and intelligent, can't help thinking of his young wife as something of an insect, and persistently urges her to accept this view of herself so long as she remains essentially passive, blandly submissive, compliantly meek. In each case, characters are forced to confront deeply unpleasant realities, and if they are unequal to the task of doing anything about them, as is usually the case, they are forced to acknowledge the failure, however little they are able to grasp the enormity of that failure. A man in Ginzburg may accept that truly he was not much of a father to his son without adequately registering what that says about him, but he is made to live with an unmistakable burden of failure, with the sense that he has never earned the right to regard himself as a grown-up.

In none of my own stories did I set out with a clear sense of what I hoped to accomplish, and in most cases the point of a story would reveal itself to me very slowly, gradually, in several instances over a number of years. I began the title story of what became the collection *Excitable Women, Damaged Men* soon after the death of my mother, herself an unusually "excitable" woman, complicated, driven, irritable, unstable, a kind of truth-teller who specialized in punishing, deeply unsettling partial truths guaranteed to make no one comfortable or happy. In building a narrative around her I am sure that I did not think at all of Ginzburg, though there must have been, in the proverbial "back" of my mind, the example of Ginzburg's remarkable portraits, in particular the unforgettable one of the father in the memoir *Family Sayings*, a portrait of another one-of-a-kind figure subject to mood swings and rages and definite opinions and a species of household tyranny. But then Ginzburg's father was not in any obvious way a pathological figure like my own mother, and Ginzburg did not portray herself as someone who developed as she did precisely in response to, or in fear of, her father.

Not having a clear sense of what I wished to accomplish, I soon discovered, six or seven pages into "An Excitable Woman," that though I had made a very good beginning, I did not know how to proceed. The central figure had been set up in a vivid and compelling way, and her potential effect on others had been suggestively evoked as well. But what, I wondered, could be the importance of such a portrait where the character is clearly not fully responsible for her actions, where she is, unmistakably, disturbed? In this case, moreover, the exaggerated features of the character's irrational behavior had much to do with her inability to accept that her husband of thirty years had suddenly left her for a younger woman, so that the mother figure had not merely a grievance but a seeming justification, however specious. Surely, I saw, the importance of my story could not be made to lie in the domain of what used to be called "marriage and morals." I knew that I had no wish to compose a story commenting upon the culture of divorce. My story was not driven by issues of any kind, and I knew that there was something else I needed to identify if I was to proceed. That something else, in fact, turned out to be the specter of inadequacy that had always informed my relations with my mother.

In the early draft of my story I had drawn the thirty-year-old son of this ferocious mother as a person fundamentally innocent and acted upon, a plausible victim subject to a stronger person's bullying and fits of temper. But I saw after a while that this would not do, that there was a dishonest sentimentality in this depiction of the youthful character. His benevolence toward the mother was perhaps not entirely a mask, but he was allowed too entirely to keep it up and enjoy it with something just short of voluptuous self-approval. What was wanted was a growing intimation of something else. The mother, after all, deserved not merely to be pitied and tolerated but to be feared and even hated, and the revulsion she could inspire needed to be registered, acknowledged, without my allowing it to become fatally disabling for the son or allowing him to appear to himself and to others perfectly blameless. The further the full, complicated range of emotions might be let in, the further the young man would necessarily be made to revise his own sense of self and taste, sharply, his own failure to effectually alter the trajectory of his mother's descent into misery and derangement.

"Only in our dreams," Ginzburg had written, "did we succeed in conducting ourselves competently." Often, she wrote, we love "to perceive in others amazement about ourselves," about our benevolence or resilience or depth of conviction. Such observations were so entirely a part of me by the time I began to write fiction that I have no doubt they guided me in the shaping of stories and, more especially, in the revisions I determined, again and again, to make in works that seemed to me, in one way or another, not fully honest. Such was the case with "An Excitable Woman," where, with considerable reluctance, I revised my portrait of the son so as to make him a well-intentioned but ambiguous accomplice in the mother's free fall.

Of course, writers often believe that in the imaginary worlds they invent they are free to do what they please, to use real people (or characters based upon real people) according to their own needs—"like so many objects," as Ginzburg once wrote. But though Ginzburg often acknowledged the sheer pleasure involved in making things up and trying things out, she was alert to the distortions enforced by the will to delicious self-approval, and she understood that in writers she admired there was always some discernible "obedience to [an] instinctual darkness" that went against the grain of the usual desire for happiness. Fearful of that darkness in myself, and strongly committed to the gift for equanimity that has rarely left me, I learned from Ginzburg—so I believe—to forego some of the pleasure I routinely derived from insisting upon the essential innocence of characters in whom I was personally invested.

By the time I published my first few stories in the mid- and late 1990s, Peg was at work on her Ginzburg poems, often reading them aloud to me and discussing with me the peculiar, elusive accent or tonality that would convey Ginzburg's sensibility. Was the quality of irony expressed in a poem built around Ginzburg's relations with Pasolini or Hemingway not in fact more peculiar to Peg herself than to Ginzburg? Was the attitude toward children expressed in another poem not rather more unforgiving than was usual in Ginzburg's work? Absorbed as we were in addressing such questions, over several years, it was not possible for me to write my own stories without having Ginzburg somehow there, in the ether, haunting my thoughts. And though Peg rightly noted that the manic velocity of my stories—their tendency to shuttle rapidly between external narration and interior monologue—as well as their fondness for characters dangerous or deranged, made them feel utterly different from Ginzburg's fiction, she also supported my belief that, had Ginzburg lived long enough to read the stories I wrote under her influence, she would have recognized the influence at once, and written me a letter acknowledging our curious spiritual affinity. An idle thought, to be sure, but then, who would deny himself the sort of occasional self-indulgence that Ginzburg anatomized with merciless insistence and with an unfailing sense of the ridiculous?

FATHERS

Jay Cantor

L ike most stories in my life, the one about me and the great Jewish American writer Bernard Malamud begins with my relationship with my father. Of course, to understand my relationship with my father, you have to understand *his* relationship with his family—and so on, probably, back to Abraham and Sarah.

But for the moment, let's tarry with Abraham (Cantor) and his wife, Fanny. These two, and their five children, came to the United States from Poland, and then settled in Syracuse, New York, which city I can only assume they'd chosen because they were attached to their previous pain and this seemed the part of New York most like Poland. Mercifully, no Cossacks (though my cousin believes our grandfather had to pretend to be Republican to hide his socialist past), but it had dismal weather surely, and (to my childhood eyes) a gray quality of a province of the provinces, a place where they dream of moving to where Chekhov's characters live and dream of Moscow.

Anyway, it's 1913. The Cantors have just arrived in a New World that I imagine they've made painfully, comfortably old again. They celebrate. Schnapps? I doubt it. The two or three times I saw my father . . . well, not drunk, but a little bit *not completely sober*, was at the end of the Passover meal, when he would sing a little, and speak fondly and angrily of Syracuse and Sinai. But with or without wine or peppermint drinks, a pregnancy results. My grandmother, who already has five unaffordable children, had thought all that blessed bother behind her, and seeks out someone she believes could perform an abortion. This wise woman, perhaps seeing regret in my grandmother's eyes, says, "No. Have the child. He'll become a doctor, and take care of you in your old age."

Doctor the baby became, and in record time. Along the way, he was elected to all the honorary societies (ask me, I can tell you which ones), and then became a man known for his books on ambulatory surgery—which isn't a surgery done as the doctor ambles around, but an operation performed in such a clever manner that the patient doesn't require a long hospital stay. This was, unfortunately, not a technique useful for the cancer that killed my grandmother. Nonetheless, I think that abortionist's directive continued in my father's sense of things, passed on to me, that medicine was almost the only menschlike of professions.

In the early years of my own life (and, come to think of it, in the current ones, too) I was very grateful for doctors. Among His other gifts to me, God had implanted in my body a gimpy immune system, and some oddly shaped tubes in my ears. Yes, yes, I know everyone has earaches as a kid, and fewer die of them than of heartbreak. But I swear from the time I was born, mine hurt like a motherfucker. They were *special*.

Ha! After all, if there's one thing that everyone can and does do, it isn't peeing or making babies, it's common, and pointless, suffering. As the hero of Malamud's novel *The Fixer* says, "what suffering has taught me is the uselessness of suffering." Still, it's a lesson: the mensch's job is to put an end to it.

Which is what doctors try to do, no? Soon I saw the Earology Man at Mount Sinai—and it was, I got the feeling from my parents, almost an honor for me to be sick if the Top Specialist in the field would see me. The doctor shook his head sadly and said I'd definitely be deaf by twelve. The Mayo Clinic, as a last desperate measure, suggested radium implants. My father, thank God, nixed the sci-fi stuff. Thus, another reason to be grateful that I had a doctor for a father: he could protect me from doctors. This reminds me that my dad also found an error on a chart that a doctor had scribbled a command on when I was in the hospital once, and saved me from some fatal dose of something. In fact, all things considered, I don't see how any of you who didn't have a doctor in the family made it to puberty. But the further point I want to make is that in addition to any kid's perhaps outsized admiration for his father, there was also this: this child was attached to his father for dear life.

And so, as if out of love and gratitude to his mother for his life, he became a doctor, and out of love and gratitude to him for mine, I was chosen, ordained, and required to continue paying the debt. The family myth is that to prepare me for my career my dad taught me all the bones of the body, and that, age five or so, I'd recite them at parties. (I now very much doubt the *all*. There are a huge number of the things, almost as many as there are mitzvahs to fulfill.) Before I was eight, my father had also given me a stethoscope, a microscope, and a strange device called "a suture board," which was, as I remember, a hidelike substance attached to a block of wood, so one could pull a large needle through the thin leather and learn how to close an incision. At the same age, my father began to show me movies of operations, to prepare me for the whirligig of guts, the not quite perpetual motion of the heart that was to be my playground and work world. Of course, I know now that this story, like my earaches, isn't the least bit uncommon; since time began doctor fathers have wanted doctor sons, and I hope by now doctor daughters as well, for why shouldn't girls, too, get to share in this blessing. Yet I still believe there was a little extra energy applied to the project in the Cantor household. Of course, I bet every one of those sons believes something similar, each of us attached to the special suffering that makes us special, each in our own particular Poland.

Even so, by the time I was fourteen, I'd wandered from the path. And like everything else in the story, this may have something to do with my father. He'd written medical texts and, like some other melancholy people, self-help books—sometimes locking himself in his study and completing one in a weekend. They included guides for cancer treatment, or weight loss, or a contented life, though my father was far from content with his. I suppose he wrote self-help manuals thinking that if enough people saw him as judge and benefactor that might heal him, too, or put him above and beyond life. What I remember, though, is a man nearly crushed by it, lying on the floor of his paneled study trying out relaxation exercises for the books, and all the while producing a black fog of melancholy that seeped throughout Great Neck, and over to Little Neck, Long Island, and perhaps Roslyn.

But my father's face looked lively, tender, and passionate as he talked about the books he truly loved, and that he himself couldn't write, complicated novels, like the ones by John Barth or Thomas Pynchon, or the less overtly intricate but powerful and heartrending work of Saul Bellow and Bernard Malamud, whose sandwiches of realism, sour-rye wit, and fable could make the past appear suddenly present again in the Long Island or Syracuse here and now, a magical conjunction of times and realms, of wandering Jews and talking crows, that released a precious if often ominous instruction.

My father liked to talk to me about these books, and in my childhood we would wander about Great Neck ourselves, discussing them, or making up plots for me to perform as school skits. In those days, he treated me (though I knew this was just a skit) as someone like an equal, and even—if he really wanted to wow me—said I was, or someday would be, intellectually his superior. My father sometimes had the overly precise manner of a slightly antic Adolph Menjou, but in those years he was always easy and fond with me, generous with his time, with praise. And he was, of course, the person whose praise I most wanted—I still felt like my life depended on it. I can see now that he, too, like many the melancholic with his child, clung to me for dear life.

My father's love of stories confirmed what I already felt. Or maybe what I was, through stories, able *not* to feel. For me, as for many others, there was a druglike quality to books. Novels were—just as for anyone riding the subway while turning the pages of a page turner—*forgetting*; when I read I was not in pain, even if that pain was mostly earaches, accompanied by a smattering of pneumonias. The world, that is to say, was not much worse for me than for others, and better in one way: I could leave it and find another one, its replica, inside me.

Novels were the best stuff for me for this—who knows why? such tastes feel almost metabolic—but I also loved plays, musical comedies, comic books, films, situation comedies, and the glimpses of Bazooka Joe's life that came wrapped around bubble gum. It wasn't just that a story took me elsewhere, but that the web of colored words of a story showed more *elsewheres* nested around it, more webs of words (of philosophy, theology, science), like heavenly spheres arrayed around, above, and below the story, ready with a slight bit of thought to show new connections between them, ones I could wander among contentedly for hours.

For my father, producing at least some forms of this drug was among the world's most honorable pursuits. I tried, in skits or rhyming songs, in stories soon, and discovered that there was an even better anodyne than reading. The pleasure of writing a narrative, of composing the right words for a story, going where they lead and/or the writer leads them was like becoming the boat and the wind, and forever departing from myself. During the time I scribbled, *I* wasn't.

On the surface I remained, as doctors say of patients who follow directions, *compliant*. I took the usual high school courses someone who might someday need a suture board would take (though I didn't do well at them—a case of self-sabotage, my father was sure), and when I arrived at Harvard College in 1966, I still thought at least that I *should* be a doctor, though I knew beyond doubt that I *wanted* to be a writer. For a good Jewish boy like myself, *should* was the glue of the personality, and I'm not sure how this story would have gone on if Bernard Malamud hadn't just come to Harvard for two years, to teach (such was the university's odd largesse) only freshmen. At Harvard, though, there would always be barriers and selections. After all, if there weren't rows and rows of discerning gatekeepers to be impressed, how could you know yourself at the end of the process as truly among the special, the deserving, the chosen?

I rejoiced at being admitted to the course, but I don't think the goose (who is the goose here, by the way, me or my dad?) was roasted until the afternoon I opened the door to a sterile seminar room near the top of Holyoke Center and met Bernard Malamud himself, a short, very self-contained man, with a close-clipped graying mustache (my father's hadn't begun to gray yet), wearing a gray and restrained manner. It wasn't love at first sight, mostly because he wasn't looking for love from us, but for admiration and understanding, and even then, only in small doses that wouldn't knock a person off balance.

Malamud laid out the way the course would operate. We would give him a copy of our story at his office in Kirkland House, and leave a copy in a shoebox in one of the periodical rooms of Widener. Each student would visit the shoebox, and read all the stories for the next week, when the authors would read them aloud in the seminar. Discussion to follow. He had also put some recent books of stories on reserve in the library for us. I remember Bruce Jay Friedman and Ivan Gold were among them. They weren't perfect (what is?) but we should make ourselves familiar with our art—what he assumed, that is to say, we *hoped* would be *our* art.

This is all writing class Standard Operating Procedure (except for the homey shoebox in the high-ceilinged, marbled Widener room, which was a nice Malamud-like touch: the shoebox in its cardboard ordinariness radiated power, and the big room lost its standing, became hollow in its pretensions). So, why did his ordinary dictates make this group of students at once so sober and so inebriated—as if we were, in our drunken excitement, doing our best to imitate the sobriety of the serious writer? That was the Malamud effect. In part it was the glow of his reputation, but more than that, it was his mien. Even as he laid out the usual boilerplate, we were impressed with his seriousness and his will. Once, talking about his own penchant for rewriting, Malamud told an interviewer, "I have a terrifying will that way." The interviewer, Israel Shenker, said he found him not so terrifying, but for the life of me I can't imagine why not. People talk of self-made men, meaning, usually, a broad-shouldered fellow who bulls the world into submitting to his desire. Malamud, small and narrow-shouldered, was more like someone who'd made *himself* submit so he could find and then express in words his own vision of the value of submission. To the craft of writing, first of all.

Over the weeks, his seriousness drew out the seriousness in us, made that seminar room a place where we were on our best behavior, which at Harvard meant we sometimes tried to work together to unriddle each other's stories, rather than finding inventive, witty ways to cut each other's throats. The students from that year became (and have remained, in fact or in imagination) my competitors and my comrades—because we shared that experience of taking writing very seriously.

Too seriously? Perhaps so. Once, nearly two decades later, we were having lunch, and Bern said, "I feel sorry for your generation. When I was young, writers were like gods." Then, after lunch, we went for a walk in Cambridge, and, as if to add some ironic punctuation, a Chinese man on the street bowed to him. "He's here from Peking," Malamud said, "to work with me on a translation of my work." It made him smile.

A little, anyway. One mustn't let such things cause one to wobble too much. Case in point: About three months into the seminar year, we opened the door to find photographers and television cameras. Malamud's latest novel, *The Fixer*, based on a case of blood libel against a Jewish odd-job man in Czarist Russia, had received the National Book Award, and now the Pulitzer Prize. Malamud's mood was tinged that afternoon with something antic, but only barely. He was tickled, I guess, but not enough to laugh. After all, the next day would return him to the empty room, the black manual typewriter, the blank page, his own debt to existence (he'd survived his mother? he hadn't gone mad like his brother?) that could only be repaid by a properly composed sentence, a story that clicked shut at the end, that had, he would say that year, fulfilled its form.

I think by that November I already knew that Malamud was himself the jailed Fixer. He pushed the pages under the door. The world returned prizes, food, and (in the case of his daughter, Janna, I'm sure) a love that he most certainly returned. But how much really can fit under a door? And he carried that room around with him; he was bound and a little isolated wherever he went. A great many people are locked up one way or another; many people remain piously attached to a suffering and constraint, a Syracuse, a Mount Sinai Hospital, or a Poland. Malamud, when he worked (though perhaps not always when he *lived*), had made his binding mean something more than complaint; and in his imprisonment, and often about imprisonment, he'd written harrowing fiction, filled with impossible (because in the modern world we're all Freud's patients, after all, not prophets) wry wisdom.

Malamud could crack wise because he seemingly had a reformed or revised (post-Freudian) Talmud all his own, which was somehow the gift of the room. It had directed him, I think, to keep rebuilding that room and to continue to sit in it working. God Himself might have been analyzed away, but you still had to obey at least the important directives (how could you tell which they were, by the way? I forgot to ask), and by a ferocious effort of will overcome in yourself whatever would have preferred to break free of the room and caper, raven, or embrace. And you could tell Malamud also found time to regret what he'd given up by way of capering, etc. It was painfully palpable that, like Chekhov's Masha, he was in mourning for his life.

On the other hand, always judging himself meant he was authorized to judge others, that maybe being the one pleasure the obedient alrightnik always finds it all right to enjoy. His contract with the twelve of us was this: he would help us understand our own stories, learn how they might be fixed, and then he would pronounce sentence on us; he would tell us if we might someday become writers who could make a decent sentence — which to him was almost the most menschlike of professions. The Malamud effect was also this: we all soon actually believed he was entitled to make that judgment.

So each Tuesday, in that room at Holyoke Center, Malamud either praised our stories or sliced through our thick Harvard presumptions. As he did so, he was sometimes on the edge of pomposity himself; after all, the risk in a Malamud story is that without the right fablelike setting, the perfect ironic sour-rye twist—the Malamud touch—wisdom can taste like sententiousness. But mostly he spoke of writing, his or ours, in a matter-of-fact way. Or maybe his trick was more profound: it was to speak of the very exultation of fiction in a matter-of-fact way; to have in mind always its particular moral sublimity was a matter of a craftsman's choices.

At the moment, it feels almost ridiculous to talk of writing as a moral enterprise, let alone of "moral sublimity," but at that time in American Jewish writing (and not just there, of course; after all, think of Flannery O'Connor), that was the goal. Malamud, like Bellow, or Mailer (with the usual signs reversed in his case, bad become good, etc.), wanted to provide usable knowledge. The novel was a self-help book of sorts, even if the help it offered was to tell you that you might as well stop kvetching, there is no help possible. All of those writers, that is to say, are in the judging business.

And as judges go, Malamud proved himself that year to be a mostly generous one. When we succeeded, he spent the session pointing out the story's excellences, savoring its jokes, admiring its chiming of style and theme. When we failed, however, he laid out in a sad, even tone, at whatever length he deemed necessary, what our stories lacked, and *why*. And that part could and did bring tears to a young writer's eyes, because the basic failure of the story turned out not to be wordy, vague sentences, or incoherent character, but that the writer hadn't grasped the themes (the questions, imperatives, desires) of his one and only life, had preferred to think himself the Prince of Great Neck instead of a schlemiel who trips on his own conflicted desires. Your real concerns, once you'd boiled out the illusions, could be alchemized into the stories' themes as well. Fail in self-knowledge, though, and you'd fuck up the fiction; and its monstrous, mismatched parts—now diagrammed by Malamud on the chalkboard for all to see—would show everyone that you hadn't had the courage to look clearly at yourself.

Know thyself—only an eighteen-year-old, or a genius, could be impressed with *that* advice. Besides, the reward for seeing yourself and so your story clearly was, strangely enough, more hard labor. It meant you could imagine the unremitting work by which you (maybe by writing about your characters) and then the characters in their fictional worlds could heal themselves and begin to act humanely to others.

Which I would do *why*? Well, because, dear child, if you're a mensch, then it's your mission impossible to heal the wounded *holiness* of life. I use

34

that slightly ridiculous word because one afternoon in the seminar Malamud said, with an uncharacteristically relaxed self-praise, "Bellow and I
are the writers who know that life is holy." And thus, I think, the talking
animals in his stories: such words sound less ridiculous coming from the
horse's mouth. I might have asked the horse: "Holy? But without God?"

For Malamud, God seemed mostly abscondus, though the Angel of
Death was certainly still around, had perhaps even been left in charge.
And along with death, God had left his little brother, guilt, like a black
fog over Little Neck. Malamud felt that the sting of guilt was precious,
it marked where you've failed a moral law that you should, even must,
obey. Must? I mean, if there's no God, why was obedience to the moral
law so ferociously important? Without God in the picture, morals are just
people's ideas of the good, and so nothing special. Why not go to therapy
or take a pill, and then have what *you* want, what the law denies you? If
God not only isn't around now, but never existed at all (in the Old, or even
in the reformed "life is holy version"), then the person who values moral-
ity and guilt so highly can seem like a fool, the sort of person who (like
Frank in *The Assistant*) will end up circumcising himself. Malamud knew
that, and much of the horseradish humor of his stories (and the pathos of
his life) comes from acknowledging that uncertainty, the wry humor of
an American Jew, a person still bound to his tradition, yet far from sure
anymore about its origin on Sinai.

Whether he was a holy fool, or just foolish, I knew soon into that first
year with Malamud that I wanted to have a room of my own, one just like
his, wanted to have God lock me in it, before He swallowed the key and
disappeared. Because for all the worry about Bern's judgment, or because
of it, for all the seriousness of the class, or because of it, writing was no
less a pleasure to me than before, though "pleasure" may not be quite the
right word, for the very idea of pleasure seems to me to involve someone
experiencing it. When I worked, *I* was often on the edge of disappearing.
("You get to a point in your career," Bern told us once, "when you're working, really concentrating, the radiator coughs, and you nearly have a heart
attack.") What Bern's moral imperatives offered me was a way to turn the
thing I *wanted* to do into the thing that I was kind of in a way *required* to
do. He helped me make the enterprise of writing *moral*, the sort of thing a
grown-up *should* do. And he gave me something more, as well: he played
the rabbi who had the authority to choose me for that work. Without that,

I would have ended up belonging to my father, to his mother and the abortionist. What he said in that line was always a little equivocal. After my first book came out, for example, he and I were walking in Manhattan, and he said, "You know, you're not really a writer until the second novel." That book came out two years after he had died, but I'm sure if he'd been there, he would have said, "You know . . . really . . . the third one." One is never a writer, perhaps, only almost about to become one. Still, my freshman year he provided a vision of a profession that was as menschlike as medicine, and a license for me to do it from the wonder-rabbi himself. I was ready, then, to go about the business of grievously disappointing my father.

I dropped Natural Sciences Five (the pre-med bio course) when the teaching assistant said, "If you go on like this, you'll be carrying a gun soon." I'd imagined replying, "You know who the first person I'll shoot will be." I didn't say it, though, because my failure wasn't the assistant's fault. I wanted out; this schlemiel had finally realized that he wanted to trip over his own feet. My father's voice on the phone when I told him about the end of biology, the end of my becoming a doctor, had in it a ferocious mixture of anxiety (how would I earn a living?) and anger at my betrayal of him, and his own powerlessness to stop it.

After that first year, I tried to keep in touch with Malamud. I was smart enough to know about valuable contacts, but, honest, it was more than that. When asked what he taught young writers at Black Mountain, the poet Charles Olson said, "Posture." I was studying how a writer carries himself, what he noticed in his daily rounds, how he talked about and to his friends. There was, I was sure, a secret to the business Malamud hadn't told me yet. (Actually, along the way, he did tell me the secret to being a writer, but, as in a Malamud story, it looked so *gemütlich*, so much like a shoebox, that I missed it. "Put some words down on the page," he said. "Then you can move them this way and that until you can go on.") During the years that I courted him, Malamud saw things I wrote for the *Harvard Crimson*, and he sent a review I'd done of Updike's *Couples* to the arts editor of the *Atlantic*, Robert Evett. This led, comically enough—Bob, I think, drank too much—to my being the movie reviewer of that magazine for a month or two. Later, Malamud sent Updike himself my sophomore thesis on *Of the Farm*. (Updike found it good, but thought my ideas about how his themes worked themselves out in the book a little more programmatic and neat than he'd felt the novel was. That, too, was a lesson—not everything need lock itself up as tightly as Malamud's own work did.) And after college I sent Bern my stories as I finished them. His responses were terse, but always usefully to the point. A teacher now myself, I know what a burden all that was to him, how truly kind he was to pay attention—all the more so as each student he'd praised in that freshman class, and probably in many classes at Bennington as well, also went on sending him stories, or came to him for advice, because as one of the most lavishly talented students from that freshman year said, "he was the closest thing I knew to a wise man." Malamud also arranged for me to go to Yaddo when I was all of twenty-two, and when it came time for me sign contracts for my first book, he arranged for me to meet his agent, Tim Seldes—who in grace and charm is a Fred Astaire of representatives (but that's a subject for another piece). In a way, Malamud had become Bern, and though we would always remain teacher and student (two roles with which we both felt all too comfortable), we also, to some extent anyway, had become friends.

My father (who nursed both a grudge toward Malamud and probably the fantasy that I would change my mind, even ten years out of college, and reenroll in Natural Sciences Five) wasn't pleased with any of Bern's generosity to me. By this time, though, I had a job teaching, could earn a living, so his concern, I felt, wasn't any more for my financial well-being but for feeding his own hungry ghosts. Still, we spoke almost every week— but, no, we didn't speak, not really; we avoided speaking, so we wouldn't say anything unforgivable, and would still be able to speak-but-not-speak more the next week.

Then, soon enough, it was clear that the weeks we could play this game were running out. In 1982, age sixty-nine, my father began a long, wasting death from lung cancer: Around then, I got the galleys of my first novel, and was disappointed that Bern wouldn't consider a blurb ("too many other requests would follow," he said, meaning too many interruptions, too many heart-attack-inducing knocks at the door to the room). With my father, though, things went better and, of course, much much worse. The bound galleys of the book, which was dedicated to him, arrived when he was still at the edge of lucidity. Though in a great deal of pain, he read the novel with care, and I can only hope the story helped him to be not there, not in his body for a while. He spoke fulsomely well of it. It was, after all, the kind of risky, difficult enterprise he'd taught me to value most.

Alas, by then the long struggle we'd been locked in for fifteen years or so had changed me, and not for the better. From long practice, I'd come to think that I couldn't let his words matter to me. Now, as in some fairy-tale curse, his praise fell under that same sullen edict. His words did and do matter, of course, yet somehow even today I can't reach the pleasure they should give me. It's one of the things outside the room where I've locked myself up.

Soon enough, my father grew thinner, weaker, and then from drugs and lack of oxygen, his mind went; the past overtook the present, and he thought we were in Egypt, building the Pyramids.

As for Bern, he wouldn't blurb my book, but he did eventually, with extraordinary generosity, offer me a kind of diploma. He and I would visit twice a year or so, sometimes in Cambridge, but mostly at his house in Vermont. On one of these visits, near the end of his too short life, he showed me a story he'd been working on. It was very good, I thought, yet not quite right; its meanings didn't ring clearly enough for a Malamud story. It needed, I had the temerity to say, a sentence. Two years before, Bern had had bypass surgery at Stanford, and a stroke had followed from that. Words came hard to him after that, against a resistance, a darkness and bafflement stronger than any repression, or any moral injunction to get things right. "Like what sentence?" he said. I tried to say what the sentence would do. That wasn't what he wanted. "What sentence?" I constructed it as best I could—after all, I'd studied his structures, his sentences for years. He changed a word. I changed one. And so on. Whose sentence was it? Whoever may have chosen the words, it was his really.

But later, he told Tim Seldes, "Jay wrote a sentence in this story." Then Tim told me Bern had added, "Try and guess which one."

Myself, I've looked at the story in the years that followed. I can't guess myself. This time, in a small way, I've disappeared into a story, just as I'd always wished.

And my ears are fine now, thanks for asking. Doctors, what do they know, they're no better, or worse, than fiction writers.

Mentors in General, Peter Taylor in Particular

John Casey

I'm going to try to be serious before Lola gets here. Actually that's not fair. In a lot of ways Lola is more serious than I am. Certainly more focused. Last week I thought she wanted me to be her mentor. Now I'm pretty sure I was flattering myself.

Mentor. The *American Heritage Dictionary*, the *OED*, and the other *OED—Online Etymology Dictionary*—all mention Mentor, the character in the *Odyssey* who's a friend of Odysseus and who guides Telemachus in his search for his father. Sometimes Athena disguises herself as Mentor and lends a hand. But all three dictionaries reach further back and suggest that a common noun came before Homer's naming a character. If you Google "mentor, etymology," you find either Indo-European root *men*, to think; or Sanskrit, *man-tar*, one who thinks; or, my favorite: "an agent noun of *mentos* which means intent, purpose, spirit, passion."

LOLA, the INTERLOCUTRIX: Hello, hello, sorry I'm late. I heard that last bit. Greek, Sanskrit. Come *on*. Less ivory tower. More here and now.

The *American Heritage Dictionary* adds: "The word has recently gained currency in the professional world, where it is thought a good idea to have a mentor, a wise and trusted counselor, guiding one's career, preferably in the upper reaches of the organization."

But it occurs to me that a mentor in the arts isn't quite the same thing as, for example, a mentor in the CIA, an organization with upper reaches and where career guidance is more practically crucial.

So I don't *need* a mentor?

Some writers do, some don't. But like that part of college life that is neither lecture notes nor wild oats, a mentor can give you a context for what you're learning, can suggest to you what more you're capable of—but, most of all, a mentor can level out the sine wave of arrogance / helplessness / arrogance / helplessness that is often the initial flight path of a writing career.

Hey, I'm not helpless. I'm not arrogant. I think I just need a muse.

A muse is trickier. A mentor, a decent mentor, won't trick you. When a muse is being helpful, a mentor steps aside. But when a muse is whimsical, a mentor can keep you from going into tailspin. In the Bhagavad Gita, Krishna, in human form, starts off as a mentor, gives advice to Arjuna. But then Arjuna asks Krishna to show what he's like as a god. Krishna shows him the energy of all creation. It's more than Arjuna can bear.

There you go with ancient myths again. Something less mythic.

Rudyard Kipling called his muse a "daemon."

Okay. Glad to hear you mention an actual writer of prose fiction. Get back to *mentors*. An example of a writer who's a mentor of a young writer like me.

Flaubert took Maupassant under his wing. I've heard that Flaubert set Maupassant a useful exercise. The two of them used to sit at an outdoor café, I think in the early evening. Lots of the same people passed by every day. Flaubert had Maupassant write one-sentence descriptions. The next day, if Flaubert picked out the right people, Maupassant got a gold star.

Anton Chekhov helped out Maxim Gorki. Read Chekhov's letters to him.

Samuel Beckett was James Joyce's private secretary. (I don't know what they talked about. I hope it was more artistically useful than the conversation Joyce had with Proust when someone got them together. They talked about their respective health problems.)

So Flaubert had Maupassant do exercises. So a mentor is just like a coach, like a personal trainer?

No. Not just. It's not just straight how-to. *Some* things can be taught straightforwardly. *Hunters of the Northern Ice* is a book about the Inuit around Cape Barrow, Alaska—before their life changed with the introduction of rifles, outboard motors, and snowmobiles. There is a description of an older hunter teaching a younger hunter how to find a seal breathing hole in the ice, and how to harpoon a seal. It is probably word-for-word what the older hunter was told years before. It is not a seminar. It is not a Socratic dialogue. It is not a dialogue at all. Look, this is how you can see a breathing hole is in use and not an old breathing hole. There are not enough seal-holes or seals for practice sessions.

Other skills can be taught with more margin of error, but there is still no question of what error is, in, say, canoeing. You either are upside right or not. You either get where you're going or not. The man who taught me how to catch fish—

No, no, no. Enough with wildlife. Get back to mentors. *Writing* mentors.

The first time I got stuck writing—really really stuck—I ran into a well-meaning friend. He said, "Writer's block? Hey, you don't hear plumbers going around talking about plumber's block."

So he's a mentor . . .

No. I went for a walk with Peter Taylor. My mentor. I moaned a bit. Peter nodded but began to talk about a small, remote farmhouse he'd bought. Peter bought houses. It was his vice. It was a less harmful vice, as he pointed out, than gambling, drinking, or running around with fast women. Peter described the house, nothing in it but a table and chair. He loved the view. "But the best thing," he said, "is that nobody sees me, nobody hears me, nobody knows what I'm doing. After a time, who knows how long, I'll go home and write in the basement."

That's it? That's not much.

Perhaps not. Or perhaps a drop of balm.

Tell one with more of a punch line.

Okay. Peter and I had a mutual friend, a very good poet. The poet wrote a short story. He gave a copy to Peter and me. Peter and I went for a walk. I said, "It's elegantly written." Peter said, "Oh yes, it's beautifully written." "I don't know what it is," I said, "but something's missing." "Yes," Peter said—"It lacks that low vaudeville cunning."

I guess I did ask for a joke.

It's not just a joke.

It sounds like a joke. You take it seriously?

I take it seriously *also*. Low vaudeville cunning. It should be on the list with Truth and Beauty.

So what does it mean?

It means, among other things, that you, the writer, should pounce.

Pounce?

Pounce. Have you watched a cat hunt? You know something is going on — the cat gets low and creeps. The tail twitches. The rear end wags and then, *pounce*.

Get back to what the writer does.

After you've pounced, you go back and make sure the reader has a chance to pounce. Making sure of *your* pounce is the cunning. Making sure the reader gets a chance to pounce is the vaudeville.

And the low?

That's the word that made it sound like a joke. It's also the word that makes you remember the whole thing . . . I had a housemate, a smart, earnest woman, an animal-rights activist, member of PETA. She acquired a beagle. She named it Bagel. I like most dogs. I tried with Bagel. I made a trail of dog biscuits on the lawn and lay down. Bagel got within five feet and then ran back under the porch. But every day Bagel got one dog biscuit closer. Finally he took one from my hand. Mary-Ann said, "Oh Baggie! You see? I told you he was a nice person just like you."

I said, "Jeez, Mary-Ann. Let's just get him to be a *dog*," and Mary-Ann said, "You'd be that way too, if you'd been abused by an Amish farmer."

I see. Key word "Amish." The key word is the "pounce." But can we leave the cats and dogs, the fish, the seals, for God's sake? What is it with you and animals? I don't want to write for *Animal Planet*.

It's not just animals. I wouldn't write fiction if I didn't read a lot. But I also wouldn't write fiction if I didn't spend time bumping into the physical world.

You're certainly easily distracted by it.

I'm easily interested.

Well, right now I'm interested in a practical matter. What about an agent? Isn't an agent a kind of mentor?

Sometimes. But the starting point of that relationship is contractual. It's a business deal, which may or may not include friendship or long-term wise counsel. At the bad end there are sad stories. I've heard that Nelson Algren got fleeced by an agent. At the good end there's Alice Munro and Ginger Barber, who used to be Munro's agent. A dozen years ago Alice Munro told Ginger that she, Alice, was all written out. Ginger did not cry out or keel over. She mulled it over in a sympathetic way. After a bit Ginger suggested that she and Alice spend some time together. Ginger's idea was that she and Alice could look over all of Alice's published work with an eye to putting together a book of selected stories.

By the way, *The Selected Stories of Alice Munro* is a great way to start if you're not already a fan. It begins with some of the lyric single-voiced stories that are like piano or violin sonatas. It moves on to the more complex dramatic stories that are like string quartets. I wish there were a tape recording of the discussion Ginger and Alice had. But, perhaps because they know each other so well, it wouldn't be clear to anyone else. I'm thinking of Wittgenstein's remark: If a lion could speak, we still wouldn't understand him.

I don't know how long the discussion went on, but not long afterward Alice Munro was writing new stories. *The Selected Stories* came out in 1996, dedicated to Ginger Barber, "my essential support and friend for twenty years." *Queenie* came out in 1999. *Hateship, Courtship, Friendship* in 2001. *Runaway* in 2004. *The View from Castle Rock* in 2007.

I don't think Ginger was sure it would turn out that way, but she had an intuitive sense that was better than shrewdness. It was wholehearted empathy. Here is the part of me that is closest to you.

That's nice. So how do I find an agent like her?

Here's what you can do to narrow your search. Find out what agents represent writers you admire, writers whom you resemble or hope to resemble.

I don't know that many agents—most writers know two: the one they fired and the one they hired. And most writers don't expect the Ginger Barber kindredness. They're happy to have a good agent. I have a very good agent. I'm very fond of my agent, I love our yearly lunches, but if they were the only meals I ate . . .

Then what about editors?

The main job of an agent is to find not just the publishing house that is good for your work but the editor in that house. That requires a thick Rolodex and a lot of intuition. It's a hard job—but it's selling to one person at a time. Editors have to think about selling to the public. Or to the reading public. Or at least to enough of the reading public to turn a profit.

Once upon a time it may have been that an editor could say to herself, "I love this book, and surely there are 37,000 people like me and all we need are five good reviews in national newspapers, and Bob's your uncle."

Ask an editor if this is the case now and hear him laugh. Or weep. And then he'll say, "If you're a writer, you don't want to know."

It could be that what he doesn't want you to know—leaving aside the input from the publicity department or even the sales staff—is that he's flying blind. He's in a business that doesn't have a business model. There's no brand. You don't hear "Ballantine Books Build Bodies Eight Ways." Each book is its own brand. It's an impossible business.

Editors are torn between loving your work and selling your work—trying to *guess* how to sell your work. Sometimes they're telling you to make changes that they think will get them to love your work more, and sometimes they're suggesting changes that they imagine will help it sell more. Sometimes they can't tell the difference. Sometimes *we* can't. It's a mess.

I'm sorry I asked.

And yet. And yet. My editor is one of the smartest people I know. And, unlike some, she really edits. Once we sat side by side at her desk and turned every page of a 500-page manuscript one page at a time.

Although, on the second day, somewhere around page 300 she tapped her finger on a sentence and said, "That line. Were you drunk?"

Was she right?

She has a good ear for bad notes. A line here, a line there—that's okay. When she cuts off a bigger hunk I go into shock. I wish she were more of a believer in cheering the troops on.

"The more we love our friends, the more we criticize them." Molière said that.

Wrong. Molière *wrote* that. Alceste *says* it. Molière is making fun of Alceste. Alceste is the title character in *The Misanthrope*. It is true that of all the title characters Molière makes fun of—the miser, the would-be gentleman, the affected woman, or Tartuffe, the pious hypocrite—Alceste is the one you can kind of admire. He's very smart. His fault is that when he sees a fault in someone else, he jumps on it. He's right, but he's wrong to be so fiercely right.

You mean he's someone who says things like, "That line. Were you drunk?"

Yeah.

Or someone who says things like, "Wrong! Molière *wrote* that. Alceste *says* it."

Oh. I'm sorry.

I hope so . . . So, when your smart editor is pulling your novel to pieces, do you argue? I'll bet you do—I'll bet you get up in her face.

No. No—I'm mute. I'm paralyzed. It's back to the lowest part of the sine wave: helplessness. Then I get depressed for months. Then I think of arguments. I have arguments with her in my mind. I get her in the witness box and cross-examine her. In my mind I'm a terror. "Isn't it true that when I showed you the third rewrite, you said, 'I don't like X. Get rid of her'? And yet here's the fourth rewrite and you're saying, 'I like X. I want more of her.'" But *arguments*, even if you win them, don't help. If someone, if *anyone* says, "It's not there yet. Make it better"—of course she's right, even if the suggestions aren't ones that make it better but just move things sideways. So you're on your own, and you're paralyzed, depressed, and muttering arguments to yourself that take up all your time and keep you from writing.

So what do you do?

Aside from violent exercise, there are two things that can help. One is to remember that when editors say, "Change X to Y," very often a slight variation of X is all they really want. I've had a couple of experiences of that kind—for example, an editor says, "Page three of your fifteen-page story is way too long." You puzzle over it, rewrite two sentences, change the font, and the editor says, "Good." It's actually frightening when that happens. But considering the whirl of manuscripts that is an editor's life, it's not surprising they suffer from amnesia.

And there's another possibility. The most cynical dictum to come out of the school of thought called Legal Realism is this: Law is what the judge had for breakfast.

So what's the second thing to do?

In the case of paralysis, depression, and fruitless anger, get a second opinion. I'm lucky to have a friend, a retired professor of comp. lit., whose taste and judgment I know. We pass books back and forth for each other to read. We've team-taught a couple of courses. We both went to Peter Taylor's memorial service.

Twenty years ago, Tony used to render opinions that were so compressed they were like particles of antimatter he'd found in a black hole. An example: I loved James Salter's *Light Years*. I gave it to Tony. Tony's review in its entirety: "Luminously depressing." After he retired, he began to write stories. His son grew up to be a very good fiction writer. Tony's opinions became less terminally adamantine.

He's read my current manuscript. Another 500-pager. He typed an eight-page, single-spaced commentary, chapter by chapter. He had some minor cautions, more notes of satisfactions, one major reservation ("The ending is both too elegiac and too hasty"). But he gets the point of all the characters, gets the coherence of the world they live in. What he *conveyed* was: I have considered the matter for all I'm worth and you should get back to work.

So, how do you people find each other? How did Alice Munro find Ginger Barber? Or Gorki find Chekhov? Maupassant find Flaubert?

Affinity.

And that means?

On the same wavelength. First you intuit affinity from a few clues. Then you confirm it by shared reading, shared reactions, shared storytelling. Some people think friendship and even love is based on shared taste. I don't think that's necessarily so. I know lots of people who have friends who share almost none of their tastes. And there are a few people who share tastes but who aren't friends. But it's nice if there's an overlap. It's nice if you can say we share a "final vocabulary." That's a phrase of the philosopher Richard Rorty.

So it was affinity that got Peter Taylor and you together?

Yes. But there was something else. An odd coincidence that started us on a thirty-year friendship. During my third year of law school I signed up for a writing course Peter Taylor was teaching. In those days you could take an extra course in the Arts and Sciences. I submitted a novel I'd written during summers when I should have been clerking at a law firm. Our first conference was very short. Peter said, "If I'd known from the beginning that this was a comic novel, I believe I would have laughed a good deal." And then—"You should write some short stories."

After a month or so of writing every weekend from Friday noon until Sunday evening, I turned in two stories. I showed up for our second conference in my Army uniform. I said, "I'm sorry. I forgot I had a Reserve meeting. I can't stay long."

Peter said, "This won't take long." I sat down. Peter said, "Don't be a lawyer. You're a writer." I was speechless. Peter said, "We must conspire about this later. As it happens I have to go out, too. Some friends are taking me to a party to watch the election returns."

"As it happens . . ."

As it happened, the party Peter's friends were taking him to was the huge party my parents gave every four years on election night—a mix of my father's old political friends and academic acquaintances and a variety of other people whom my mother and a brother of hers knew, and people these people knew. That sort of party. Peter, after a swirl through the crowd, found himself trading stories about Tennessee politics with an equally enthusiastic teller of stories about Massachusetts politics. The Massachusetts man's wife changed the subject long enough to find out that Peter was a writer, spending a semester teaching a fiction writing course at Harvard. "Can you teach writing?" she asked.

"Perhaps all one can do is encourage," Peter said, "Just this afternoon I told a young man, 'Don't be a lawyer, you're a writer.'"

"Yes," my mother said. It was indeed my mother, eager to join Peter in abstract loftiness. "If someone has a talent, he should pursue it no matter what."

As it happened. As it happened, I had finished my Army Reserve meeting, taken the MTA, and at that very moment was making my way through the room. Peter saw me first. He said, "There he is! That's the very young man . . ."

Every few years after that, either Peter would ask me or I would ask him if it really happened that way. Yes, all the details dovetailed.

So, forget affinity. It was just dumb luck. Without your Peter Taylor you'd be working at some white-shoe law firm.

Possibly. More likely government work. Some years later I told William Maxwell that story and several other less inadvertent instances of Peter's guidance. William Maxwell then sent me one of his habitually short notes—"You are fortunate. Few writers are as generous as Peter Taylor."

So it *was* dumb luck? You wrote a couple of good stories and you got a godfather. What are the odds? Like getting struck by lightning.

I'd written a pile of stories and a novel. But you're right, it was luck that I found Peter, that he was an encouraging teacher. He was a tutelary spirit.

Tutelary spirit. I had a great-aunt Ida who talked like that. Look—I just want a mentor who's been around the block, someone who looks out for me, someone who writes me recommendations, someone who finds me a job, someone who finds me a publisher. Is that too much to ask?

It's not asking too much; it's not asking enough. The part you want is the way it was with Roman senators and their clients, the way it still is with a lot of politics and business—"Okay, you're a smart kid. Maybe we can help each other out"—a quid pro quo. That's the relationship for people who read neo-Machiavellian how-to books that say things like, "Don't make friends, make allies."

Isn't that the real world? Maybe you're living in a dreamworld.

Maybe. Maybe. The editor of the first story I sold was William Maxwell. He was a wonderful writer as well as an editor. I didn't meet him face-to-face until he'd edited three stories. We did it by mail, except for the time he telephoned to ask me to read a paragraph out loud. He wanted to hear if a sentence in it needed a comma. When we finally did meet for lunch, we talked about Conrad. He'd considered Conrad in detail. After lunch he suggested an experiment in writing that he thought might lead me into a new cycle. He understood how cycles work, and his guess was that I was nearing the end of a cycle. He'd read seven stories and had bought three. This was disinterested advice, as he was about to retire. It was good advice, so carefully offered it was eventually irresistible.

Eventually?

Yes. It took a while to think it over. What I did right away was to reread a lot of Conrad in light of what he said. It's the by-the-way parts—

You really like the by-the-way parts—

Yup. The man who taught me how to catch fish—

You're going there no matter what—

—taught me the first parts in very narrow detail. He was like an Inuit seal hunter. I was living on a four-acre island not far from the mouth of Narragansett Bay. He said, "See those rocks out to the southwest? When the sun gets low, when the bottom part gets orange and when the top half of the tide is running, cast your plug out there." That worked. Next week he said, "See that one big rock to the nor'east? Get yourself some clamworms. Go out in your boat at sunset, top half of a dumping tide. Drop your anchor. Bait your hook. Put a cork on your line an arm's length up. Let your line out about a stone's throw."

I said, "Exactly how far is that?"

He said, "About as far as you can throw a stone."

First you're all Hindu myths. Now you're all quaint New England.

This instruction went on for a year. We caught striped bass, bluefish, flounder, fluke, tautog, squeteague—

I've got the picture.

No, you don't. Not yet. One evening just as it got dark, he showed up at the end of the dock in his boat. I said, "I'll get my fishing rod."

He said, "Nope. Just get in." We went out a ways, and he cut the motor. We drifted in the dark. He said, "Look down there."

What had happened was that the incoming tide had brought in whole banks of phosphorescent plankton. When something brushed them, they lit up. It was like looking at an X-ray, a living X-ray of everything that was going on down there in the salt water. Big fish made pale green outlines of themselves, then swam off and left dwindling trails of light. An eel made a quick bright wiggle, then vanished. Most likely hid under a ledge. There were other flashes and shimmerings. I couldn't tell what. That part was as if the Northern lights were in the sea. My point is by-the-way. Of course a mentor helps in practical matters, is an adviser. I'm not saying that isn't so. I'm just saying there is something more important. A mentor points out things he has seen that are wonderful in themselves. A mentor points these things out to someone he hopes will go on seeing them.

A Life in Books

Maud Casey

An American Romance[1]

It was one of those first date throwaway questions; really, I just wanted to hear him talk.

"What's it like to be a twin?" I asked the man who would eventually become, in real estate parlance, my joint tenant, and with whom I would raise two very strange cats.

"I don't know," he said. He paused to sip his beer. He understands the value of the dramatic pause. "I've always been a twin. What's it like *not* to be a twin?" He also understands the value of the conversational judo flip.

It was the first time I truly understood why it felt nearly impossible to answer the question I've been asked over the years: What's it like to be the child of writers? I don't know. I've always been the child of writers. What's it like *not* to be the child of writers?

But this is a meditation on influence, and while a conversational judo flip may be a surefire way of piquing the interest of the lady you're trying to woo, it remains a clever way of avoiding the question. It's the end of the story, not the beginning.

---

[1]   *An American Romance* by John Casey (Atheneum, 1977).

Double Lives[2]

He went home that night and read my father's novel based loosely (in TV docudrama terms, "inspired by true events") on the end of my parents' marriage.[3] Like the end of most marriages, theirs was no cakewalk.

The novel moves back and forth between a third-person point of view—the father—and a first-person point of view—the eldest daughter. Last time I checked, I was the eldest daughter.

"Fiction!" I hear my father calling across the pages of the book you're holding in your hands.[4] "It's *fiction*. You know how that works. You're a *writer*." My boyfriend isn't the only one who understands the value of the conversational judo flip.

"Talk about an open book," my boyfriend said. "You and your family give literal meaning to that phrase."

"*Fiction*," I protested. "It's *fiction*."

"With a little triangulation . . ." He smiled, raising an eyebrow. Did I mention the wicked smile? The raised eyebrow? "Between his books[5] and your books[6] and your sister's books[7] and your mother's books,[8] I can skip the whole getting-to-know-you part."

Graham Greene famously said that a writer must have a sliver of ice in his heart.

A whole family of writers with slivers of ice in their hearts? The family dinner table can get a little chilly.

But this is still not the beginning of the story. It's only the tip of the cardiac iceberg.

---

[2] *Double Lives* by Jane Barnes (Doubleday, 1981).

[3] *The Half Life of Happiness* by John Casey (Knopf, 1998).

[4] See "Mentors in General, Peter Taylor in Particular," his essay in this book.

[5] See also *Testimony and Demeanor* (Knopf, 1979); *Spartina* (Knopf, 1989).

[6] *The Shape of Things to Come* (William Morrow, 2001); *Drastic* (William Morrow, 2002); *Genealogy* (HarperPerennial, 2006).

[7] *Unholy Ghost* (William Morrow, 2001) and *An Uncertain Inheritance* (Harper-Collins, 2007), by Neil Caroy.

[8] See also I, *Krupskaya, My Life with Lenin* (Houghton Mifflin, 1974).

GENEALOGY[9]

What was it like *not* to be the child of writers?

I needed a point of comparison and I decided to interview my parents. My father responded to my query with a riveting two-page e-mail that read like a short story; my mother sat down for a gripping three-hour conversation that included forays into Keats's death in obscurity and the irony of another man dying with one of Keats's odes on his lips; a discussion of Kafka's story "The Hunger Artist"; and Mary Gordon's poem "Prayer for Those Whose Work Is Invisible," in which there is a line my mother is particularly fond of that calls us to pray for the people who paint the bottom of boats.

Still, though my parents' parents weren't writers—my paternal grandfather was a congressman from Massachusetts,[10] my maternal grandfather was in the CIA back in the day[11]—they were avid readers, as were both of my grandmothers, and they moved in the kind of glittering social circles that intersected with the literati. My father's e-mail included sentences such as "I met Irwin Shaw when my mother and I were in Rome when I was fourteen." And "Arthur Schlesinger, Jr. was a family friend." And "Uncle Drew worked for Bennett Cerf, head of Random House." And most fabulously, the mention of a book found among Uncle Drew's possessions when he died, inscribed by Noël Coward—"Drew, darling—that night in Antibes!"

John O'Hara was the second husband of my mother's Aunt Catherine, and the novelist Louis Auchincloss was a distant cousin of my maternal grandfather.

Still, even in e-mail (where there is no tone) there was a sweet, child-like innocence to my father's list of the books he first fell in love with:

---

[9] Ibid.

[10] See Joseph Casey in William Shannon's *The American Irish: A Political and Social Portrait* (University of Massachusetts Press, 1990).

[11] See Tracy Barnes in Evan Thomas's *The Very Best Men: Four Who Dared: The Early Years of the CIA* (Simon & Schuster, 1996), and "Through the CIA Darkly," an essay by Jane Barnes (winner of the Illinois Council Prize for nonfiction).

Howard Pyle's *Book of Pirates, Under Storm Canvas* by Armstrong Sperry or was it Sperry Armstrong? Probably *Captains Courageous* by Rudyard Kipling. A lot of Raphael Sabatini: *Captain Blood, The Return of Captain Blood. Moby Dick* in fourth grade because I had to do a paper on whaling. Emil Ludwig's biography of Bismarck about the same time. Why? Beats me. A lot of science fiction. *Anne of Green Gables* (the woman at the bookstore in Spring Valley didn't want to sell it to me because it was for girls. I persisted). Edgar Rice Burroughs—not the Tarzan books but the Mars books. Particularly *Thuvia, Maid of Mars*, tho' also John Carter, *Warlord of Mars.* Very early (I was four) my father used to *tell* us Sherlock Holmes stories—I remember one about Holmes getting a guy to confess by tickling his feet with a feather—of course the old man was making it up.

When did he want to be a writer? "Early. 10? 11? After finishing a page of a book, I used to write a sentence on a notepad and think, If they put that on that page, maybe no one could tell the difference."

My mother's response to a question about her early influences suggested an appealing rebelliousness: "Coover and his satiric inclinations. Updike. I got out of books the sense of a purposeful inner life and, more than that, the sense that an inner life went on below the surface of the everyday. It helped define me as a bohemian against the social dazzle of my parents." There's the story of when she was an aspiring writer as an undergraduate at Sarah Lawrence where she knew Gates Gill, the son of Brendan Gill, a staff writer at *The New Yorker.* One night Brendan Gill took her out to dinner and she was so nervous she went to the bathroom six times before the meal came.[12] "With *Krupskaya*," she said, referring to her first novel, "the hum in my head was Lytton Strachey." And "I remember reading that James Baldwin said a writer is someone who couldn't do anything else."

I don't remember the moment I thought: *I want to be a writer.* I've never had a swift answer to that dinner party question: when did you know?

---

[12] See Jane Barnes's essay, "An Affair to Forget," *Mirabella* (December–January 2000).

True, I've never been very good at dinner parties. Still, even in the private cave of my mind, I have trouble answering the question. What I remember is the moment at about age ten, well, okay, eighteen, when I realized, with some shock, that I wasn't going to grow up to *be* my parents. The hum in my head for years was *them*. It was the story of their lives as writers.

TESTIMONY AND DEMEANOR[13]

I was born with a reading list I'll never finish. I was a nervous kid. A worried kid. The kid with the upset stomach who is embarrassed when her gregarious father sang in public or flirted with the waitress. Where my mother wanted to define herself as a bohemian against the social dazzle of her parents, I yearned for invisibility. I yearned for propriety and decorum. I didn't want anyone's messy inner life to spill out onto the lawn. Nothing like wild parents to turn a kid into a prude. Shouldn't we children be in bed by now? I wondered primly, as the grapefruit-selling hippie poets splashed in the bathtub late into the night and some novelist gave a whiskey-soaked soliloquy on top of the dining room table.

In Thomas Lux's poem "The Voice You Hear When You Read Silently," he describes that voice as a combination of the author's words and "your voice/caught in the dark cathedral/of your skull." Your private voice, in other words, amplified by a kind of communion with the words on a page. But for me—nervous, worried, neurotic child—books were trammeled territory. My parents had always been there before. There was a kind of invisible marginalia, the imprint of their reading minds. When I read silently, it was a trifecta of voices: me, the author, and my parents. In large part this came from my parents' generosity in the realm of passing books on—they gave me countless books and often read aloud to me (I had the luxurious pleasure, for example, of having much of Jane Austen read aloud to me). There was, though, a feeling of chasing my parents' shadows through books. There they were, flitting up ahead on the next page. And when I read the books they had written, it was as though I had walked into the strip club of their imaginations.

---

[13] Ibid.

It took going to an MFA program in Tucson, Arizona, land of saguaro cactus, where black widows and scorpions made themselves at home in the desert dust-ridden corners of my Old Barrio apartment, to find a book not on my parents' shelves.

Even then, there was another hoop to jump through on the way to that book. My first workshop was taught by a writer I idolized. My adoration was of the youthful, big, beating heart worn dangerously on the sleeve variety. Within a week, she was dangling my stories by their corner as if they were soiled toilet paper and asking, "How should we discuss this posturing scrabble?" Within a month, she began class with, "I'd like to go around the room and have everyone choose a word that should never be used in fiction. Mine is *rigor mortis*." The first sentence of my story included *rigor mortis* (wasn't *rigor mortis* two words?). I wept in the bathroom.

After class one day a fellow student approached me. He was on his way to the Arizona Inn, where the anointed went for postmortem cocktails. "Didn't your father win the National Book Award?" More weeping in the bathroom. I got into my long-bed pickup truck (I was vigilant about escaping the East Coast), arms weary from parallel parking without power steering, and drove into the saguaro-filled landscape. There were days when the desert looked mysterious and beautiful, but that day it looked like Mars, frightening and desolate. And yet I stayed. I'm not sure why. It was one of those nondecisions, which later reveals itself to have been a good nonmove.

The next semester, my former idol co-won a fellowship with my father, a genius grant of sorts, requiring the recipients to give up teaching for five years in order to devote themselves entirely to their writing. My former idol left town and I took a workshop with a kinder, gentler teacher who, one day after workshop, suggested I read a book by Barbara Comyns called *Sisters by a River*. "Who?" I asked. I was confounded by the idea of an author whose books I'd never seen on my parents' bookshelves. "From what I've read of your work, I suspect you'll really like her," said this kind, gentle teacher. That someone suspected something, anything, of me based on my writing was even more of a thrill.

Sisters by a River begins: "It was in the middle of a snowstorm I was born. . . . Mammy rather liked having babies, it was one of the few times she was important and had a fuss made of her but Granny used to interfeer [sic] a lot, and an old woman called Mrs. Basher who lived in a round cottage used to come too, but she didn't when I was born because of the snow." From the start, it is rollicking chaos, but the wild ride is carefully crafted in the pitch-perfect loopy language of an imaginative young girl caught in the swirl of a riotous family.

Comyns hadn't intended to publish this novel, her first. On the eve of World War II, in order to get out of London before it was bombed, she took a job as a housekeeper in a Hertfordshire manor house. The owner of the house was often away, and Comyns began to write the story of her childhood as a series of odd vignettes. There was plenty of material. She was born in 1909, one of six children, in Bidford-on-Avon, Warwickshire, to the managing director of a chemical plant, a man with violent tendencies, and a much younger woman who suddenly went deaf at the age of twenty-five and who owned a pet monkey. They lived in a rambling, ramshackle house on the banks of the Avon where, aside from the governesses who often fled, the children were left to their own devices. A friend of Comyns eventually discovered the vignettes in a trunk filled with old photographs and encouraged her to send them out, leading to their original serial publication by Lilliput Press under the title "The Novel Nobody Would Publish." *Sisters by a River* was published in its entirety in 1947.

Comyns went on to publish nine other novels and a memoir, but it was *Sisters by a River* that most captivated me, a young, yearning, unpublished writer, with its eccentric cast of characters, its strikingly original phrasing. It was the first book I read where the voice I heard inside my head was a fusion of my own and the author's words. Just me and Comyns, no parents.

There's a section in it called "Gather your hats while you may," just after the narrator's mother jumps out a window to escape the brutality of her father, and immediately following a scene in which the narrator's sister mistakes another sister stricken with rheumatic fever for a ghost and pushes her down the stairs. The narrator lies in bed with yet another sister and, suddenly, the sky starts to rain hats of all shapes and sizes and colors. Comyns once remarked to Ursula Holden, another not-acclaimed-enough British woman novelist, "I think we lose a lot when we grow up." Comyns's child narrators exist in a world separate from the catastrophe of adulthood, attuned to the magic in inanimate objects, a magic that is invisible to the inevitable blind spot in the grown-up eye. Something opened inside me when I read Comyns that first time. A space was cleared for childlike wonderment. There it was, akin to my father's exuberance, my mother's rebelliousness. The hum in my head was Barbara Comyns.

Oh Dad, Poor Dad, Mama's Put You in Her Novel and I'm Feeling So Sad[14]

But Comyns comes later in the story; I still haven't reached the beginning.

My father is a pipe smoker. Watching him choose the right pipe, which seems to involve a complicated and mysterious alignment of the moon, the stars, and the rings of Saturn, watching him run a pipe cleaner through it, tamp the tobacco with the corner of a matchbook, and, finally, light it is one of my most vivid childhood memories. The ritual choosing of the pipe has, over the years, been made more and more complicated by the hundreds of pipes he's amassed. Even when I was a kid he had a legion of them lined up along the windowsill of the bay window in his study. From the backyard, where the neighborhood kids and I played—*whatever you do, do not disturb your father when he's working*—we could see the pipes lined up like chorus girls waiting for the music to begin. Inevitably (I mean, what do you expect if you tell a kid not to make noise under any circumstances and, whatever you do, don't make it *right there*?), one of us shouted right outside the bay window, and my father would come roaring out, wearing earphones the size of an air traffic controller's and a tattered bathrobe.

"Do you know what Mr. Casey does?" a neighborhood mother asked her son, the one unfortunate enough to have the most distinctive shout, after she received the call from Mr. Casey.

"Yeah," her son said. "He makes pipes."

What *was* he doing in there? From where we crouched in the bushes, writing looked a lot like playing solitaire in a ratty bathrobe. It looked a lot like staring out the window. It looked like making pipes.

In order for my mother to make her pipes, she too had to beat back the family noise, find a room where no one else was, barricade herself inside, and perform something that looked a lot like chewing gum (a habit that had replaced cigarettes) and staring out the window.

What was *she* doing in there?

In his essay "My Father's Suitcase," from his 2006 Nobel Lecture, the Turkish novelist Orhan Pamuk writes: "When I speak of writing, the image

---

[14] See Nell Casey's essay of the same title in *Elle* (April 1996).

that comes first to my mind is not a novel . . . it is the person who shuts himself up in a room, sits down at a table, and, alone, turns inward." Here, finally, is the beginning of the meditation on influence, the beginning of the story.

There is so much my parents gave me that made writing possible: all those books; an understanding of the value of art and the fresh beauty of idiosyncratic eccentricity; the sense that I didn't need to run away to join the circus because they were the circus. But the most profound gift, the most essential inheritance, oddly, is a restless discontent. The sort of restless discontent that leads one to the solitary turning inward required to write. (Maybe this is what Greene meant by that sliver of ice?) It causes you to suspect that the world in front of you isn't all there is, and so you beat back the very family you've worked so hard to gather around you precisely to stave off loneliness. You voluntarily seek out the sometimes terrifying deep-space silence of solitude, and, on a good day, you transcend the world in front of you to find the invisible world shimmering behind it.

When I find myself still in my pajamas on the days I'm not performing that bizarre alchemy otherwise known as teaching writing, when I find myself chewing on a pen and staring out the window and defending my little cave of silence in a world of noise, when I find myself turning away from my beloved joint tenant and our strange cats and calling it writing, calling it *work,* I have my parents to thank for showing me that this seeming madness is part of the deal. This, they showed me, is how you create the conditions under which you might catch a glimpse.

And, if I'm lucky, there is a flicker, and then suddenly I'm no longer chewing my pen and staring out the window because there is no window. There's only that shimmering invisible world. It's delicate and fleeting, and like all things fragile and wondrous, it's not something you should talk too much about because it might disappear altogether, and because you start sounding like an asshole. That I can write that sentence and know that my parents know exactly what I'm talking about is part of what it means to be the child of writers.

In that interview with my mother, she described writing as "inchoate reaching in heartfelt darkness." That I know exactly what she is talking about is also what it means to be the child of writers.

Thanks a lot, guys.

Seriously, thanks a lot.

ANNIE DILLARD AND THE WRITING LIFE

Alexander Chee

I

Dear Annie Dillard,

My name is Alexander Chee, and I'm a senior English major. I've taken Fiction 1 with Phyllis Rose and Advanced Fiction with Kit Reed, and last summer, I studied with Mary Robison and Toby Olson at the Bennington Writers Workshop. The stories here are from a creative writing thesis I'm currently writing with Professor Bill Stowe as my adviser. But the real reason I'm applying to this class is that whenever I tell people I go to Wesleyan, they ask me if I've studied with you, and I'd like to have something better to say than no.

Thanks for your time and consideration,
Alexander Chee

In 1989, this was the letter I sent with my application to Annie Dillard's Literary Nonfiction class at Wesleyan University. I was a last-semester senior, an English major who had failed at something else—being a studio art major—and an English major by default.

As I waited for what I was sure was going to be rejection, I went to the mall to shop for Christmas presents and walked through bookstores full of copies of the Annie Dillard boxed edition—*Pilgrim at Tinker Creek, American Childhood, Holy the Firm*—and the *Best American Essays of 1988*, edited, yes, by Annie Dillard. I walked around them as if they were her somehow and not her books, and left empty handed.

I didn't buy them because if she rejected me, they would be unbearable to own.

When I got into the class, in the first class meeting she told us not to read her work while we were her students. Some people looked guilty when she said this. I felt guilty, too, for not having read her at all.

I'm going to have a big influence on you as it is, she said. You're going to want to please me enough just for being your teacher. So I don't want you trying to imitate me. I don't want you to write like me. And she paused here. I want you to write like *you*.

I didn't know her work, I just knew it had made her famous. This felt shallow, but I was there because my father had always said, Whatever it is you want to do, find the person who does it best, and then see if they will teach you.

I'd already gone through everyone else at Wesleyan. She was next on my list.

I can still hear her say it. *Put all your deaths, accidents, and diseases up front, at the beginning. Where possible. Where possible* was often her rejoinder.

The accident is that in the spring of my sophomore year, I fell asleep in the drawing class of the chair of the Art Department and woke to her firm grip on my shoulder.

My professor was an elegant, imperious woman with a formal but warm manner.

Mr. Chee, she said, tugging me up. I think you should do this at home.

I felt a wet spot on my cheek and the paper beneath it. I quickly packed my materials and left.

Before that, she had loved my work and often praised it to the class. Afterward, I could do nothing right. She began marking assignments as missing that she'd already passed back to me, as if she were erasing even the memory of having admired my work. I left them in her mailbox with her clearly written comments, to prove my case, but it didn't matter—a grade of B− from her put me below the average needed for the major. I was shut out.

I spent the summer before my junior year wondering what to do, which in this case meant becoming a vegan vegetarian, cycling twenty miles a day, working for my mother as the night manager of a seafood restaurant we owned, and getting my weight down to a hundred forty-five pounds from a one hundred sixty-five. I turned into a brown line drawing, eating strawberry fruit Popsicles while I rang up lobsters and fries for tourists. And then in the last days of August, a school friend who lived in the next town over called me at home.

Do you have a typewriter? he asked.

Yes, I said.

Can I borrow it? he asked. I need to type up this story for Phyllis Rose's class, to apply. Can I come by and get it this afternoon?

Sure, I said.

After I hung up the phone, I wrote a story on that typewriter in the four hours before he arrived that I can still remember, partly for how it came out as I now know very few stories do: quickly and with confidence. While in high school, I'd won a poetry prize from a national poetry foundation, and had a play from a "gifted and talented" workshop read by real actors at a real stage company, but was an amnesiac about my accomplishments, and my basic sense of my own worthlessness was unmoved. This first short story satisfied in me the idea that I could write in a way that these other things did not.

I made something with some pieces of my life, rearranged into something else, like an exercise from that drawing class, combining three life studies into a single fictional tableau. I made a story about a boy who spends the summer riding a bicycle (me), who gets hit by a car and goes into a coma, where he dreams constantly of his accident until he wakes (this happened to my dad, but also, the fateful art class). When he wakes, he is visited by a priest who wants to make sure he doesn't lose his faith (me with my pastor, after my father's death).

Lorrie Moore calls the feeling I felt that day "the consolations of the mask," where you make a place that doesn't exist in your own life for the life your life has no room for, the exiles of your memory. But I didn't know this then.

All I could tell in that moment was that I had finally made an impression on myself. And whatever it was that I did when writing a story, I wanted to do it again.

My friend arrived. I closed the typewriter case and handed it over. I didn't tell him what I'd done. Somehow I couldn't tell anyone I was doing this. Instead, I went to the post office after he left, a little guilty, feeling like I was doing something illicit, and sent the story.

I saw your name on the list, my friend said, weeks later, back at school, with something like hurt in his voice. Congratulations.

When I looked, I saw he wasn't on the list. I felt like I'd taken something out of the typewriter before I gave it to him, and wanted to apologize.

I didn't think I'd gotten in because of what I'd written.

I went on to get an A in that class, which I didn't understand, not even when a classmate announced he'd gotten a B. I didn't feel like I knew what I was doing. I did, though, apply and get into Kit Reed's advanced fiction class for the next semester—twenty pages of fiction every other week—and won from her another of these mysterious A's. I applied to and was accepted at the Bennington Writers' Conference, studied with Mary Robison and Toby Olson and met Jane Smiley's editor at Knopf, who offered to read a story of mine and then returned it with a note that said if I could turn it into a novella, she'd buy it.

I had no idea what a novella was or how to write one, and the excitement I felt as I read her note turned to confusion and then sadness.

Great and enviable things were happening for me. Another student in this situation would have gotten Mary Robison or Kit Reed to help him understand what a novella was so he could write it, and would have been published at age twenty-one, but that wasn't me. I thought I could choose a destiny. I wanted Jane Smiley's editor saying, *Go be a visual artist and forget about this writing thing, kid.* I was someone who didn't know how to find the path he was on, the one under his feet.

This, it seems to me, is why we have teachers.

II

In my clearest memory of her, it's spring, and she is walking toward me, smiling, her lipstick looking neatly cut around her smile. I never ask her why she's smiling—for all I know, she's laughing at me as I stand smoking in front of the building where we'll have class. She's Annie Dillard, and I am her writing student, a twenty-one-year-old cliché—black clothes, deliberately mussed hair, cigarettes, dark pop music on my Walkman. I'm pretty sure she thinks I'm funny. She walks to class because she lives a few blocks from our classroom building in a beautiful house with her husband and her daughter, and each time I pass it on campus, I feel, like a pulse through the air, the idea of her there. Years later, when she no longer lives there, and I am teaching there, I feel the lack of it.

The dark green trees behind her on the Wesleyan campus sharpen her outline. She is dressed in pale colors, pearls at her neck and ears. She's tall, athletic, vigorous. Her skin glows. She holds out her hand.

Chee, she says. Give me a drag off that.

She calls us all by our last names.

She lets the smoke curl out a little and then exhales brusquely. Thanks, she says, and hands it back, and then she smiles again and walks inside.

Lipstick crowns the yellow Marlboro Red filter.

I soon know this means there's five minutes until class starts. As I stub the cigarette out, I think of the people who'd save the filters. At least one of them. I feel virtuous as I kick it into the gutter.

In that first class, she wore the pearls and a tab collar peeped over her sweater, but she looked as if she would punch you if you didn't behave. She walked with a cowgirl's stride into the classroom, and from her bag withdrew her legal pad covered in notes, a thermos of coffee, and a bag of Brach's singly wrapped caramels, and then sat down. She undid the top of the thermos with a swift twist, poured coffee into the cup that was also the thermos top, and sipped at it as she gave us a big smile and looked around the room.

Hi, she said, sort of *through* the smile.

One hundred and thirty of you applied, and I took thirteen of you, Annie announced.

A shadowy crowd of the faceless rejected formed around us briefly. A feeling of terror at the near miss came and then passed.

No visitors, she said. Under no conditions. I don't care who it is.

The class had a rhythm to it dictated by how she had quit smoking to please her new husband. We were long distance, she told me, at one of our longer smoke breaks. We met at a conference. He didn't know what a smoker I was until we shacked up. She laughed at this, as at a prank.

At the beginning of class she would unpack the long thin thermos of coffee and the bag of Brach's singly wrapped caramels—the ones with the white centers. She would set her legal pad down, covered in notes, and pour the coffee, which she would drink as she unwrapped the caramels and ate them. A small pile of plastic wrappers grew by her left hand on the desk. The wrappers would flutter a little as she whipped the pages of her legal pad back and forth, and spoke in epigrams about writing that often led to short lectures but were sometimes lists: Don't ever use the word "soul," if possible. Never quote dialogue you can summarize. Avoid describing crowd scenes but especially party scenes.

She began almost drowsily, but soon went at a pell-mell pace. Not frantic, but operatic. Then she might pause, check her notes in a brief silence, and launch in another direction, as we finished making our notes and the sound of our writing died down.

Each week we had to turn in a seven-page triple-spaced draft in response to that week's assignment.

Triple-spaced? we asked in the first class, unsure, as this had never been asked of us.

I need the room to scribble notes in between your sentences, she said.

The silence in the room was the sound of our minds turning this over. Surely there wouldn't be that much to say?

But she was already on her feet at the chalkboard, writing out a directory of copyediting marks. *Stet is Latin and means let it stand . . . When I draw a line through something and it comes up with this little pigtail on it, that means get rid of it.*

There was that much to say. Each week we turned in our assignments on a Tuesday, and by Thursday we had them back again, the space between the triple-spaced lines and also the margins filled with her penciled notes. *Sometimes you write amazing sentences,* she wrote to me, *and sometimes it's amazing you can write a sentence.* This had arrows drawn that pointed toward the amazing sentence and the disappointing one. Getting your pages back from her was like getting to the dance floor and seeing your favorite black shirt under the nightclub's blacklight, all the hair and dust that was always there but invisible to you now visible.

In her class, I learned that while I had spoken English all my life, there was actually very little I knew about it. English was born from Low German, a language that was good for categorization, had filled itself in with words from Latin and Anglo-Saxon, and was now in the process of eating things from Asian languages. Latinates were polysyllabic, and Anglo-Saxon words were short, with perhaps two syllables at best. A good writer made use of both to vary sentence rhythms.

Very quickly, she identified what she called "bizarre grammatical structures" inside my writing. From the things Annie circled in my drafts, it was clear one answer to my problem really was, in a sense, Maine. From my mom's family, I'd gotten the gift for the telling detail—*Your Uncle Charles is so cheap he wouldn't buy himself two hamburgers if he was hungry*—but also a voice cluttered by the passive voice in common use in that part of the world—*I was writing to ask if you were interested*—a way of speaking that blunted all aggression, all direct inquiry, and certainly, all description—the degraded syntax of the Scottish settlers forced to Maine by their English lords, using indirect speech as they went and then after they stayed. And then there was the museum of clichés in my unconscious.

I felt like a child from a lost colony of Scotland who'd taught himself English by watching Gene Kelly films.

The passive voice in particular was a crisis. "Was" only told you that something existed—this was not enough. And on this topic, I remember one of her fugues almost exactly:

You want vivid writing. How do we get vivid writing? Verbs, first. Precise verbs. All of the action on the page, everything that happens, happens in the verbs. The passive voice needs gerunds to make anything happen. But too many gerunds together on the page makes for tinnitus: Running, sitting, speaking, laughing, inginginginging. No. Don't do it. The verbs tell a reader whether something happened once or continually, what is in motion, what is at rest. Gerunds are lazy, you don't have to make a decision and soon, everything is happening at the same time, pell-mell, chaos. *Don't do that.* Also, bad verb choices mean adverbs. More often than not, you don't need them. Did he run quickly or did he sprint? Did he walk slowly or did he stroll or saunter?

The chaos by now was with her notebook and the wrappers, the storm on the desk, a crescendo fueled by the sugar and caffeine. I remember in this case a pause, her looking off into the middle distance, and then back at her notebook as she said, I mean, just what *exactly* is going on inside your piece?

If fiction provided the consolations of the mask, nonfiction provided, per Annie's idea of it, the knowledge that what was underneath the mask, your own individual sensibility, *that* was irreplaceable and potentially of value. The literary essay, as she saw it, was a moral exercise that involved direct engagement with the unknown, whether it was a foreign civilization or your mind, and what mattered in this was you.

You are the only one of you, she said of it. Your unique perspective, at this time, in our age, whether it's on Tunis or the trees outside your window, is what matters. Don't worry about being original, she said dismissively. Yes, everything's been written, but also, the thing you want to write, before you wrote it, was impossible to write. Otherwise it would already exist. You writing it makes it possible.

Narrative writing sets down details in an order that evokes the writer's experience for the reader, she announced. This seemed obvious but also radical. She spoke often of "the job." If you're doing your job, the writer feels what you felt. You don't have to tell the reader how to feel. No one likes to be told how to feel about something. And if you doubt that, just go ahead. Try and tell someone how to feel.

We were to avoid emotional language. The line goes gray when you do that, she said. Don't tell the reader that someone was happy or sad. When you do that, the reader has nothing to see. She isn't angry, Annie said. She throws his clothes out the window. Be *specific*.

In the cutting and cutting and the *move this here, put this at the beginning, this belongs on page 6*, I learned that the first three pages of a draft are usually where you clear your throat, that most times, the place your draft begins is around page 4. That if the beginning isn't there sometimes it's at the end, that you've spent the whole time getting to your beginning, and that if you switch the first and last pages you might have a better result than if you leave them where they were.

One afternoon, at her direction, we brought in our pages, scissors, and tape, and several drafts of an essay, one that we'd struggled with over many versions.

Now cut out only the best sentences, she said. And tape them on a blank page. And then when you have that, write in around them, she said. Fill in what's missing and make it reach for the best of what you've written thus far.

I watched as the sentences that didn't matter fell away.

You could think that your voice as a writer would just emerge naturally, all on its own, with no help whatsoever, but you'd be wrong. What I saw on the page was that the voice is in fact trapped, nervous, lazy. Even, and in my case most especially, amnesiac. And that it had to be cut free.

After the lecture on verbs, we counted the verbs on the page, circled them, tallied the count for each page to the side, and averaged them. Can you increase the average number of verbs per page? she asked. I got this exercise from Samuel Johnson, she told us, who believed in a lively page, and used to count his verbs. Now look at them. Have you used the right verbs? Is that the precise verb for that precise thing? Remember that adverbs are a sign that you've used the wrong verb. Verbs control when something is happening in the mind of the reader. Think carefully—when did this happen in relation to this? And is that how you've described it?

I stared, comprehendingly, at the circles on my page, and the bad choices surrounding them and inside them.

You can invent the details that don't matter, she said. At the edges. You cannot invent the details that matter.

I remember clearly, in the details that matter to this, going to the campus center on the morning before one class in the middle of the spring, to pick up my manuscript for that week. We turned them in on a Tuesday, and she returned them to us on Wednesday, by campus mail, so we could have them in time for Thursday's class. This particular essay I'd written with more intensity and passion than anything I'd tried to do for the class thus far. I felt I finally understood what I was doing—how I could make choices that made the work better or worse, line by line. After over a year of feeling lost, this feeling was like when your foot finds the ground in the dark water. Here, you think. Here I can push.

I opened the envelope. Inside was the manuscript, tattooed by many, many sentences in the space between, many more than usual. I read them all carefully, turning the pages around to follow the writing to the back page, where I found, at the end, this postscript: *I was up all night thinking about this.*

The thought that I'd kept her up all night with something I wrote, that it mattered enough, held my attention. Okay, I remember telling myself, if you can keep her up all night with something you wrote, you might actually be able to do this.

I resented the idea of being talented. I couldn't respect it—in my experience, no one else did. Being called talented at school had only made me a target for resentment. I wanted to work. Work, I could honor.

Talent isn't enough, she had told us. Writing is work. Anyone can do this, anyone can learn to do this. It's not rocket science, it's habits of mind and habits of work. I started with people much more talented than me, she said, and they're dead or in jail or not writing. The difference between myself and them is that I'm writing.

Talent could give you nothing. Without work, talent is only talent, promise, not product. I wanted to learn how to go from being the accident at the beginning to a writer, and I learned that from her.

III

By the time I was done studying with Annie, I wanted to be her.

I wanted a boxed set of my books from HarperCollins, a handsome professor husband, a daughter, a house the college would provide, teaching just one class a year and writing during the rest of the year. I even wanted the beat-up Saab and the houses on Cape Cod. From where I stood, which was in her house on campus during a barbecue at the end of the semester, it looked like the best possible life a writer could have. I was a senior, aware that graduation meant the annihilation of my entire sense of life and reality. Here, as I balanced a paper plate stained by the burger I'd just eaten, here was a clear goal.

I had given up on vegetarianism, it should be said.

If I've done my job, she said in the last class, you won't be happy with anything you write for the next ten years. It's not because you won't be writing well, but because I've raised your standards for yourself. Don't compare yourselves to each other. Compare yourself to Colette, or Henry James, or Edith Wharton. Compare yourselves to the classics. Shoot there.

She paused here. This was another of her fugue states. And then she smiled. We all knew she was right.

Go up to the place in the bookstore where your books will go, she said. Walk right up and find your place on the shelf. Put your finger there, and then go every time.

In class, the idea seemed ridiculous. But at some point after the class ended, I did it. I walked up to the shelf. Chabon, Cheever. I put my finger between them and made a space. Soon, I did it every time I went to a bookstore.

As Thoreau, someone she admires very much, once wrote: "In the long run, we only ever hit what we aim at." She was pointing us there.

THE SNOW GLOBE

Jonathan Safran Foer

I

I was sixteen when I first met the poet Yehuda Amichai. It was the summer after my junior year of high school. I was still the star of the film of my life, then, and a soundtrack followed me wherever I went. If I'd met Amichai at another moment—even a year earlier, when I was too little formed to be so radically changed; or a year later, when I was already well into my solidification—it's unlikely that I'd be writing about him now. Or writing at all.

I was traveling across Israel that summer, on a program intended to foster a generation of young Jewish leaders. We saw sights, smoked a fair amount of pot, played a fair amount of the Jewish version of basketball (characterized by a lot of arguing over esoteric rules), and endeavored to couple.

In the course of the summer, we met with an eclectic cast of Israeli figures: politicians, artists, activists, archeologists, soldiers, kibbutzniks, and theologians. Our summer's final meeting was with Amichai. It's hard to imagine why he agreed to spend time with us. Perhaps the fellowship was paying him. Perhaps it was a personal debt he owed to one of the organizers. Perhaps he actually bought into the premise of the thing, and genuinely believed—as we never could, thank God—that we were Future Jewish Leaders, that his words might redirect us, if only by a few thousandths of a degree, toward some version of Jewish Leadership that he found palatable or even inspiring.

I had never heard of Amichai before that day, and by that point in August had had my fill of imparted wisdom. We were herded into a small, humid classroom: a grid of plastic seats with metal legs and wood veneer, chipboard desks for righties. I was sitting beside a young woman, R, with whom I'd been frustratingly trying to mate all summer. I don't know to what extent that frustration—that life-affirming, joy-denying, self-making-and-destroying frustration—influenced Amichai's impact on me, but I doubt that afternoon would have been so important to me if I'd entered the room contented.

I've kept exactly one diary in my life, and that only because it was one of the conditions of the Israel program. The diary began on July 6 with these words: "I am on a plane heading for Israel. I am sitting next to R. She is beautiful and extremely amiable."

Four days later, on July 10, I wrote: "Last night, R and I talked together on a hill overlooking the Old City. It became clear after a short period of time that we had a lot, in fact almost everything, in common. She is fantastic. I feel 100% comfortable talking to her about almost everything, from our families to music to God. I sincerely hope that our friendship doesn't end with the summer."

On July 14, eight days after meeting her, I wrote: "R had a minor asthma attack today. We sat next to each other on the bus and I asked her if she didn't, hypothetically, have a boyfriend, would we be lovers? She thought so, as did I. I won't pursue it. Maybe I should get my head shaved as some sort of metaphor for this relationship."

The afternoon of July 29, shortly before meeting Amichai, I came back to the dorms and opened my journal to write in it. I found the following: "Dear Jonathan, Don't worry, I didn't read your journal. I am sixteen going on seventeen. I hear you on the stairs and I can't write any more."

What does it mean to tell someone you haven't read his journal? That you were tempted to read it, but chose not to? That the thought never crossed your mind, but because journals are so potentially nuclear, you want to set his mind at ease? That in fact you read it, of course you did, but by saying you didn't, you and he can continue with a charade of mutual ignorance?

She hadn't read my journal. I was in love with her precisely because she was the kind of person who would not read a journal whose pages were sure to be filled with statements of love for her. Which meant I was never able to state that love to her, because I couldn't do it in life.

An hour after walking out of that meeting with Amichai, I could remember very little of what he said. Ten years later, I can remember—or feel that I can remember—virtually every word. Impressions usually work in the other direction—they diminish with time. Memory always seems to. Nietzsche said that everything we have words for is already dead. To follow this path, the people we speak to become the coffins for our words. This feels true most of the time. But Amichai was a great exception in my life. I became a greenhouse for his words.

I've returned to many, many things he said that afternoon, but one has stood out: "I wish there were two more commandments. The eleventh would be: *don't change*. The twelfth would be: *change*." (In an only slightly altered form, it wound up in my first novel.) We were sixteen going on seventeen, and he was asking us to always stay sixteen, to always be so frustrated, so unsatisfied, romantic, angered by boredom, inspired by uncertainty, demanding, disappointed, and unrealistic. And at the same time to become men and women. That afternoon has changed and stayed the same for me, remained still like a city in a snow globe, while also moving with me into my present, through my fingers and onto this page.

II

The second time I met Yehuda Amichai was in my sophomore year of college. I was twenty, a long four years older than when we first met. He had come to Princeton to give a reading. In anticipation of his visit, I made a small, sculptural gift for him out of a snow globe I'd emptied and refilled as a kind of surreal diorama. I intercepted him in the hallway, reminded him of our first meeting in Jerusalem, told him how much his words had come to mean to me, and presented him with the gift.

He took the box and nodded. I don't know what I was expecting, but that wasn't enough.

"You can open it now," I said.

He removed the tissue paper from the box, and the snow globe from the paper. After examining it from all sides, he said what I thought was a very earnest "Thank you." And then he put it back in the box.

What was I expecting? I didn't know. Perhaps if I'd developed a clear image of how I wanted him to respond, I would have been able to dismiss it as preposterous. Instead, I was left with the feeling that he didn't sufficiently appreciate my appreciation, that the gift hadn't meant anything to him. He turned and walked away. At the reading, he spoke with great beauty, and at great length, about nothing in particular. (And not that it matters, but he didn't repeat a single thing I'd heard in Israel.) I remember the buzz as people left the room. We had witnessed something special, something life-changing and contagious. I can only imagine that many went home to write or have sex.

Among the dozen poems he read that afternoon was "A Man Doesn't Have Time," the poem I had used as my yearbook page upon graduating high school halfway between our two meetings. It's an argument against Ecclesiastes: we don't have time for every purpose and so must, in the same moments, laugh and cry, hate and forgive, remember and forget, throw stones and gather them together.

A man doesn't have time. The easy (and not incorrect) interpretation is that life is short, and so we must pack our experiences tightly, often one atop another. We shouldn't expect the seams to hold.

But I like to think he also meant something different, more nuanced. Man doesn't have time because he exists outside of it, changing and unchanging, always returning to his past and engaging with his future. We were never sixteen going on seventeen. We were sixteen going on sixteen, and three, and seventy-seven. In 2000, five years after I gave him the snow globe, Amichai died at seventy-six years old. There was still one more meeting ahead of us.

III

My first son was born on January 25, 2006. The following January, my family moved to Berlin for four months. While there, I gave a phone interview to an Israeli journalist, on the occasion of the Hebrew translation of my second novel. As we were getting off the phone, she said, "I almost forgot. One more thing. Do you know any Israeli literature?" Among the writers I mentioned was Amichai. And for whatever reason, I then told the story of the snow globe I'd given him. It was the first time I'd mentioned it to anyone, as it felt so unimportant, and there was something embarrassing about the imbalance of regard. I'd spent hours making the thing, and rehearsed what I wanted to tell him. He received it with a nod, and for all I knew, proceeded to toss it in a garbage can.

A few weeks later, I received this e-mail:

> Dear Jonathan,
> Please let me introduce myself: my name is Hana Amichai and I am Yehuda Amichai's widow. I read your interview in the Israeli paper Maariv, and was very moved by your words on Amichai. I wanted to tell you that he brought home your glass object, saying he got it in one of his readings. My children liked it and got hold of it. I do not know where it is now.
> Thank you,
> Hana Amichai

Two years after that, I returned to Israel, this time as a professional writer participating in a literature festival. My wife and I spent an afternoon with Hana at her home in Jerusalem. We ate almond-stuffed dates in her living room, drank cappuccino from her new machine, had the history of our view of the Old City explained to us, heard the story of Amichai's death. I kept thinking some version of *Why didn't I know then what I know now?*

Why didn't I write him letters? Why didn't I insist on another meeting, which could have been done easily enough. (I've since heard of a number of people who got to spend time with him this way.) Why didn't I realize that he wasn't going to live forever?

Because I was too young? Because he did live forever?

R, who is one of my closest friends, wrote me the following in 2004, ten years after I met her on the plane to Israel: "But still, I find myself not quite happy, but invigorated, realizing that while I might not leave the world a better place, I am, every day, committed to acting like I can. This fills me with a bigger-than-myself swelling, the swelling that has been keeping me up at night: the world never seems to get dark enough for me to sleep easily these days."

Did Amichai meet with us that afternoon because he wanted to leave the world a better place? Is it ridiculous even to wonder such things? What motivated his writing? Why did he meet with us that afternoon in Israel?

My first son is named Sasha, after my wife's grandmother. In a few weeks he will be three years old. One week ago today, my second son was born. We named him Cy Amichai Foer—Cy for my wife's grandfather, Amichai for the poet. A good friend of ours, who was a good friend of the poet's, sent us a book of Amichai's, which Amichai had inscribed to him: "For Leon / with love, Amichai." Below this inscription our friend wrote: "For Amichai / with love, Leon." I've never encountered a more powerful expression of the declension of life, the generational giving and taking, the reading and writing of each other that has no beginning or end, yet is all the time beginning and ending. The book's title is *Time*.

WHEN JULIE MET DEB . . .

Julia Glass

Fiction writers feed off their fantasies: not just those they create for readers but those they conjure for themselves. And while the fantasies we whittle into stories may demand a respect for realism, the private ones do not. They tend, in fact, toward the grandiose.

The tale of how I found my muse is, like the books I write, long. Ultimately, it's a tale of the grandiose fantasy denied, expectations fortuitously dashed, pretentions unmasked. It's like the archetypal romantic comedy in which the protagonist pines over one ill-chosen paramour after another only to turn around in the nick of time and see that the best friend, the most familiar person of all, is and always was the one true love. (Well, it's sort of like that.)

I came to writing fiction sideways. I have always been a lover of books, of language, of playing with words as if they were tiles in a sprawling iridescent mosaic. Yet in school I chose to aim my aspirations at the visual arts. Through my twenties, I was a painter who paid the rent as a wordsmith. (I failed—thank heaven—the tray-with-six-soupbowls test to become a waitress. I failed *gloriously*.) I worked as a proofreader and then a copyeditor, tackling book manuscripts, magazines, speeches, and financial reports. Among multifarious clients, from *Cosmopolitan* magazine to Barclays Bank, from an art dealer to a publisher of ersatz travel guides, I inspired respect and fear as a verbal vivisectionist, queen of the grammar gestapo: smiter of dangling modifiers, defender of the en dash, deployer of ellipses correctly spaced. By night, I turned to my "real work," toiling away on large, extravagantly colorful canvases, most of them depicting people engaged in mysterious activities in rooms full of curious objects, with windows open to equally curious views. (I look at these paintings today and laugh: Did this painter long to tell stories or what?)

And then, like one of those Loony Toons anvils that falls on Baby Huey's head, spins him around, and simply turns him in a different direction (rather than turning him into chicken paillard), George Eliot knocked me widdershins. Why oh why, my aching heart asked me as I closed the back cover of *Daniel Deronda*, weeping for Gwendolen Harleth and the difficult future she would face, was I not a teller of tales?

There began my conversion, which was anything but easy. On an IBM Selectric passed down from my dad—a machine with the heft and vigor of a Volkswagen Beetle circa 1968—I began to make stuff up. I wrote ungainly, overpopulated stories featuring urbane, intelligent, angst-ridden thirty-something heroines. I subscribed to *The New Yorker* and *The Atlantic*, eagerly and devoutly reading the fiction in each and every issue. (Back in the 1980s, *The New Yorker* published two stories a week, *The Atlantic* one or more per month. Remember those days?) I began sending my stories to editors at these magazines, as well as a slew of quarterlies and literary contests.

Something surprising happened. In response to the first story I submitted, I received letters from editors at both *The New Yorker* and *The Atlantic*. They were rejections, but they were personal, encouraging rejections, thoughtful critiques of my earnest heroine and her modest adventures of love run amok. My *New Yorker* respondent told me I had "talent to burn." (Quite the ego snack, as a friend of mine likes to say.)

Over the next seven years, these editors responded personally to more than a dozen stories I sent their way (though, ironically, I never received so much as a hastily scrawled "Try us again!" from any of the smaller magazines). I continued to work alone, on my IBM jalopy, too stubborn to take classes or go for an MFA. Sometimes I longed for a mentor or muse, yet those two faceless editors kept me hopeful. I became certain that sooner or later I would publish a story in one of their gilded magazines. Then I would publish many more, and the world would marvel: I'd be the next Alice Munro or McDermott—or at least the next Ethan Canin (even if I wasn't a doctor) or David Leavitt (ditto gay), two twentysomething wunderkinds who'd burst onto the pages of those magazines, whose stories I loved. . . . I'd publish a collection—with Knopf or possibly FSG. Defying the usual expectations, it would hit the *New York Times* bestseller list and perch there, like a golden bird, for weeks. (All the people who'd ever scorned me would see that golden bird, high in those vaunted branches, and would they ever regret their callow behavior!)

Not that I'd reach this pinnacle alone. I would have a tough-as-jerky editor who'd cluster-bomb my prose and leave me breathless with humility. The process would be ruthless. We would sit together for hours in a stuffy, windowless room at the publishing house, between us a table strewn with the pages of my embattled manuscript, broken pencils, ashtrays overflowing. (Never mind that I'd never smoked and saw pencils as instruments of drawing, not writing. When I wrote by hand, I used a pen.) Without tact or courtesy, with only my soon-to-be-immortal literary soul in mind, my editor would eviscerate and temper the steel of my prose (and unmix my torrid metaphors).

That editor would, of course, be a guy. This wasn't a sexist thing; I was the sort of woman, back then, who insisted on female doctors, who turned to female friends for important advice. But the only iconic fiction editors I knew of were Maxwell Perkins and Gordon Lish. (I'd read an article about what it was like to work with Lish, how authors were gratefully reduced to tears.) In fact, the editor at *The New Yorker*, whose letters had become increasingly blunt, a shade impatient with my never quite crossing the bar, was a man. Rumor had it that he, too, was tough.

In fairy tales, seven is a magic number. So, fittingly, after seven years of submissions, I saw my first story published—not in a magazine or quarterly but in the pages of the *Chicago Tribune*; I had won a runner-up prize in the paper's annual fiction contest. Soon after, two quarterlies published two more of my stories.

At the same time, it became clear to me that if I ever wanted to publish a book, I'd have to write a novel. And so, to make a long story short, I took a short story—one admired by my two loyal if never quite affirmative pen pals—and made it long. Or longish. At 75 pages, it seemed to arrive at a natural end, so I submitted it to a novella contest. It won. This gave me the courage to make it longer. I called it *Three Junes*. To condense another saga, I got an agent. (The first one to look at my work, she has turned out to be one of the greatest blessings in my life as a writer, but that's another story.)

I was in my early forties by now; all those fantasies of becoming a young, even youngish, literary star à la Canin or Leavitt had necessarily vaporized. (Was I a has-been without having been?) But I had not surrendered my core vision: the conference room filled with ashtrays, pencils, and the vitriolic inspiration of my Perkinsy/Lish-ish editor. By strange coincidence, the editor from *The New Yorker* who had kept me hopeful for so many years had recently become a book editor at a major publisher.

Would my agent send *Three Junes* to him? She agreed to do this, though he was not one of the half dozen editors she had in mind. She described each one to me; some were men, some women. There was one at FSG, but none at Knopf.

"Not Knopf?" I asked wistfully.

"Well, if you want, sure," she said. "You're the boss. But if you don't get the right editor there, or if your book's on a list including one of the biggies—John Updike, Anne Tyler, Jane Smiley—you can fall right through the cracks."

She ventured that she had a hunch *Three Junes* would fit well at Pantheon—which belonged, I learned, to the "Knopf Group." She'd sent my novel to the editor in chief at this illustrious house. He edited books by, among other esteemed writers, Charles Baxter. I had just finished (and was crazy about) *The Feast of Love*; this was an omen! Although he seems to eschew the customary jacket photo, I could nonetheless picture an ascetically handsome Charles Baxter in that windowless conference room, sweating rusty nails under the chain-gang discipline of said editor.

Meanwhile, my old pen pal from *The New Yorker* wrote from his new post. How bittersweet to read a letter that differed not at all from the letters he'd written me over nearly a decade: He praised my talent, admired my characters, wished me luck, but . . . once again, not quite. (Those two words are the bane of many a talented but unpublished writer's existence.)

A week or two later, my agent called. Good news: Pantheon was potentially interested. First, however, Baxter's editor wanted to meet me.

Meet me?

This was not part of my projected scenario. Furthermore, I was less than a week from the due date for my second baby. I could barely make it two blocks to the grocery store, let alone dress up and haul myself to midtown for what might be the most important meeting of my life.

"Call him. Tell him your situation. If you can't make it there because you're having a baby, he'll understand. But call him," said my agent. She gave me a phone number.

The man I spoke with sounded . . . lovely: enthusiastic and cheerful. It was Friday when we spoke; I told him that we could make a date for Monday, but I might be otherwise occupied. I might be giving birth. He laughed warmly and said, "Well then, just do this one thing for me: As soon as you get off the phone, put my number in your labor bag. That way, someone can call if you can't make it."

"You know about labor bags?" I said.

"Oh sure, I've been there," he said. "I have three sons!"

I got off the phone elated but baffled. This guy was no man-eating tiger. He was, if anything, a pussycat.

Monday came and the baby did not. I put on the only dress that still fit me—a charcoal-colored burlap sack—and decked myself in large Mexican jewelry (baubles so dramatically chunky, you hope they'll hide the fact that you are, too). With all the grace of a Zamboni, I maneuvered myself into and out of a yellow cab.

I waited in an intimate lobby surrounded by glass cases displaying first editions of literary giants spanning a century. My size notwithstanding, I felt like Alice shrinking.

I was greeted by not one but two editors: the man with whom I'd discussed labor bags and a slim, striking young woman—certainly younger than I—with soft, pale features and a slightly crooked smile.

What I remember, however inaccurately, is this: that she greeted me with a remark akin to "Look at you! When are you due? I just got back from maternity leave after having my second." Or maybe she said this to me after she'd told me how much she loved my novel. It doesn't matter. I felt, yet again, like a cartoon character brained by a falling piano or bathtub. Dizzy on the verge of concussion or enlightenment, no half measures.

We sat down at a small conference table; or, rather, they sat while I cantilevered my anatomical mass into a chair. For an hour, I listened to these two kind, articulate people—each leaning over a copy of my manuscript on the table—tell me what they found so remarkable about my book, why indeed they thought it could *become* a book. They also told me where they felt it could use more work; I knew they were right, and together we pondered what that work might be.

Only after I'd left (still dizzy, my head a swarm of stars) did I understand that if they bought my novel, the young woman—who'd spoken most directly, forcefully, eloquently about my novel—would be my editor.

How ashamed I am now to confess that I felt, at that instant, a pang of disappointment. Not only was she a *she*, but she was so obviously and thoroughly *nice*. She would never mock my clichés, mass-murder my darlings, wipe the floor with my vanities. Unless . . .

Unless some transformative process took place once the ink dried on a contract. And the ink did dry, a month or so later. In the meantime I had a baby, who kept me close to home (it was the dead of winter) and, in cahoots with his older brother, made sure that domestic matters ruled my life, body, brain, and soul.

One day the phone rang.

"Hi! It's Deb! How are you? How's the baby?" Her voice rose with a lilt of innate, effortless joy at the end of each utterance. She asked in detail about both of my sons; in return to my answers, she offered stories about her own children, a pair of girls who fell, in age, between my boys. And then we talked about possible revisions to the end of my book.

Deb spoke about the lives of my characters as if they were our friends and acquaintances. At first, it felt as if there'd been some sort of prison break; for years, these make-believe people had inhabited only my brain. How had they escaped? Yet this other person, whom I barely knew, whom I'd met exactly once, knew everything about them. And she knew what they needed to live more fully in the world of my novel. She knew where their flaws were too hazy, their virtues unproven, their connections weak, their convictions unconvincing. I wasn't sure which felt more real: discussing our flesh-and-blood families or the members of this Scottish family, the McLeods, who lived inside my novel.

"When do you need me to finish my revisions?" I asked.

"No rush," Deb assured me. "Enjoy your baby. This is such a special time."

I protested that I wanted to make the revisions we'd discussed as soon as possible. I'd already learned how to nurse my son, Oliver, while typing one-handed on my computer (long surrendered, that monstrous IBM).

Shouldn't we make an appointment to meet again? I asked.

"Oh no," said Deb. "You don't have to go to that trouble. You can call or e-mail anytime, send me attachments if you like. We can talk on the phone."

Editing by e-mail? What about the conference room lit like an inter-rogation cell? The flurries of eviscerated text, red on black on white? But I am a generally cooperative person, and I didn't want to make waves. I worked on my novel, baby in the crook of my left arm, right hand peck-ing the keys. When I'd finished revising those last few chapters, I attached them to an e-mail and clicked *Send*. How anticlimactic.

Only a few days passed before Deb called to tell me how much she loved what I'd done—though perhaps the reader needed to see, a bit more clearly, why character X had fallen so hard for character Y. My heart sank; this would be no small endeavor.

As if reading my mind, Deb said, "You know, all you really need is a single flashback from the early days of their being together. Something special they shared that she has never forgotten."

With surprising ease, I dreamed this young couple onto a vast red vel-vet couch rescued from a New York City curb (and inspected for vermin by the endearingly fastidious boyfriend). They read on that couch, feet to feet, legs tangled. They played badminton, at night, in a Queens backyard that belonged to the boyfriend's brother. Three paragraphs total.

"Perfect," said Deb when I sent them by e-mail.

Perfect? Did Lish or Perkins ever tell a writer that anything was perfect?

Deb soon mailed to me her annotated copy of my entire manuscript. I ripped open the puffy envelope the minute I had it inside my apartment. There was a brief cover letter, but I set that aside and flipped through the pages, bracing myself for a bloodbath of ink, the sort of markings I still lavished on bank brochures and galleys of women's magazines.

In delicate pencil and a generously girlish script, I saw a minor deletion here, a query there. For pages on end, my writing remained pristine, untouched. *Maybe a bit much?* Deb might jot beside a melo-dramatic turn of phrase I'd missed. *Do you mean to repeat this word three times? . . . Remind us that he's an ex-boyfriend of hers?* Her notations were nearly always questions, rarely revisions made without permission, almost never an admonition. (Though I will never forget Deb's uncharacter-istic *EWWWW!* penciled beside a sentence where, in some benighted moment, I'd described a character as experiencing a sorrow like "an ice-pick to her heart.")

I called Deb. "I can't believe how little you've changed!" I told her, realizing at once that it sounded as if I were scolding her. (Was I?) She came as close as she ever does to indignant (that is, still several miles away) when she said, "Julie, you're a wonderful writer. Your writing doesn't need my help. That's part of what we love about you! That's why we're publishing your book!"

I absorbed this compliment. Oh.

Would I like to meet her for lunch? She'd like to take me somewhere special. Special: This was a word my editor used often, always sincerely.

I put on a dress—for possibly the first time since I'd met Deb, months before—and joined her at a restaurant that was, like her, quietly stylish, a place conducive to conversations between people who know how to listen. She wore something simple: white blouse, beige skirt, black boots. There was nothing elaborate or fancy about this woman: not her clothing, her hair, her jewelry (if any), not even the plain, solid nickname she preferred to Deborah.

For most of our lunch, we spoke about our children and our mates. We shared the absurd agonies of applying to preschools, of helping children negotiate their first friendships. I found out that Deb was married to her high school sweetheart from the Midwest, that he was a scientist turned lawyer. They lived in New Jersey. I learned, too, that she had worked at *The New Yorker* for fourteen years, starting in the secretarial pool after college and working her way up to editing fiction. Nothing had given her more pleasure, she said, than discovering a talented new writer and changing that writer's life by publishing a story in *The New Yorker*.

I thought wistfully back on the decade during which I had clung to that very dream, during which I submitted work to that magazine without ever gaining entry. Did she know the editor who'd written me all those years?

"Oh yes!" said Deb. "He was my mentor."

All at once I had this strange retrospective vision of a much younger Deb plucking one of my carefully addressed manila envelopes out of the slush pile, opening it eagerly, reading my story . . . and passing it on to her boss. "Read this one, I think it's special," she might have said. Something uncanny was happening here.

I went home and something even more uncanny happened. I happened to pick up a recent issue of *Poets and Writers* magazine—and there she was, my editor, interviewed as a *poet*. It turned out that Deb had recently published a successful volume of poetry. I strapped baby Oliver to my chest, went to my local bookstore, and bought it. That night, I read it cover to cover. I loved it.

I was mortified. I called Deb the next day to thank her for lunch and to tell her I'd read her book, that I hadn't realized—

"Oh God, don't worry about that," she said. "I'm here as your editor. Our relationship is about your writing. Don't even think about mine."

About a week later, my life turned upside down. A small lump in my right armpit turned out to be malignant, a recurrence of cancer for which I'd been treated seven years before. On a long list of fears, I panicked that if my publisher found out about this recurrence, they'd write me off as a goner and make little effort to promote it.

It took me a week to tell my agent. A protective, nurturing person, she said we could handle it however I chose—but she assured me that the people at my publisher would have nothing but sympathy, that they believed in my book no matter what.

Finally, I called Deb. I tried to tell her my news without crying, but I failed. "Oh Julie, oh Julie," she said, and I heard such genuine sorrow in her voice. "Of course we won't change any of the plans we have for this book. Of course not." If, however, I wanted to keep my condition close (I would have chemo and very shortly lose all my hair), we could continue to do everything over the phone and by e-mail. She talked to me at length about my health and my family.

Over the next eight months, I went through physical hell. My book's planned publication date in May, a year later, was the proverbial light at the end of the tunnel. By then, my oncologist ventured, I should have just enough hair to shed my colorful turbans and caps.

Every time Deb called—about jacket design, blurbs, galleys, copyediting, marketing, a possible change of title—I got off the phone feeling calm and reassured. When my chemo ended, I began to write a new book. The main character was a woman filled with confidence and joy in life, a character unlike any I'd created before.

Just before *Three Junes* was published, a reporter from a book magazine called to interview me. He asked me a few of the questions writers expect to be asked, and then he said, casual as you please, "So I've read that you had cancer and lost your only sibling to suicide. Can you talk about how those things influenced this novel?" I felt as if I'd been punched. How did he know these things?

"I Googled you," he said.

This was in early 2002, and I had never heard that word as a verb before. I found out that an essay I'd written a few years before, published in a transient newsprint journal, had found its way online. My voice trembling, I told the reporter that I didn't want to talk about these things, that I didn't see them as relevant (though, as I came to realize later, of course they were).

Gently, he pressed me; his editor would never forgive him if he didn't.

We spoke briefly about these events in my life, and then we went back to the kind of conversation I'd expected to have.

The minute I got off the phone, I began crying. Almost without thinking, I called Deb, who listened carefully before she spoke.

"Tell me what you're afraid of," she said.

"That people who read this article will come to my readings and know these things about me!"

"Well," said Deb, "if this article makes people go to your readings, that's a good thing. And if they make that effort, do you think they'll be feeling anything but sympathy for you? Don't you think they'll be on your side?"

I thought about that. "But," I said, "what if they ask me about those things and I lose control and I cry?"

"If you cry," said Deb, gravely yet with a hint of humor in her voice, "you'll sell ten more books."

When I hung up, completely consoled, not the least bit worried about that reporter and what he might write, that's when I knew that I was the luckiest writer in the world, to have this woman in my life—not just a very fine editor but a guardian and a friend.

I could—and would love to—go on for pages with stories about how Deb Garrison has stood by me at the most turbulent as well as jubilant moments over eight years and three books; how she's guided me—like a midwife rather than a surgeon—to make those books the best books they can be; how we've had conversations intended to be about catalog copy or a typeface choice that ended up as emotional gabfests about household pets, sibling rivalry, telling our kids about sex; how she called me, while in labor for her third child, because she wanted so badly to be the one to tell me about an honor my first book had won; even how Deb's mother (whose nature explains a lot about her daughter) always rallies the troops when I give a reading in Deb's hometown.

The night of the National Book Awards in 2002—at the beginning of the evening, when I was still a finalist, sure I hadn't much of a shot at winning—Deb introduced me to the dozens of editors and other bookfolk who congregated around her. (I met, face-to-face, the editor at *The New Yorker* who'd never said yes to my stories yet kept me striving.) At one point, I was left briefly alone with one of these people. "Isn't Deb wonderful?" he said.

"Yes, she is!" I said. Nervously, I added, "My only fear is that when I give her my second book, it might not be good enough, and she might have to reject it." I'd heard such chilling stories from authors more seasoned than I.

The man shook his head, smiling. "Oh no," he said. "Not Deb. If that book has problems, Deb will tell you what they are and show you how to fix them."

"Really?" I said.

"Absolutely," he said.

He was right.

Seven years have passed since that night. Deb has shared in all the best moments of my life as an author (as she should, having made me one in the first place), but she's helped me through the worst as well: how to right myself after a cruel review; how to negotiate a petty feud with a fellow author; how to rise above a rejection from a teaching job I wanted badly; how to know which favors to grant and how to say no to the ones I can't.

Perhaps she sounds too good—too sweet, too kind, too giving—to be true. If so, I have failed to convey her strength of conviction as well as heart, for Deb is nothing if not gutsy. Only recently have I realized that what makes her intelligence so rare as well as acute is this: she resists the easy cynicism that preys on most people involved in "creative" pursuits. To some, that makes her appear naive or eager to please. Hardly. She will readily express her outrage or scorn, and she is fully aware of the ironies rife in what it takes to succeed in the world she negotiates so well. She is a straight shot: honest, outspoken, and shrewd. But when she errs, it's always on the side of generous. That is a gift—of hers and to others.

As I work on a new book, I look forward to finishing it in part because I know that's when she'll come fully back into my life, not just as the editor who will help me follow and strengthen the complex psychological threads in the tapestries of my characters' lives but as someone whose company and fellowship make me feel invigorated, inspired, filled with a luminous energy in all aspects of my life. There is no part of my life in which I would not eagerly turn to Deb for advice.

A few years back, while we were in the thick of working together, Deb told me she'd be out of town for a grandmother's birthday. The grandmother was well into her nineties and going strong. We had a conversation about longevity and genes. I volunteered that on both sides of my family, reaching eighty is a stretch.

By then, I'd learned that Deb is a decade younger than I am, so I joked, "Hey, if you live into your nineties and if I'm gone by eighty, and *if* by any chance there's such a thing as reincarnation, I could come back as one of your grandkids. But boy, would I have to earn a lot of good karma for that!"

We laughed, Deb with the nervousness of someone truly modest.

I look back now and realize that over all those early years of working in such writerly isolation, of hearing no again and again, I came to assume that the guidance I yearned for would come in the guise of a taskmaster, a disciplinarian, a scold. I was sure that I wanted tough, but—bless the literary cosmos—what I got in the end was tender. How could I have known, even in my loftiest daydreams, sitting at my two-ton typewriter, writing my earnest letters to magazines that would never publish a word of mine, that all this persistence and patience (and, let's face it, denial) would bring me such good fortune?

THE TIGER AND THE PELICAN

MENTORS ELIZABETH HARDWICK AND JANICE THADDEUS

Mary Gordon

I arrived at Barnard on a brilliant September day; the year was 1967. It took less than an hour from my mother's door to the gates of Barnard Hall, but I might have crossed an ocean or a continent—or indeed a galaxy—so different were the worlds separated by less than twenty miles.

I had got to Barnard through sheer will and drive and ignorance. Educated to that time entirely in Catholic schools, I knew, though I didn't know why, that I had to get out. In large part it was because I was obsessed with Salinger's *Franny and Zooey* and *Raise High the Roof Beam, Carpenters*, and *Seymour: An Introduction*. I was utterly convinced that I was a long-lost member of the Glass family, and that to meet my kind (bookish hyperarticulate Jews with a bent for mysticism and show business), I needed to go where Seymour had gone to college: Columbia. It wouldn't have occurred to me to go where Franny had gone—Radcliffe—because I knew I couldn't leave home. My mother was a widowed polio victim and I was an only child. It was thought that I would go to Fordham or to St. Joseph's College for women—both within commutable distance, both Catholic. I balked. I could have gone to Queens or Hunter, to both of which I applied, and to both of which I was admitted, but some sort of siren song, whose tune I would never have dreamed of naming as class snobbery, class ambition, was the only register I could take in. I talked my two best friends into applying to Barnard with me. The principal refused to send in our applications. With a fearlessness I wish I could recapture, I phoned the Barnard admissions office and they phoned the principal. The applications were sent. We were admitted. The principal greeted the news with the dire words, "I once met a Columbia professor who boasted that within a week, he could make a Catholic girl lose her faith, her virginity, and all her political convictions." We didn't have the nerve, but if we had, we would have asked for his name.

My mother's annual income was low enough so that I got the full amount of a Regent's scholarship, enough to pay my whole tuition if I could come up with an additional five hundred dollars—a princely, but not impossible sum. I worked that summer as I had the one before. I was a secretary for the Republican-based Nassau County Board of Supervisors: I typed, I collated, I made filthy mimeograph copies of the weekly calendar. I worked from the day school got out until Labor Day. My mother's boss had got me the job. With it, I could save three hundred dollars and still buy a Villager dress and a pair of Pappagallo loafers and a Pendleton jacket. I thought I was dressed for success.

It is difficult to convince people, but it is entirely the case that, until that first day at Barnard, I had never had a serious conversation with a non-Catholic. And the conversations of any sort—serious or not—that I had had with people who could find themselves categorized properly as "middle class" could have been counted on the fingers of one hand. It didn't occur to me that that would be a problem when I got to Barnard. I had always been the best English student in my class: I was *the* school writer . . . I had started the first literary magazine. The magazine's publication was threatened because I wrote an essay in praise of Allen Ginsberg. I saved the magazine by appealing to Father Daniel Berrigan, not yet a public radical, only a prized priest-poet. And so I was not only the school's only writer, I was the most daring (therefore the coolest) girl in school. I was used to everyone's deferring to my literary gifts; I had never dreamed I might be overwhelmed in the area I felt I owned.

But in my freshman English class, I met girls from Brearley, Spence, Milton, and Concord Academy, girls from honors schools in California and Washington, girls who had spent their summers not cleaning mimeograph ink off their fingers but sunning themselves on the Amalfi coast or a place on Long Island I had never even heard of, something called the Hamptons—the only part of Long Island they had ever been. I did not get automatic A's—and I drowned in French classes and history classes, sinking in the wake of students infinitely better prepared than I. Still, I wrote poetry as easily as I sweated: I knew that was who I was, and in the world of writing I could not be made to feel unsure. In other areas, I was not so firm, however. I found that my one Villager dress was nothing: others had a closetful, and Pappagallo shoes not just in black but in many colors. And then, no one was wearing dresses or flats; everyone was in jeans and boots, and the revolution was happening, and if you had to leave a demonstration to get to your typing job—well, that was a thing you kept to yourself.

I had been advised not to take a writing course until my sophomore year, and it was poetry I wanted, so I applied for Janice Thaddeus's poetry class in the spring of my sophomore year. It was a chaotic time; the Columbia riots had changed my political consciousness; I had lost my virginity out of impatience with its symbolic weight; I was in love with a homosexual who was the pet of someone who regularly frequented Andy Warhol's Factory. Two years before, I had been in a procession crowning the Virgin Mary with a wreath of roses. The only thing that seemed firm to me was my hunger for writing. I knew that in Mrs. Thaddeus's class, I would come into my own, move from my position as undistinguished duckling to radiant literary swan.

My first encounter with her happened before the class met, and it happened secondhand. I had seen her in the halls: unmistakable for the mane of chestnut hair that hung down to her waist. I had never spoken to her: I wanted her to know me only as the writer of my work.

My best friend had a regular babysitting job caring for two little boys. I didn't know that Janice Thaddeus was also the mother of two young children. She came up to my friend one day and said: "I've watched you in the park with those kids for some time. You're very good with children, and I know you're a Barnard student. Would you like to babysit for my two sometime?" My friend told her I was about to study with her. "Oh, yes, she's very good. Tell her I said she's very good."

I had left high school thinking that e. e. cummings was the greatest world poet; my freshman English course had moved me into a T. S. Eliot phase, and I had a strong appetite for Yeats and Baudelaire. All that was large and lush drew me; none of my models was female. I thought I knew who I was as a writer and the way I wanted to say what I believed needed to be said.

The class was full of good writers, but I felt I held my own. What was remarkable, though, about Janice Thaddeus as a teacher was that she made it clear that there were no favorites, that each person's work was to be regarded on its own merits and honored on its own terms. And when I handed in my first assignments, I was shocked at the number of question marks and slash marks that were on the pages she returned. She encouraged me to try difficult forms in order to deal with what she thought of as "my fondness for purple poetry." I wrote villanelles and sestinas and triolets. She suggested I read a poet who scared me: Sylvia Plath. She told me that the work of Louise Bogan would be important to me: one could be both passionate and rigorous, she said. Her midterm assignment was to choose a poet whom we loved, and do an imitation of him or her. With her consultation, I chose Auden.

Rigor, restraint, precision—I had not been drawn to any of them. My sense of the world was that larger and looser was better: I had been too confined by the narrowness of Catholic thought and practice. But Jan pointed me toward a kind of restraint that was freeing rather than limiting, a precision that was not denying but enabling. She would look at endless drafts of endless poems . . . her corrections in pencil in an italic hand I later learned she had taught herself as a discipline because someone had told her that illegible handwriting was a burden to others. She was demanding, but never discouraging: you can do more, she would say, it can be cleaner, sharper, more exact. But you are on the right track. Her hand on my shoulder, between the blades of my scapular, was light but constant.

When I was through with her class that semester, she asked if I would consider being her regular babysitter, watching her children two afternoons each week. Half in love with her, her elegance, her kindness, her delicious sharpness, I was honored. Her children were two and five when I first met them; a remarkably precocious little girl who was reading long books and inventing story cycles, an angelic blond boy who stood on the corner of Riverside Drive, his eyes closed in ecstatic pleasure, repeating to himself, "The wind, the wind."

I had never before spent time in a middle-class household, to say nothing of one like Jan's: a demesne of intellectual and literary aristocracy. I didn't know that Jan's father was John Farrar, the first Yale Younger Poet, the founder of Farrar, Straus & Giroux, and that her mother was one of the first to create the form of the crossword puzzle. Jan's husband was a distinguished physicist. The walls were covered with books; every item in the house was carefully considered, carefully chosen; nothing was ostentatious, everything pleased the eye and the hand. As a teacher, she was engaged but removed; as a mother, she was intoxicated. I watched as she would drop her book bag, her long hair almost sweeping the floor as she fell to her knees to embrace her children. She was a genius at maternal inventiveness: observing her two children and acknowledging their strengths and differences; negotiating Eva's willful brilliance, her sibling rages; nurturing Michael's dreamy visions; encouraging him to hold his own against his dynamic sister. She wrote stories and poems with them, she took them to piano lessons, to concerts—they drew and painted and sewed and cooked. They put on plays and had elaborate picnics with their friends in Riverside Park. She included me in all this, and I, hoping one day to be the kind of mother she was, studied everything I saw her do with her children, as I studied the comments she made on my poems Each week, when I left the apartment, I would leave her a new poem. Each week, along with my salary, she would hand back a poem marked with her attentive corrections. Students are narcissists, even the best of them; it never occurred to me how generous she was to read my poems when she had a clutch of official students—and two young children—and her own poetry to write.

She would ask me questions about my life and my background. I was as exotic, as unfamiliar to her as she was to me. She asked me what I was doing for the summer. I told her I was working as a typist. "But where will you go on holiday?" she asked. I blinked; it had never occurred to me that I would do anything but work. I told her I'd only worked all summer since I'd been fifteen. She shook her head, as if I had said something unbelievable or obscene. The next week, she gave me an application for a Barnard summer grant. Barnard was giving out a few grants for summer study. "Wouldn't you like to go somewhere and study something?" In days I had come up with a plan: I would go to Harvard to study Italian.

I don't think she understood the significance of that change: it was a clue to me that I could imagine intellectual life, the creative life taking precedence over working-class financial anxieties. More: that I had the right to take the risk of doing something with my mind, assuming that it was of enough value that it deserved financial remuneration. And she did it quietly, without ever telling me she was sorry for me, or that my life was hard, harder than hers had been. She simply made it happen, as she airily sometimes assured me that I had to take an extra five dollars with my pay because she just didn't have the change. Only later, when I learned how important Yankee penny-pinching was to her, did I realize the extent of her gift.

I went to graduate school at Syracuse, but I still sent her all my poems, because her criticism was the one I valued most. And, still unaware of the outsize nature of my demands, I accepted her criticism, never imagining how kind it was of her to go on reading and commenting on my work when I was out in the world and ought to be asking people who were paid to read me. And in graduate school, I switched from writing poetry, the area of her mastery, to prose, where she was a novice and an amateur. But I was a member of the family now, a friend. I showed her my first stories, and she responded, tentatively—admitting that she hadn't any more expertise than many others but delighted at my new turn, a turn that would take me away from her.

She was a fine and accomplished poet but she didn't write much, publishing one excellent book which won a competition for older, unpublished poets. She would speak, ruefully, in a puzzled, somewhat abashed way about her own lack of ambition and what she thought of as my endless appetite for work—and for publication. She felt pressure to use her PhD in eighteenth-century literature, and though she didn't enjoy scholarship, she wrote an excellent biography of Fanny Burney. She died at sixty-eight, of a stroke; she had gone to the hospital to have her blood checked. Typically, her physical crisis caused the least possible inconvenience to those she loved. She had collapsed in the hospital and shortly after, gave up the ghost, her husband reading her poetry as she left this world.

In my senior year at Barnard I wanted to take another course with Jan, but she suggested that I work with Elizabeth Hardwick, who was also teaching in the department. I was reluctant; I wasn't a prose writer, and I didn't want to work with "Robert Lowell's wife." I had read those poems about her which made her seem like someone to stay away from. I hadn't really been paying attention to *The New York Review of Books*, and she had yet to publish her most praised essays, later to be collected in her remark able *Seduction and Betrayal.* I had yet to experience the seduction of her voluptuous prose, its thrilling thrusts and parries. But Jan knew her work and her place in the literary world. She said, "Well, if the Dark Lady were a fine writer, you wouldn't refuse to take a course with her. You mustn't miss this. She'll push you to a different place."

The difference in Jan's and Lizzie's physical presentations was a kind of metaphor for their difference as teachers. Jan was radically unadorned: her astonishing hair was the only adornment she needed; she never made up and wore no jewelry; her clothes were muted, unspectacular. Lizzie had Lucille Ball red hair, arranged in ringlets and deliberately unnatural-looking. She wore mascara, which was smudged by the end of the day, and dark lipstick. Her clothes were excitingly designed, and she wore high heels with interesting bows and buckles. Where Jan made a point of not having favorites in class, Lizzie picked me as her favorite and would say things like, "Nobody has written anything interesting this week but Mary, so we'll only read her." I would later learn that the word "interesting"—which she pronounced "innerresting," to rhyme with "arresting"—was the most important criterion by which worth would be judged. She told me to stop writing poetry, which was "so boring," and encouraged me to write stories. I wrote my first story in her class, which she said was "innerresting," and she returned it with not one mark on the page.

She invited me to her house for tea, and to meet her daughter. Lowell had just left her and he had returned home to see Harriet, their daughter, who was ten. I was mortally embarrassed to be in the room with the two of them, and even more embarrassed to see this icon of female accomplishment scurrying around to do her betraying husband's bidding. "Lizzie, get me a handkerchief," he said. I don't think he snapped his fingers, but he might as well have. She literally ran around the apartment looking for a handkerchief. "Cal, I think we only have Kleenex," she said, abashed. "Oh, Lord, Lizzie, what have you come to," he said. He looked at me and out of nowhere said, "Do you know who Theodore Watts-Dunton was?" For some miraculous reason, the kind of thing that made my mother believe in the Holy Ghost, I did know. I said he was Swinburne's companion and an expert in the early Elizabethans. He looked me up and down. He looked at Lizzie, who was beaming. "So, Lizzie, is this one a comer?" he asked. "Oh, Cal, of course she is," she said. I walked out onto 67th Street, anointed.

She took me with her to hear Rostropovich, whom we met backstage, and to see Sam Shephard, who walked into the audience to kiss her. I had dinner with Adrienne Rich and heard gossip about Mary McCarthy. She liked me to spend time with Harriet; she said I was one of the only "normal" people she could trust her child with. I didn't know whether that was a compliment or not. From a poor background herself, she liked stories about my working-class family; with her, I turned my mother from an anguishing burden to a comic character. She loved hearing my gossip; all my men troubles interested her much more than anything I was working on. I visited her, but I never brought her any manuscripts.

When I finished my first novel, I asked if she would give it a read. She was mildly encouraging. I remember some notes she made—nothing textual but an idea: "You are looking for the thing by which the nun in every Catholic girl is created." She also said I should change the book from third to first person. "You can always tell . . . if every other word is 'she thought,' or 'it seemed to her,' you should be writing first person, but you're afraid."

I did rewrite it, in first person, but I knew she didn't want to see another draft. Living in England, I met Margaret Drabble, who read and liked the book and sent it to her agent. Lizzie had never offered to help me in the slightest way. When the book was published, she gave me a publication party but refused a blurb, telling my editor, "One day she might write something we'll be proud of."

I knew I wasn't writing the kind of work she liked. At that time, she was over the moon about Renata Adler's *Speedboat* and Joan Didion's *The Book of Common Prayer*. She wasn't interested in fiction with a strong narrative line: that was "borin," a word which, when she said it, was made up of six or seven deadly syllables. She never praised anything I wrote; she sent me a letter when my novel *Men and Angels* came out saying, "It will never be my favorite of your books."

But I visited her regularly; she was always exciting to be with. Once, when I was being unfaithful to my first husband, I said I was with her and he, suspicious, phoned her. I called her in an anguish of embarrassment. "Honey, I love covering up, but you have to give me warning," she said, making me feel glamorous rather than tainted. She was excited when I was pregnant, grandmotherly with my babies. We never spoke about my work. She encouraged me to write criticism, saying that would give me a "luster that would set you apart from all those others."

In 1986, when I had known her for sixteen years, we were both invited to a writers' conference in Sicily. I was happy to carry her bags and order her cappuccino; she had no Italian and I was younger and fitter than she. I was happy to sit next to her on the bus and "dish" the others. But then, one night at dinner, she mentioned a writer whose work she liked. I said, "I don't think her sentences are very interesting." Lizzie had had a lot to drink; she was drinking more and more as she aged. "What would you know about it?" she said to me. "You've never written an interesting sentence in your life."

The company was shocked, and went silent. I managed to hold my tears until I got to my bedroom, then wept myself to sleep, calling my husband—international rates—for comfort. The rest of the trip was destroyed.

By the time I got home, I felt I had to break with her. I felt she was a danger; I feared she would convince me I had no right to go on. We didn't speak for twenty-one years. I kept being afraid that she would die without my seeing her, and I didn't want that. I felt great gratitude for what she had done for me at the beginning. With the help of my friend and colleague Saskia Hamilton, who had worked for Lizzie and won her approval through her masterful editing of Lowell's letters, I made contact with Lizzie. She said she'd be glad to see me. "We had some kind of falling out," she said to Saskia. "I just don't remember why."

When I saw her, she was sitting in a wheelchair, her hair bound in a fillet, like an English flapper's. She asked about my family; she said she'd always found my mother "inneresting" and was sorry to hear she'd died. She said she liked my hair and that my complexion was wonderfully young. We said nothing about writing. I went to visit her once again; the conversation was similar, although she repeated herself more.

And then, I learned that she had died. Something enormous had gone from the world, I knew, but something cruel had gone too, and though I mourned the loss of brilliance from the world, I mourned as well the pain that she had caused by her appetite for malice. She could have given me everything that she gave me, she could, indeed, have gone on not liking my work. But the cruelty: that added to nothing, that was unnecessary.

Jan Thaddeus and Elizabeth Hardwick: the tender mentor and the terrifying one. Jan, who pointed me to writers who would feed me for the rest of my life, who gave me a standard that would stay with me forever, from whom I learned not only lessons of writing but essential lessons of ethics and maternity, whose self-effacement gave me the freedom to find my own way, but made it impossible for her to acknowledge her own talent and ambition. Elizabeth, who could not forgive me for not writing in her image and likeness, but who gave me the courage of ambition and large daring, and whose literary suggestions, carelessly, almost randomly bestowed, gave me the form that made my first novel publishable.

This is how I think of them: the tiger and the pelican: Lizzie the tiger, brilliant, careless, destructive, and exciting, crashing through the underbrush heedless of the damage in her wake. And Jan the pelican. In medieval iconography and legend, the pelican plucks her own breast and feeds her young with her own life's blood. My gratitude to them both is complex and contradictory; they showed me who I could be, and what I wanted not to be.

THE MOMENT

Arnon Grunberg

(translated from the Dutch by Sam Garrett)

When the reading is over and the inevitable question-and-answer session begins—and there's nothing wrong with that, of course—the
question invariably arises: "When exactly did you start writing?"

As though that could be traced back to an exact date and time. Like
one's first cigarette, or the loss of one's virginity. The interlocutor tends to
adopt an expression that demands a painstakingly precise answer: "September 20, 1986. Immediately after dinner." But mightn't a classroom
essay, written with no matter how great a lack of enthusiasm, be considered the start of writing? Or an awkward love letter? Perhaps even a poem
written for an uncle's silver wedding anniversary?

If called upon to pinpoint the moment when I began writing, I suppose I would have to say that it was the moment when I—of necessity, and
prematurely—ceased to attend the Vossius Gymnasium in Amsterdam.
Yet even that can't really be called "a moment," for like so many estrange-
ments, my estrangement from high school was a long, drawn-out affair
that lasted weeks, yea even months.

Perhaps, then, the birth of my writing career—if you'll excuse the pre-
tentious tone—is to be found not so much in my farewell to the Vossius
Gymnasium as in my decision not to enroll in another, somewhat easier
high school where no Latin and Greek were taught, as I was advised to do
from all sides. I decided, in fact, that I no longer wanted to go to school
at all. To me, the fact that I was thereby effectively putting an end to all
prospects of an academic career seemed merely the icing on the cake. I
was going to be an actor, and no university was needed for that.

When I tell this story after readings, I usually explain to my audience that I locked myself for twenty-four hours in the bathroom of my parental home, where I still lived at the time, in order to show my parents that I was serious about putting an early end to my academic career. That is, I fear, a form of mythologization, an activity that comes naturally to the writer. But a writer, in my view at least, is also well advised to then turn around and do a little demythologizing as well.

To convince me that I must not fritter away my life at an early age, my parents exerted emotional pressure on me, and I undoubtedly exerted emotional pressure on my parents to convince them that frittering away my future was, as far as I was concerned, the only way to create enough room for my own life. And if my memory serves me well, during this mutual exertion of emotional pressure, I did indeed lock myself in the bathroom, but definitely not for twenty-four hours. Three hours, max, it couldn't have been more than that.

My father did, however, succeed in pushing through orders that I would allow myself to be tested by a psychological consultancy in Utrecht, half an hour from Amsterdam.

The consultancy promised to tell its customers what it was they were good at. What the consultancy did not mention was that some of those customers might very well prove to be good at nothing. At that stage in my own life there was, with the exception of acting, nothing at which I wished to be good, but my father was bound and determined to let the psychological examination have the final say. It was a desperate, last-ditch attempt to dissuade me from my foolish plans.

The test took all day. There were a few young people in the room, but most of those being tested were men in their forties who, despite years of job market experience, still seemed to have no idea where their own strengths lay. The mood was somber and a little tense, like in a crematorium.

Four weeks later, the test results arrived. My arithmetical skills were somewhere around average, but my language skills lay below that. Exactly what it was that the consultancy advised me to do with my life I can no longer recall. All I know is that my father was deeply disappointed by the agency's recommendations, and hid away their report in the bottom drawer of his desk, from which it reappeared only after his death.

Meanwhile, my attempts to get ahead as an actor were being systematically nipped in the bud. For any number of reasons, no theater school wanted to have me, and in the world of film, I made it no further than as a sort of glorified extra. A few of these experiences I was later able to incorporate in my novel *Silent Extras*.

After a couple of years on the sidelines of film and theater, two things became clear to me. First of all, when you are a glorified extra, everyone is allowed to humiliate you with impunity. The second conclusion was a more personal one: I was not an actor. I lacked the fire that burned deep within. And probably the requisite talent as well. I no longer wanted, in the middle of the night and at freezing cold locations, to perform stunts that never made it into the movie anyway, and that at wages barely exceeding the minimum.

My father told me: "I don't care what you become anymore, not even if it's a shoeshine boy. But you have to become *something*." For once I thought he was right. Being an extra was not a profession, merely a hobby at best, and one you had to stop doing before it was too late.

I responded to an advertisement asking for unskilled administrative personnel, and my acting career came to an end. On second thought, however, that is a form of mythologization as well. My acting career guttered out. I no longer bothered auditioning indiscriminately for bit parts, and soon enough the casting agents stopped calling.

A vestige of that dream, which in retrospect seems more like an attempt to elude my parents and their expectations, took the form of dance lessons. Classical ballet lessons to be precise. Every Monday evening from eight to ten. A theater school had informed me politely but matter-of-factly that my motor skills and the musicality of my movements were not exactly the cat's meow. Without receiving any commitment whatsoever that they would accept me once my motor skills had improved, I decided to go to work on it.

I had an acquaintance—someone with whom I had once performed in an amateur theater production—whose mother, Jolanta Zalewska, gave dance lessons. I signed up. Born in Warsaw, Jolanta had fled the Communists and ended up in Amsterdam. Her son said she had once been offered a job as choreographer with Amsterdam's prestigious National Ballet, but was struck down by a crippling case of nerves the day before she went in. She polished off two bottles of vodka and arrived at the interview in a woeful state of inebriation. That was the end of her career as choreographer with the National Ballet.

Later it turned out that she had not so much fled communism, but had come to Amsterdam for the sake of love. Those are details. Writers are not, by the way, the only ones with a talent for mythologization. It's also worth nothing that it is often extremely unclear just where running away from communism (or whatever) begins and love ends.

In any event, I will never forget the day I met Jolanta. She was little and volatile. She spoke Dutch with a heavy Polish accent and smoked greedily, with abrupt gestures. It was as though she kept forgetting that she was holding a cigarette, then suddenly remembered and, with thinly disguised irritation, took a drag of it.

Ballet lessons were indeed her métier: jazz ballet and classical. She recommended that I begin with classical.

The Monday evening sessions were attended by a number of students, including a number of attractive coeds after whom I lusted to no avail, each and every one of them, as well as a few older academic types: a philosopher, a general practitioner, a theater director.

Our pianist, Roman, was also a Polish refugee, but unlike Jolanta he never spoke. At the stroke of eight he would appear, lift the lid of the keyboard, and begin to play. At the stroke of ten he would stop, close the piano, and disappear without a word.

One day he was dead, and Jolanta placed a rose on the piano. From then on she used a cassette recorder.

I can no longer clearly recall why I didn't stop with classical ballet, even when I knew that my acting career was drawing to an early close. Perhaps I was ashamed to admit to Jolanta that I had abandoned hope. Perhaps there were more practical considerations at play. In those days I was not exactly what you'd call a loner, but the classical ballet lessons offered the prospect of a certain amount of social contact. When the evening was over, Jolanta, unlike Roman, always went to the café with a few of her students.

It would probably be wise to pause now and reconsider the moment when I started writing; it was not the moment when I dropped out of school, it was the moment when I decided to take classical ballet lessons, to do something about that musicality in which experts said my body was so sorely lacking.

At the end of the evening Jolanta would usually speak a few comforting words to me, something along the lines of: "Okay, you've got a weak back, but legs like a bull."

Another time she told me: "You're attractive, with those dirty glasses of yours." Not only did I deeply doubt my own talent, but I was also—like so many young men—deeply insecure about the measure of my attractiveness. All confirmation, no matter how backhanded, that my powers of attraction were up to snuff was extremely welcome.

Perhaps that is why I was always one of the last to go home. Or perhaps it was simply because there was nothing for me to go home to.

Jolanta always went home late. Sometimes she didn't go home at all.

It behooves me at this point to say something about the rose vendors who, in those days, wandered the streets of Amsterdam. They were usually Indians or Pakistanis, armed with a bouquet of roses of dubious quality and a Polaroid camera, often of dubious quality as well, who went from café to café in the hope of selling a rose and a photograph to needy romantics.

When the evening was young, Jolanta would ignore those rose vendors, but as it wore on she became increasingly friendly toward them, until the moment arrived when she would say: "Give me all the roses you've got."

Later it turned out that she maintained sexual relations with several of those rose vendors. The more she drank, the less particular she became, until at a certain point, I suspect, she would admit to herself: "Body heat is body heat."

Jolanta also had a hobby that expanded into a part-time job: she liked to borrow money. That she liked to borrow money, of course, had to do with the fact that she liked to spend money as well, and preferably more than she earned. Her ability to keep on borrowing money can only be ascribed to her charm and powers of persuasion. There were a number of cafés and restaurants where she was able to eat and drink on credit. And there were establishments where that no longer worked. Having said that, it is important to note that she borrowed money only from people who, in her eyes, already had enough of it. In those days I had little money myself, and she never borrowed much from me.

She was also extremely generous. With other people's money, to be sure, but that is a talent in its own right.

Despite this shifting field of interests, there were few things she took more seriously than art in general and dance in particular. In the midst of a café conversation about politics, wine, or roses, she might suddenly launch into an analysis of another customer's body language. She also liked to talk about the difference between the way Dutch people and Poles moved. "The reason Dutch people walk funny," she told me once, "is because they ride bicycles so much."

Jolanta's son, Redbad, also brought me into contact with another Polish émigrée in Amsterdam: Ewa Mehl.

As a baby Ewa had been found along the tracks in wartime Poland, and was therefore almost certainly Jewish. She had been raised in a foster home in Wroclaw, the former Breslau.

She was an artist, a ceramicist to be more exact, and she had a studio in downtown Amsterdam. Redbad suggested I stop by and visit her sometime.

Ewa Mehl welcomed me to her little studio with the words: "So, you want to become an actor?"

"Well," I said, "to be honest I'm not so sure about that anymore."

"Well, then, what *do* you want to be?"

A brief silence followed.

"What do you do now?" she wanted to know.

I told her that I performed unskilled administrative duties.

Her next question, whether I hoped to continue performing unskilled administrative duties for the rest of my life, was not hard to answer.

"I write, too," I said.

That was not a complete lie. I had written a couple of plays, one-acters to be precise, albeit more in the hope that those plays would further my acting career than that they would lead to a breakthrough as a playwright. At the age of fifteen I had, almost by accident, won a playwriting prize for young people. I was honored, but still a bit disappointed that it wasn't a prize for my acting abilities.

For the rest, I wrote letters. To the waitresses and salesgirls I lusted after. I believed that those letters might do what the body itself had failed to do: seduce. That the letter would cause the faulty musicality of the body to be forgotten by focusing all attention on the musicality of the language. My confidence in the written word must, in those days, have bordered on the insane. Especially seeing that I did not limit myself to one letter, even though the only reaction was silence: no, I kept writing.

As a letter writer I lived a life of serial monogamy. This time it was a salesgirl at the grocery store, the next time an actress I had met and who had started talking to me. Most of all, however, I wrote letters to a waitress at a cheap Italian restaurant in Amsterdam. Her name was Mariëtte, and even now I cannot think about her without an echo of lust and longing. Through the grapevine I have heard that she recently gave birth to her first child.

I told none of this to Ewa Mehl. All I said was: "I write, too."

To which she replied: "So show me something you've written."

The first person who took my writing seriously and provided it with criticism was a Polish immigrant in Amsterdam whose Dutch was only so-so.

Her criticism was fairly scathing. "Write about people you know," she said. "Write about me, write about Jolanta, write about your parents. Don't write about revolution, because you don't know shit about revolution."

From that day on, after performing my unskilled administrative duties, I would cycle to Ewa Mehl's studio, where I received a cup of tea, a bowl of borscht, and where we talked about art.

Was that, then, not the moment when I started writing? That moment in Ewa Mehl's studio when I said: "I write, too"?

Ewa and Jolanta were friends, but they had a complicated relationship. Someone told me that when Redbad was little she would drop him off at Ewa's place with the words: "Watch him for a little bit, okay? I'll be back in ten minutes."

Then she would disappear for days on end.

One afternoon Ewa said to me: "You know who you should read? Marek Hlasko."

He was a Polish writer. I had never heard of him. But, I will freely admit, there were not an awful lot of Polish writers I *had* heard of back then. And there were no Dutch translations of his work available back then, but in a bookstore called *Die Weisse Rose* I found Hlasko in German.

I started reading. Although he wrote about a world that could not have been farther away from my own, it all seemed familiar to me. Hlasko wrote about the Poland of the 1950s, at the height of Stalinism. One of his most famous stories, "The Eighth Day of the Week," is about two young people in Warsaw who can't find a place to make love. I admit "outlook on life" is a horrible term, but there was something about Hlasko's outlook on life that I thought I understood, feelings I could share, and I had never come across that in quite the same way with any other writer. The desolation,

104

the rage, the disgust, the naive—who knows, perhaps spurious—faith in love.

Whenever I seemed about to lose my way during the writing of my first novel (*Blue Mondays*), I turned to Hlasko.

Recently I reread what is perhaps his finest book, *Killing the Second Dog*. It is about two Polish émigrés in Israel. One of them is a director, the other an actor. The actor seduces older women on the beach at Tel Aviv, in the hope of finagling them out of their money. The director comes up with the texts; the actor recites them.

The book has faults not a few, yet I can still recommend it heartily to one and all. It is about seduction as a game, and the ironic fact that the game more or less ceases to be a game as soon as one starts taking it seriously. It is about the power of the word and the negation of the cliché, at the moment when the cliché is used to a different end and so takes on a new ambiguity. Perhaps it is also about how, if one looks carefully, almost everything boils down to the art of seduction, even though that art often presents itself in a different guise.

What these three Poles—Jolanta Zalewska, Ewa Mehl, and Marek Hlasko—taught me in the end had to do perhaps with the attractive power of destructiveness. About how discovering that power within yourself and taking it seriously may very well be a precondition for the ability to construct, to create.

The romanticization or mythologization of self-destructiveness is not what I am advocating here, simply the recognition that that destructiveness is there and that it can be crucial for the writer to make friends with that peculiar, magnetic power within.

But let there be no misunderstanding: generally speaking, I have no problem whatsoever with the acquisitions of a bourgeois existence.

Marek Hlasko committed suicide on June 14, 1969, in Wiesbaden, Germany.

Jolanta Zalewska was found floating in an Amsterdam canal in the mid-1990s. Sometimes it is hard to say where alcoholism ends and suicide begins.

Shortly afterwards, Ewa Mehl died of leukemia.

In 1995, shortly after my first novel appeared in the Netherlands, I moved to New York.

During the final years of their lives I had little contact with Ewa and

Jolanta. I may have allowed myself to become a bit carried away with the success of my first novel, with success in general, even though I should have known that success was an illusion.

When my second novel came out, Ewa Mehl sent me a packet of powdered borscht. There was no note attached.

I am writing this text in the Ukraine, where I am accompanying a group of American men each in search of a Ukrainian bride. I act like I am searching too, but I am here to write about them for the newspaper. And who's to say where the acting ends?

Never, since the days when I would pop down to the café with Jolanta after dance lessons, have I drunk as much vodka as I have here.

This morning I awoke with a head of iron, and I felt it, an almost physical sensation. They are very close to me, Jolanta Zalewska, Ewa Mehl, and Marek Hłasko.

ONLY PLUMP THE PILLOWS

Margot Livesey

"Only plump the pillows," Roger admonished, "and the Muse will come." We were talking on the telephone—he in the small Scottish town of Aberfeldy, where he lived until Monday, July 28, 2008; I in Cambridge, Massachusetts, where I sit now, writing this. I must have been complaining about my struggles with my current novel. Roger spoke with enthusiasm, and when I teased him—did he even know how to plump a pillow?—he laughed. Until his last days he had a laugh that invited whoever his audience was to share his delight in a story, an idea, a situation. I did not tell him then that my muse was already there, courtesy of a satellite, at the other end of the phone. We went on to talk about other matters: William and Dorothy Wordsworth perhaps, or Keats and Coleridge, each, for different reasons, striding across the Scottish hills, or William Morris's relationship with Dante Gabriel Rossetti. Or we might have gossiped about the family, or the upcoming Tay Valley bicycle race.

How do we know when a story begins? If Roger were writing this, he would have an answer, probably several answers, to that question. He was hugely interested in how stories come about, in life and in art: where they start and where they end. Also in serendipity, which he regarded as a major force in his own life. But we would both, I think, be united in regarding a boys' private school on the edge of the Scottish Highlands as playing a crucial role.

Founded by the future British prime minister William Gladstone in 1847, Trinity College, Glenalmond (as it was then called), is situated on the banks of the river Almond about fifty miles north of Edinburgh. As one drives up from the main road, the countryside grows rougher and wilder until, coming over the final hill, one sees the valley, the school and the river hidden between the trees, and beyond the fields rising up to the line of bare hills. "I never see that view," Roger said, "without my heart lifting," and so it seemed utterly appropriate that on the morning of his funeral—a beautiful August day—we all, in separate cars, without consultation, drove from Perth crematorium to Glenalmond. As we made our way down the school drive, the opening line of Wordsworth's sonnet about London ran through my head: "Earth hath not anything to show more fair." Of course it was Roger who first read, or perhaps recited, the poem to me. During World War II, he committed a good deal of poetry to heart.

The oldest part of the school is a heroic red sandstone edifice with turrets and battlements and a flagpole. The bleak moors and hills in the distance only make the surrounding lawns and playing fields seem more verdant. From the main building, the Front Avenue winds up past the velvety cricket pitch, the tennis courts, the school infirmary (run by first my mother and then my stepmother), and various large houses occupied by boys (and nowadays girls) and smaller houses occupied by masters. Almost a mile from the school is The Cairnies, the boys' boarding house of which Roger became the housemaster in 1953, and where he and his wife Merril lived with their four children. A few hundred yards beyond The Cairnies is Bell's Cottage, where I lived with my father and stepmother.

How did two Englishmen as different as Roger and my father end up in what was then a rather remote part of Scotland? My father, too young for the first war, too old for the second, was teaching in the Lake District before he came north to be the geography master at Glenalmond, in the early forties. He spent the next two decades teaching boys about countries he had never visited. As for my mother, Eva, she arrived at the school in 1946 or '47, after spending the war nursing in London. A former pupil had recommended the school's peaceful situation, and she became the school matron.

While my father was drawing maps of Africa and scything the fairways of the school golf course (the horses used to pull the lawn mowers had been requisitioned), Roger was fighting in India and Burma, a bloody and little-known front of World War II. On his twenty-second birthday, he lost nineteen close friends. For most of his life, until the last decade, he seldom spoke about those years except in terms of the books he loved. He would describe reading the complete plays of Shakespeare on the voyage out to India, or almost missing a vital landing—he was an officer in a parachute regiment—because he was absorbed in *Jane Eyre*.

After the war, Roger returned to England to study literature at Balliol College, Oxford. During his second or third summer vacation, he acted in a touring production of Aristophanes' *The Clouds*. The company performed at various schools, and at one of these a housemaster told Roger to get in touch if he needed a job after graduation.

Roger spoke often, with awe and appreciation, of how this chance meeting shaped his life. The housemaster went on to become the warden of Glenalmond, and Roger did need a job. He had met Merril Brady, who was studying philosophy, politics, and economics at Oxford, and when he asked her father for her hand, Mr. Brady responded, "Get a job." With almost no money they married in January 1949, and that summer drove north to Scotland, a country that neither of them knew but which, after two world wars, had the great virtue of seeming safe.

At that time Eva was one of the few other women at the school, and she and Merril became fast friends. Still, even Merril was surprised when, in 1952, Eva married my father, a confirmed bachelor of nearly fifty. They were happy, but not for long. Eva died when I was two and a half, and a year and a half later my father married the new school nurse. Even before the marriage, I had begun to spend as much time as I could at The Cairnies. My stepmother's arrival at Bell's Cottage only made being there more desirable; she and my father had no time for a small, noisy child. As I grew up, I started referring to Merril and Roger first as my guardians, and later as my adopted family.

For many years I thought of Eva as little more than a photograph — a carefully posed studio portrait — hanging over my bed. But one misty October morning, when the dew was still on the grass and the pheasants still foraging in the fields, Roger drove me to catch a train in Pitlochry. By this time, 1987, my father and my stepmother were also both dead, and Roger and Merril had become my main source of my first family's history. Now, as we crossed a small bridge, Roger announced, out of the blue, "The most profound experience of the supernatural I ever had was in the company of your mother."

"Tell me," I said, and he did.

He had gone to the school infirmary to use the phone (only the warden and the nurse had phones at this time). Eva had left him alone to make his call, and while he was talking, the door of the room opened. A woman in a raincoat came in, nodded to him, walked across the room, and left by the door on the far side. When Roger's call was finished, Eva returned, and he asked about her friend.

"What friend?" she said.

He described the woman—brown hair, raincoat, middle-aged—and Eva said, "Oh, her. What did she do?"

He described the woman's actions, and Eva told him to try the door.

"The door I had just seen the woman open and walk through," Roger said, "was screwed shut." He whooped with laughter as we swung around another bend. "Of course," he continued, "I always wished I'd paid more attention. Your mother had second sight. I think you do too."

"But I never see anything," I protested.

"That's because your life is too busy, too urban and too American," Roger said firmly. "What time is your train?"

On the train, I transcribed this conversation, and, by the time I reached London, I had decided to write a short novel, loosely based on the life of my mother. Over a dozen years, with many detours and dead ends, I wrote *Eva Moves the Furniture*. I did not show Roger the novel until it was published, but I often talked to him and to Merril about Eva. Merril was a wonderful source of information. From Roger I got something more intangible—a sense of how my mother's history connected to the landscape, both visible and invisible—and an unwavering faith that I could indeed write this book. When at last he held it in his hands, he announced, with great conviction, that he was sure it would find its way to readers.

"I don't think so," I said. Apart from anything else, I explained, the novel had been published on 9/11.

"No, you'll see," he said.

That night, as I lay in bed, I wondered for the first time why he too had seen the woman. Even in the asking, I knew the answer. Roger, like my mother, had second sight. Throughout his life he had a number of crucial encounters with the supernatural. His prediction about my book was not one of these but simply his usual enthusiasm. To my surprise, however, his words have proved more accurate than I had any reason to hope. Eva has, over the years, found readers who recognize in my story their own losses and longings.

As the father of four children, a housemaster, an English teacher, and a deeply hospitable man, Roger was not just my muse. I shared him—I still do—with a throng of family, pupils, neighbors, and friends. He had a great gift for communicating his love of literature and ideas, and he knew unerringly just when one was ready to meet a particular author. He introduced me to John Donne when I was fourteen, and I was totally smitten by Donne's witty, sexy conceits. Later, he gave me *Four Quartets*, and I couldn't get enough of Eliot and the fragments he had shored against his ruins. "Isn't that super?" Roger would say, after reading a poem by Gerard Manley Hopkins or reciting by heart, while striding across the moors, the great passage where Milton describes the angels falling out of heaven. After his funeral, several of his former pupils, men in their fifties and sixties, spoke to me of how Roger's enthusiasm had transformed their lives—how he had made them, too, feel that they were discovering Shakespeare and Herbert and Wordsworth for the first time.

Much of Roger's teaching was informal, but periodically he gave both his children and his grandchildren what we called—with a sense of importance and excitement—tutorials. When his older daughter Sally and I were studying Shakespeare, he would summon us to his study, a room we never normally entered, for one of these sessions. I remember him drawing the prima mobile and explaining how the divine right of kings came from their proximity to the heavens. "Look," he said, "how the Fool parallels King Lear." "Why do you think Hamlet uses the play within the play to prove his uncle's guilt?" While we sat around his desk, discussing that week's text, Roger would jump up to pull down more books from the shelves that lined the room. Here was how the critic F. R. Leavis had responded to *Lear*. And here was a more modern example of the chain of being in Thomas Hardy's *A Pair of Blue Eyes*. When the hour was over, Sally and I would return to her room with copious notes and the challenge of fitting our glittering new ideas into the conventional essays our school required.

In writing my most recent novel, *The House on Fortune Street*, I tried to dramatize Roger's belief that literature is woven into the fabric of everyday experience. I gave each of my four main characters what I call a "literary godparent." Keats, for example, shadows the character grappling with questions of romantic love and immortality. The godparents were chosen for thematic reasons: they point to the deeper concerns of the characters, but they are also all authors to whom Roger introduced me. Although he never actually said in my hearing what one of my characters claims—that

111

everyone has a book or an author that's the key to their life—I feel that he easily might have. He loved those kinds of sweeping theories.

After he retired from teaching, Roger ardently pursued various projects. He read and thought extensively about the connection between art and science in the nineteenth century; he was deeply interested in Babbage and the first computer; he explored the subversive possibilities of children's literature. We had long discussions about Charles Kingsley's *The Water Babies* and how D. H. Lawrence, in writing *Lady Chatterley's Lover*, had borrowed from *The Secret Garden*. More recently, he had been investigating William Morris and various Utopian communities.

At the same time as he delved into these topics, Roger also worked on his own novel—a hugely ambitious undertaking that drew on his many interests, and also on the lives of various people on the fringes of the Bloomsbury set. He would read me passages when I visited, not sequentially but picking out his favorite scenes and paragraphs. His very fertility of imagination made it hard, I think, for him to accept the essentially linear nature of the novel and the fact that it can, finally, only be one small branch, rather than a splendid tree of sprouting allusions. That said, one of his favorite authors was Jane Austen—who is perhaps the most robustly linear of all nineteenth-century authors. Roger's tastes, I should add, were by no means as exclusively classical as the works I've named suggest. He loved *Zen and the Art of Motorcycle Maintenance*, and he deeply admired the work of two American writers, my friends Andrea Barrett and Nicholas Delbanco.

It is only now, writing this and knowing that he will never read it, that I understand how remarkable Roger was. Not only for his panoramic knowledge and his readiness to entertain theories of all kinds, but for his willingness, as Nick Carraway comments at the beginning of *The Great Gatsby*, to defer judgment. More than most people of his generation, he understood that not everything can be solved by pulling oneself together; ordinary life can be a struggle. To an unusual degree, he regarded the people around him with the same sympathy as he brought to, say, Coleridge, with his madness and drug addiction, or Charles Dodgson, with his intense interest in young girls. As I muddled through my twenties and early thirties, slowly finding my way to writing fiction, Roger always seemed to believe,

112

with almost no evidence, that I might some day produce something of interest. But he seldom encouraged my writing directly, and my work was never the main focus of our ongoing conversation, although he did sometimes suggest possible plots. Last year he urged me to write about a renegade monastery on the Welsh border; on another occasion he told me about an early scandal at Glenalmond that he thought might prove useful.

Shortly after Roger's death, I asked Merril if he had had a muse or mentor. We were walking beneath gray skies along the bank of the river Tay. On one side lay the swift flowing brown water, on the other a field of barley.

"Not really," she said. "There was a family friend who encouraged his boyhood reading, and there were certainly people at Oxford whose conversation he enjoyed." She stepped around a clump of thistles. "No, I think he found whatever muses and mentors he needed in his books."

As she spoke, a sudden commotion in the barley brought us to a standstill. While we stood watching a crowd of mallards, thirty or forty perhaps, rose quacking, in a flurry of wings, out of the ripe grain.

We both exclaimed. "I've never seen anything like that," Merril said.

Nor had I. Watching the birds, the glossy males and dowdy females, fly down the river, I knew at once that she was right. When Roger wanted inspiration, companionship, advice, stimulation, information, he turned not to his many friends but to his beloved books. The novels and poems, histories and biographies that he piled up on his desk and around his chair were his muses: always the same, always yielding new riches.

As I sit at my own desk this autumn, struggling once again to start a novel, I've thought often of the mallards, and of Merril's remarks. In my long solitary hours, I've come to realize that death has not changed one essential aspect of my relationship with Roger: he remains my muse. Who knows if the pages I'm working on now will see the light of day, but, like everything else I've written, they are driven, in ways I sometimes don't fully understand, by his enthusiasm, by his teaching, and by his endless readiness to engage me in witty, allusive conversation. And when I can't quite hear that conversation, am at a loss to frame an idea or make a connection, I follow his example; I plump the pillows and I turn to my library.

SONTAG'S RULES

Sigrid Nunez

It was my first time ever going to a writers' colony, and for some reason I no longer recall I had to postpone the date on which I was supposed to arrive. I was concerned that arriving late would be frowned on. But Susan insisted this was not a bad thing. "It's always good to start off anything by breaking a rule." For her, arriving late *was* the rule. "The only time I worry about being late is for a plane or for the opera." When people complained about always having to wait for her, she was unapologetic. "I figure, if people aren't smart enough to bring along something to read . . ." (But when certain people wised up and she ended up having to wait for them, she was not pleased.) My own fastidious punctuality could get on her nerves. Out to lunch one day, realizing I was going to be late getting back to work, I jumped up from the table and she scoffed: "Sit down! You don't have to be there on the dot. Don't be so servile." *Servile* was one of her favorite words.

Exceptionalism. Was it really a good idea for the three of us—Susan, her son, myself—to share the same household? Shouldn't David and I get a place of our own? She said she saw no reason why we couldn't all go on living together, even if David and I were to have a child. She'd gladly support us all if she had to, she said. And when I expressed doubts, she said, "Don't be so conventional. Who says we have to live like everyone else?" (Once, on St. Mark's Place, she pointed out two eccentric-looking women, one middle-aged, the other elderly, both dressed like Gypsies and with long flowing gray hair: "Old bohemians." And she added jokingly, "Us in thirty years."

More than thirty years have passed, and she is dead, and there is no bohemia anymore.)

114

Why was I going to a writers' colony, anyway? She herself would never do that. If she was going to hole up and work for a spell, let it be in a hotel. She'd done that a couple of times and loved it, ordering sandwiches and coffee from room service, and working feverishly. But to be secluded in some rural retreat just sounded grim. And what sort of inspiration was to be found in the country? Had I never read Plato? (Socrates to Phaedrus: "I'm a lover of learning, and trees and open country won't teach me anything.") I never knew anyone more appreciative than she was of the beautiful in art and in human physical appearance ("I'm a beauty freak," was something she said all the time), and I never knew anyone who was less moved by the beauties of nature. Why would anyone want to leave exciting Manhattan for a month in the woods? When I said I could easily imagine moving to the country, not then but when I was older, she was appalled. "That sounds like *retiring*." The very word made her ill.

From time to time, because her parents lived there, she'd have to fly to Hawaii. When I said I was dying to visit America's most beautiful state, she was baffled. "But it's totally boring." Curiosity was a supreme virtue in her book, and she herself was endlessly curious—but not about the natural world. Living on Riverside Drive, she sometimes spoke admiringly of the view, especially the fine sunsets, but I never knew her to cross the street to go to Riverside Park.

Once, I showed her a story I was working on in which a dragonfly appeared. "What's that? Something you made up?" When I started to describe what a dragonfly was, she cut me off. "Never mind." It wasn't important; it was boring.

Boring, like *servile*, was one of her favorite words. Another was *exemplary*. Also *serious*. "You can tell how serious people are by looking at their books." She meant not only what books they had on their shelves, but how the books were arranged. At that time—the late seventies—she had about six thousand books, perhaps a third of the number she would eventually own. Because of her, I arranged my books by subject and in chronological rather than alphabetical order. I wanted to be serious.

"It *is* harder for a woman," she acknowledged. Meaning: to be serious, to take herself seriously, to get others to take her seriously. *She* had put her foot down while still a child. Let gender get in her way? Not on your life! But most women were too timid. Most women were afraid to assert themselves, afraid of looking too smart, too ambitious, too confident. They were afraid of being unladylike. They did not want to be seen as hard or cold or self-centered or arrogant. They were afraid of looking masculine. Rule number one was to get over all that.

Here is one of my favorite Susan Sontag stories.

It was sometime in the early sixties, when she'd just become a Farrar, Straus & Giroux author, and she was invited to a dinner party at her publisher's Upper East Side town house. Back then, it was the custom chez Straus for the guests to separate after dinner, the men repairing to one room, the women to another. For a moment Susan was puzzled. Then it hit her. Without a word to the hostess, she stalked off to join the men. Dorothea Straus told the story gleefully years later. "And that was that! Susan broke the tradition, and we never split up after dinner again."

She was certainly not afraid of looking masculine. And she was impatient with other women for not being more like her. For not being able to leave the women's room and go join the men.

She always wore pants (usually jeans) and low-heeled shoes (usually sneakers), and she refused to carry a purse. The attachment of women to purses perplexed her. She made fun of me for taking mine everywhere. Where had women got the idea they'd be lost without one? Men didn't carry purses, hadn't I noticed? Why did women *burden* themselves? Why not instead always wear clothes with pockets large enough to hold keys, wallet, and cigarettes, as men did?

She said, "Here's a big difference between you and me. You wear makeup and you dress in a certain way that's meant to draw attention and help people find you attractive. But I won't do anything to draw attention to my looks. If someone wants to, they can take a closer look and maybe they'll discover I'm attractive. But I'm not going to do anything to help them." Mine was the typical female way, hers was the way of most men.

116

No makeup, but she dyed her hair. And she wore cologne. Men's cologne: Dior Homme.

She was a great admirer of Elizabeth Hardwick's work, but she thought Hardwick was yet another woman fettered by her femininity ("I have always, all of my life, been looking for help from a man," Hardwick wrote), in this case a particularly pungent Southern brand of it. (On the other hand, in a conversation about women writers I once had with Hardwick, when I mentioned Susan, she said, "She's not really a woman.")

She thought Virginia Woolf was a genius, but to hold her above all other literary idols as I did then struck Susan as callow; predictable. Besides, something about Woolf—something I think had everything to do with Woolf's mental and physical illnesses (her weaknesses, in other words)—made Susan squeamish. The first volume of Woolf's letters had recently come out, and Susan said she could not read them. She was put off by the many intimate letters to Woolf's beloved older friend Violet Dickinson, the silly endearments and girlish prattle, and Woolf's habit of presenting herself as a cute little animal. She hated childish language of any kind and always boasted that she never spoke baby talk with her son when he was little.

She was suspicious of women with menstrual complaints. She herself had always taken her periods in stride, and she thought a lot of women must be exaggerating the inconveniences and discomforts of their periods. Or they were buying into old myths about the delicacy and vulnerability of the female body. In my case, diagnosis was simple: "You're neurasthenic." She suspected that many people exaggerated, or overreacted to, both physical and emotional pain, an attitude that no doubt owed much to her having had cancer and having stoically withstood radical surgery and chemotherapy.

Seeing me curled up in her son's lap, she fixed me with a cool I've-got-your-number look and lisped mockingly, "The little girl and her *big man*."

She was a feminist, but she was often critical of her feminist sisters and of much of the rhetoric of feminism for being naive, sentimental, and anti-intellectual. And she could be hostile to those who complained about being underrepresented in the arts, or banned from the canon, ungently

117

reminding them that the canon (or art, or genius, or talent, or literature) was not an equal opportunity employer.

She was a feminist who found most women wanting. There was a certain friend she saw regularly, a brilliant man whom she loved to hear talk and whom, though he was married, she usually saw alone. Those times when his wife did come along, though, were inevitably disappointing. With his wife there, Susan complained, the conversation of this brilliant and intellectually stimulating man somehow became boring.

She was exasperated to find that the company of even very intelligent women was usually not as interesting as that of intelligent men.

*   *   *

Over the years, I have met or learned about a surprising number of people who said it was reading Susan Sontag when they were young that had made them want to be writers. Although this was not true of me, her influence on how I think and write has been profound. By the time I got to know her, I was already out of school. But I'd been a mostly indifferent, highly distracted student, and the gaps in my knowledge were huge. And though she hadn't grown up in New York, she was far more of a New Yorker than I who'd always lived there, and to the city's cultural life you could have had no better guide. Small wonder I considered meeting her one of the luckiest strokes of my life. It's quite possible that, in time, I'd have discovered on my own writers like John Berger and Walter Benjamin and E. M. Cioran and Simone Weil. But the fact remains, I learned about them first from her. Though I'm sure she was often dismayed to hear what I hadn't read, how much I didn't know, she did not make me feel ashamed. Among other things, she understood what it was like to come from a background where there were few books and no intellectual spirit or guidance; she had come from such a background herself. She said, "You and I didn't have what David's been able to take for granted from birth."

She was a natural mentor. You could not live with her and avoid being mentored was the delightful truth of it. Even someone who met her only once was likely to go away with a reading list. She was naturally didactic and moralistic; she wanted to be an influence, a model, *exemplary*. She wanted to improve the minds and refine the tastes of other people, to tell people things they didn't know (in some cases, things they didn't even want to know but that she insisted they damn well ought to). But if educating others was an obligation, it was also loads of fun. She was the opposite of Thomas Bernhard's comic "possessive thinker," who feeds on the fantasy that every book or painting or piece of music he loves has been created solely for and belongs solely to him, and whose "art selfishness" makes the thought of anyone else enjoying or appreciating the works of genius he reveres intolerable. She wanted her passions to be shared by all, and to respond with equal intensity to any work she loved was to give her one of her biggest pleasures.

Some of her enthusiasms mystified me. As we sat in the Upper West Side's New Yorker revival house (oh vanished temples of my youth), sharing a giant chocolate bar, I kept wondering why she'd wanted to see a double feature of old Katharine Hepburn movies, both of which she said she'd already seen more than twenty times. Of course, she was *besotted* (another favorite word) with moviegoing—in the way only someone who never watches television can be, perhaps. (We know this now: if one size screen doesn't addict you, another one will.) We went to the movies all the time. Ozu, Kurosawa, Godard, Bresson, Resnais—each of these names is linked in my mind with her own. It was with her that I first learned how much more exciting a movie is when watched from a seat close up to the screen. Because of her I still always sit in the front of the theater, I still resist watching any movie on television, and have never been able to bring myself to rent movie videos or DVDs.

Among living American writers, she admired, besides Hardwick, Donald Barthelme, William Gass, Leonard Michaels, Grace Paley. But she had no more use for most contemporary American fiction than she did for most contemporary American film. In her view, the last first-rate American novel had been *Light in August* by Faulkner (a writer she respected but did not love). Of course Philip Roth and John Updike were good writers, but she could summon no enthusiasm for the things they wrote about. Later, she would not find the influence of Raymond Carver on American fiction something to cheer. It wasn't at all that she was against minimalism, she said; she just couldn't be thrilled about a writer "who writes the same way he talks."

What thrilled her instead was the work of certain Europeans, for example, Italo Calvino, Bohumil Hrabal, Peter Handke, Stanislaw Lem. They, along with Latin American writers like Borges and Julio Cortázar, were

119

creating far more daring and original work than her less ambitious fellow Americans. She liked to describe all highly inventive, form- or genre-bending writing as science fiction, in contrast to banal contemporary American realism. It was this kind of literature she thought a fiction writer should aspire to, and that she believed would continue to matter.

She was a natural mentor . . . who hated teaching. Teach as little as possible, she said. Best not to teach at all. She said, "I saw the best writers of my generation destroyed by teaching." She said the life of the writer and the life of the academic would always be at odds. She liked to refer to herself as a self-defrocked academic. She was even prouder to call herself self-created. I never had a mentor, she said. Though she must have learned something while married to her University of Chicago professor, sociologist and cultural critic Philip Rieff, a marriage that began when she was a sophomore and he was twenty-eight and ended when she left him seven years later. And she'd had other professors, among them Leo Strauss and Kenneth Burke, whom she remembered as extraordinary teachers and for whom she had no end of praise. But however else these men might have inspired her, it was not to be a great teacher herself.

Like many other writers, she equated teaching with failure. Besides, she had never wanted to be anyone's employee. The worst part of teaching was that it was, inescapably, a job, and for her to take any job was humiliating. But then, she also found the idea of borrowing a book from the library instead of buying her own copy humiliating. Taking public transportation instead of a cab was deeply humiliating. Diva-ism? She seemed to think any self-respecting person would understand and feel as she did.

I found it strange that there was this one part of her life—the teaching she did, either before or after I met her—that she never talked about. About being a student, she talked a lot. In fact, I'd never known anyone to speak with such reverence about his or her student days. It gave her a special glow to talk about that time, making me think it must have been the happiest of her life. She said the University of Chicago had made her the mind she was; it was there that she'd learned, if not how to write, how to read closely and how to think critically. She still cherished her course notebooks from those days.

Now it occurs to me that at least some of her resistance to teaching might have had to do with her passion for being a student. She had the habits and the aura of a student all her life. She was also, all but physically, always young. People close to her often compared her to a child (her inability to be alone; her undiminishable capacity for wonder; her being without health insurance in her forties, when she got cancer, even though health insurance was easily affordable in those days). David and I joked that she was our *enfant terrible*. (Once, when she was struggling to finish an essay, angry that we weren't being supportive enough, she said, "If you won't do it for me, at least you could do it for Western culture.") My enduring image of her fits exactly that of a student, a fanatical one: staying up all night, surrounded by piles of books and papers, speeding, chain-smoking, reading, note-taking, pounding the typewriter, driven, competitive. She would write that A-plus essay. She would go to the head of the class.

Even her apartment—strictly antibourgeois, unapologetically *ungemütlich*—evoked student life. Its main feature was the growing number of books, but they were mostly paperbacks, and the shelves were cheap pine board. Furniture was sparse, there were no curtains or rugs, and the kitchen had few supplies. No cooking was done there, unless it was by some visitor. No entertaining, not even on holidays. If there was a guest, he or she would be offered a cup of Café Bustelo (never any kind of alcohol), or they might be invited to join us for a frozen dinner or a bowl of canned soup. People visiting for the first time were clearly surprised to find the celebrated middle-aged writer living like a grad student. (Everything changes. In her mid-fifties she would say: "I realized I was working just as hard, if not harder, than everyone I knew and making less money than any of them." And so she transformed that part of her life. But the time I'm talking about was before—before the grand Chelsea penthouse, the enormous library, the rare editions, the art collection, the designer clothes, the country house, the personal assistant, the housekeeper, the personal chef. And one day when I was around the same age she had been when we met, she shook her head at me and said, "What are you planning to do, live like a grad student the rest of your life?")

Whenever some university made her an offer she knew she *shouldn't* refuse, she was torn. Often she turned it down even though she needed money, and then she would congratulate herself. She was amazed at those who made a much better living from writing than she did yet were still tempted by tenure. She was outraged to hear other writers complain, as many often did, about how their teaching made them miserable because it

121

interfered with their writing. In general, she had contempt for people who didn't do what they truly wanted to do. She believed that most people, unless they are very poor, make their own lives, and, to her, security over freedom was a deplorable choice. It was servile.

She believed that, in our culture at least, people were much freer than they thought they were and had more options than they seemed willing to acknowledge. She also believed that how other people treated you was, if not wholly, mostly within your control, and she was always after me to *take* that control. *Stop letting people bully you*, she would bully me.

Which brings me to another favorite story.

She said, "I know you won't believe this, but when I was your age I was a lot more like you than like I am today. And I can prove it!" It turned out the playwright Maria Irene Fornes was coming to visit that day. Fornes and Susan had been lovers almost twenty years earlier, after Susan had divorced her husband and moved to New York. When Fornes arrived, as soon as she'd introduced us, Susan said, "Tell Sigrid what I was like when you met me. Go on, go on!"

"She was an idiot," Fornes said.

When she'd stopped laughing, Susan said to me, "The point I was trying to make is that there's hope for you, too."

*   *   *

When, recently, I see that Javier Marías has said that the worst thing a writer can do is to take himself or his work too seriously, I think I understand. I think I even agree with him. I think if I had thought this way myself when I was young, my life could have been happier. I might even have turned out to be a better writer. Nevertheless, I'm grateful to have had as an early model someone who held such an exalted, unironic view of the writer's vocation. ("And you must *think* of it as a vocation. Never as a career.")

Virginia Woolf lived as if literature were a religion and she one of its priests. Susan made me think of the antiquated hyperbole of Thomas Carlyle: the writer as hero. There could *be* no nobler pursuit, no greater adventure, no more rewarding quest. And she shared Woolf's worship of books, her idea of heaven as eternal reading.

She said, "Pay no attention to these writers who claim you can't be a serious writer and a voracious reader at the same time." (Two such writers, I recall, were V. S. Naipaul and Norman Mailer.) After all, what mattered was the life of the mind, and for that life to be lived fully reading was *the* necessity. Aiming for a book a day was not too high (though something I myself could not achieve). Because of her, I began reading too fast.

Because of her I began writing my name in each new book I acquired. I began clipping articles from newspapers and magazines and filing them in various books. Like her, I always read with a pencil in hand, for underlining. (Never a pen.)

In school, I had studied with Elizabeth Hardwick, and though she was at times encouraging, I always got the feeling from her that if I gave myself over completely to the writer's life I would find more unhappiness than fulfillment. For years afterward, whenever I spoke to her, I noticed she almost always asked about my writing only after she'd asked about my love life ("Do you still have that nice young man?"). She used to tell her Barnard students that you had to be really bored with life to become a writer. Somehow I don't believe she thought this was true for men.

With Susan, I felt as if I were being given permission to devote myself to these two vocations—reading and writing—that were so often difficult to justify. And it was clear that, no matter how hard or frustrating or daunting it was—and no matter how much like a long punishment writing a book could be—she would not have chosen any other way; she would not have wanted any other life than the life she had.

"You have to care about every comma." "A writer's standards can't ever possibly be too high." "Never worry about being obsessive. I like obsessive people. Obsessive people make great art."

To read a whole shelf of books to research one 20-page essay, to spend months writing and rewriting, going through one entire ream of typing paper before those twenty pages could be called done—for the serious writer this was, of course, normal. Satisfaction? "I always think everything I write is shit," she said. But of course, you didn't do it to feel good about yourself. You didn't do it for your own enjoyment (unlike reading), or for catharsis, or to express yourself, or to please some particular audience. You did it for literature, she said. And there was nothing wrong with never being satisfied with what you did.

"The question you have to ask yourself is whether what you're writing is necessary." I didn't know about this. *Necessary?* That way, I thought, lies writer's block.

Because of her, I resisted switching from typewriter to word processor. ("You want to *slow down*, not speed up. The last thing you want is something that's going to make writing *easier*.")

One way in which she considered herself a terrible model was in her work habits. She had no discipline, she said. She could not steel herself to write every day, as everyone knew was best. But it was not so much lack of discipline as a hunger to do many other things besides write. She wanted to travel a lot and to go out every night—and to me the most fitting of all the things that were said upon her death was by Hardwick: "In the end, nothing is more touching to the emotions than to think of her own loss of evenings at 'happenings,' at dance recitals, the opera, movies."

Lincoln Center. For the rest of my life, I think, I will never hear the orchestra tuning up, or watch the chandeliers rise toward the ceiling of the opera house, without remembering her.

To get herself to work, she had to clear out big chunks of time during which she would do nothing else. She would take speed and work around the clock, never leaving the apartment, rarely leaving her desk. We'd go to sleep to the sound of her typing and wake up to the sound of her typing. This could go on for weeks. And though she often said she wished she could work in a less self-destructive way, she believed it was only after going at it full throttle for many hours that your mind really started to click and you'd come up with your best ideas.

She said a writer should never pay attention to reviews, good or bad. "In fact, you'll see, the good ones will often make you feel even worse than the bad ones." Besides, she said, people are sheep. If one person says something's good, the next person says it's good, and so on. "And if *I* say something's good, *everyone* says it's good."

She said, "Don't be afraid to steal. I steal from other writers all the time." And she could point to no few instances of writers stealing from her.

She said, "Beware of ghettoization. Resist the pressure to think of yourself as a woman writer." And, "Resist the temptation to think of yourself as a victim."

She was a natural mentor, but she was not maternal. Though she always said her biggest regret was not having had more children, I found it almost impossible to imagine her nursing, or tending to an infant or a small child. I could more easily imagine her digging ditches or break-dancing or milking a cow. In fact, she told me she never really wanted her son to think of her as his mother. "I'd rather he see me as—oh, I don't know, his goofy big sister." From the time she knew she was pregnant till the day she went into labor, she never saw a doctor. "I didn't know you were supposed to." Endlessly curious; at least one book a day—but not one book about pregnancy or child care, she said. She was the opposite of women like Michelle Obama: she was a mother last.

She liked to tell a story about the time a group of other young mothers approached her to express concern about her parenting, suggesting she needed guidance. It wasn't that they were busybodies, she said. They were just unliberated fifties women stuck with conventional ideas of what a proper woman, wife, and mother should be. I asked her if they had made her feel guilty, and she replied emphatically *no*. She had never felt any guilt about the kind of mother she was. "Not one iota."

First I moved out, then David and I broke up, and not long after that David got a place of his own. Over the next few years, a period when she was often depressed, I had more contact with her than I had with him, though it never amounted to much. Always she complained of being lonely, of feeling rejected; abandoned. Sometimes she wept. She had got it into her head that everything she ever did in her life was first of all to win David's love and respect. As if he were the parent and she the child.

While I was still in school, at Columbia, I had taken a course in Modern British Literature with Edward Said. Whenever I mentioned him, Susan would tease. "Sounds like you've got a crush." (Though Susan had probably met Said by this time, the two had not yet become friends.) There was truth to this. A lot of students were smitten with brilliant, handsome young Professor Said.

And then, somehow—I can't remember the details except that I had nothing to do with them—Professor Said was coming to visit!

I have never understood what happened that day. I remember that the four of us were in the living room, where there was only one comfortable chair. I remember that Said sat in that chair without taking off his coat, and that he had brought an umbrella, which he placed on the floor beside the chair. And the whole time, he kept reaching down to pick up the umbrella and then immediately he'd put it down on the floor again.

I remember that I didn't say anything and David didn't say anything, and though Susan did her best to engage him, Said didn't say much of anything, either. He sat there in his coat, nervously playing with the umbrella and not saying much, and when he did say something it was mumbled. He sat in the one comfortable chair, the only comfortable chair in the whole apartment, looking as uncomfortable as if he were sitting on nails, picking up the umbrella and putting it down again, nodding at whatever Susan said but obviously too distracted to be really listening. Of what was discussed all I can recall is who was and who wasn't still on the faculty at Columbia where, years before, Susan had taught, too. The entire visit, though it did not last long, was excruciating, and it was a great relief when he was gone.

And after he was gone Susan came to find me. "Are you all right?" I shrugged. "Look," she said. "I have no idea what that was all about, but I do know how you feel and I'm sorry." What was she talking about? "I know what it's like when you admire someone and then you see them in an unflattering light. I know it can be very painful."

We sat together for a while, smoking and talking. How many hours we used to spend like that, smoking and talking. To me it was unfathomable: the busiest, most productive person I knew, who somehow always had time for a long conversation.

"But that's what happens," she said. "You have to be prepared for that." It had happened to her a lot, she said. Once she started meeting writers and artists, it happened over and over. "I'd be so thrilled about meeting these people—my heroes, my idols!" And over and over she would feel let down, or even betrayed. And she was so disillusioned that she'd end up regretting having met them, because now she couldn't worship them or their work anymore, at least not in the same pure way.

One of her favorite books was Balzac's *Lost Illusions*, which she insisted I must read at once.

One of her favorite films was *Tokyo Story*. "I try to go see it once a year." (And in those days, if you lived in Manhattan, this could be done.)

She was shocked when I didn't love it. (I am ashamed to say, that first time, I found Ozu's masterpiece too slow.)

"But didn't you get it? What about the part, after the mother's funeral" — and she recited an exchange that takes place between the youngest daughter and the daughter-in-law — "Oh my God!" She clutched her throat. "Didn't that make you *weep*?"

What a dumb clod I must have seemed to her. I thought of lying just to protect her. But then she waved her hand and said, "Oh, it's just because you're too young. Years from now you'll see it again, and then you'll understand." Confident.

Actually, it didn't take years. And I didn't have to see the movie again.

Kyoko: Isn't life disappointing?
Noriko: Yes, it is.

IN THE ABSENCE OF MENTORS/MONSTERS

NOTES ON WRITERLY INFLUENCES

Joyce Carol Oates

How solitary I've always felt, in my writing life. Unlike nearly all of my writer-friends, especially my poet-friends, I never really had a "mentor"—never anyone to whom I might show my work-in-progress in anything approaching an ongoing, still less an intimate or "profound" relationship.

Even during my marriage of many years—which ended in February 2008 with the sudden death of my husband Raymond Smith—my writing occupied another compartment of my life, apart from my married life. I am very uneasy when people close to me read my writing—my fiction—as if I were intruding upon their sense of me, which I would not wish to violate; I think that the life of the artist can be detached from the life of the "art"—no one is comfortable when others perceive, or believe they can perceive, the wellsprings of their "art" amid the unremarkable detritus of life.

Since my husband was an editor and publisher, overwhelmed with reading, assessing, annotating, and editing manuscripts to be published in *Ontario Review* or by *Ontario Review Press*, I was reluctant to take up his time with yet more writerly projects of my own. I did ask him to read my nonfiction essays and reviews for such publications as *The New York Review of Books*—which, in any case, as an avid reader of that publication, he would have read when it was printed.

Rarely did he read my fiction. Not "in-progress" nor after publication. Maybe this was a mistake. I am willing to concede that much in my life has been mistaken—and yet: what is the alternative, superior life I might have led? Is there such a Platonic fantasy?

As I haven't had significant mentors in my writing life, nor have I had "monsters"—but I have had, and have now, fascinating writer-friends. It's altogether likely that these writer-friends have influenced me in ways too subtle and diffuse to examine except anecdotally.

The Rival. The day of Vladimir Nabokov's death—July 2, 1977—is firmly fixed in my memory, for on the following day Donald Barthelme said casually to me, with a puckish lift of his upper lip and what in non-Barthelmeian prose might be described as a *twinkle of the stone-colored eye* behind wire-rimmed glasses: "Happy? Nabokov died yesterday, we all move up a notch."

(And how did I respond to this? Probably with a startled or an embarrassed smile, and a murmur of mild disapprobation. *Oh Don you don't mean that—do you?*)

Well, no! Don was just kidding.

Well, yes. What is kidding but deadly serious?

We were in an Italian restaurant within a few blocks of Donald's apartment at 113 West 11th Street, New York City. We were having a late lunch after drinks at the apartment with Donald's wife Marian—Don's second wife, young, blond, attractive, and it seemed warily in love with this complex, difficult, elliptical man, who behaved much more naturally—graciously—with my husband than with me, with whom he spoke in a manner that was jocular and subtly needling, edged with irony, sarcasm. As if Don didn't know what to make of me—at least, in person. This was the first time we'd met after a friendly/ funny correspondence following a "literary feud" of sorts conducted in public, in the pages of *The New York Times Book Review* (me) and *Newsweek* (Donald)—a disagreement of the kind writers had in the 1970s, or perhaps have had through the centuries, regarding the "moral" / "amoral" nature of literature. (The following year, John Gardner would publish his controversial polemic *On Moral Fiction*, praised in some quarters as it was condemned in others.) For the purposes of writerly combat, "Joyce Carol Oates" weighed in on the side of moral seriousness; "Donald Barthelme" on the side of amoral playfulness. In an interview in the *Times* the Dada-inspired Barthelme had stated that "Fragments are the only form I trust," which in retrospect sounds reasonable enough but, at the time, at the height of whatever literary issue was raging in whatever literary publications, struck me as dubious, or in any case a vulnerable position that might be questioned if not attacked and repudiated. Subsequently, Donald "attacked" me in print, as one might have foreseen, and somehow it happened that we began writing to each other, and not long afterward we arranged to meet on one of my infrequent trips to New York, and so Donald Barthelme and I became, not friends—for we saw each other too rarely for friendship, and when we did meet, Don was so clearly more at ease with my husband than with me—but "friendly acquaintances."

Perhaps Don thought of me as a "friendly rival"—it may have been that he thought of all writers, especially his contemporaries, as "rivals"—in the combative-macho way of Stanley Elkin, John Gardner, Norman Mailer, and numerous (male) others. The notion of our being "competitors" in some sort of public contest made me feel very ill at ease, and so invariably I found myself murmuring something vaguely embarrassed and/or conciliatory, usually some variant of *Oh Don you don't mean that—do you?* with a hope of changing the subject.

With one so strong-minded as Donald Barthelme, you could not easily change the subject. You would remain on Don's subject for as long as Don wished to examine that subject, with the air of a bemused vivisectionist. As Don's prose fiction is whimsical-shading-into-nightmare, cartoon-surreal-visionary, so Don's personality on such quasi-social occasions was likely to be that of the playful bully, perversely defining himself as an outsider, a marginal figure, a "loser" in the marketplace, in contrast to others whose books sold more, or so he believed. No sooner had my husband and I been welcomed into the Barthelmes' brownstone apartment—no sooner had I congratulated Don on what I'd believed to be the very positive reviews and bestseller status of his new book of stories *Amateurs*—than he corrected me with a sneering smile, informing me that *Amateurs* wasn't a bestseller, and that no book of his had ever been a bestseller; his book sales were "nothing like" mine; if I doubted this, we could make a bet—for a hundred dollars—and check the facts. Quickly I backed down, I declined the bet—no doubt in my usual embarrassed/conciliatory way, hoping to change the subject.

But Don wasn't in a mood to change the subject just yet. To everyone's embarrassment—Ray's, mine, his wife's—Don picked up a phone receiver, dialed a number, and handed the receiver to me with the request to speak to his editor—he'd called Roger Straus at Farrar, Straus & Giroux—and ask if in fact Donald Barthelme had ever had a bestseller; and so, trying to fall in with the joke, which seemed to me to have gone a little farther than necessary, I asked Roger Straus—whom I didn't know, had scarcely heard of at this time in my life—if Don had ever had a bestseller, and was told no, he had not.

Plaintively I asked, "He hasn't? Not ever? I thought . . ."

The individual at the other end of the line whom I would meet years later, legendary Roger Straus of one of the most distinguished publishing firms in New York, said coolly, "No. He has not. Put Don on the phone, please, I want to talk to him."

Of course, Donald Barthelme was hardly a "mentor" of mine—I had the distinct idea that he'd read very little of my writing, probably not a single book, only just short stories in collections in which we both appeared like *Prize Stories: The O. Henry Awards* or magazines like *Harper's* and *Atlantic.* (It would be a long time before my fiction began to appear, not very frequently, in *The New Yorker,* in which Barthelme's wildly "experimental" short fiction had become a fixture rivaling the well-crafted "traditional" short fiction of rival John Updike. How upset Don would be were he living now, to see how George Saunders has usurped his *New Yorker* space with his deftly orchestrated, Barthelme-inspired American-Gothic-surreal short fiction . . .) In my presence at least, as on that uncomfortably hot July day in 1977 when we had lunch in the Village, it seemed important to Donald to establish himself as both a martyr of sorts—the brilliant iconoclastic / experimental writer whose books sold less than they deserved to sell—and the most strong-willed among us. Social engagements with Donald Barthelme were conducted strictly on Barthelmeian terms.

If he were still alive—he died in 1989, of cancer—Don would be seventy-six years old at the time of this writing, in December 2008. Very likely the Barthelmeian edginess would have subsided by now. Very likely even Nabokov wouldn't have been considered a rival but something like a colleague, a brother, or a friend.

The Friend. Though I was on friendlier, more relaxed and affectionate terms with my fellow western New Yorker John Gardner, who'd published an early short story of mine titled "The Death of Mrs. Sheer" in his literary magazine *MSS*—and who regarded me, somewhat embarrassingly, as a "major American writer"—like himself—it can't be said that John Gardner was a "mentor" of mine, either. John was my sole writer-friend who read my writing with enormous seriousness, which was both flattering to me, and unsettling; it sometimes seemed that John took my books almost as seriously as he took his own. His model would seem to have been the elder, didactic, somewhat tiresome Tolstoy: *Art must be moral.* Another model might have been the zealous reformer Martin Luther. For this reason, John took it as his duty to chide, criticize, scold—in particular he scolded me about my "pessimism"—my "tragic view of life"; it was John's hope to enlist me in the quixotic enterprise of writing what he called "moral fiction"— see the preacherly *On Moral Fiction* (1978). My next novel should be, for instance, a novel that John's young daughter could read and be left with the feeling that "life was worthwhile"—so John argued, with grim persistence, pushing aside his near-untouched plate of food (thick sirloin steak leaking blood) and drinking glass after glass of Scotch.

How I replied to this, as to other admonitions of John Gardner's, I have no idea.

Though John professed to admire my novels *A Garden of Earthly Delights, Expensive People, Them, Wonderland*—though he gave my post-modernist gothic *Bellefleur* a long, thoughtfully written, and generous review on the front page of *The New York Times Book Review*, and always spoke highly of me in public in venues in which he mischievously / maliciously denounced many of our cohorts—John always seemed disappointed in me. I might have been an acolyte who'd managed to elude the gravitational pull of a powerful planetary force—an American Tolstoy visionary in the mortal form of John Gardner.

With my longtime predilection for the playful experimentation of James Joyce no less than the intransigent tragic humanism of D. H. Lawrence and the absurdist surrealism of Franz Kafka, I was not likely to be influenced by my fellow western New Yorker from Batavia. I was not likely to be told what to do, still less why I must do it. Nor did I understand the passion with which John attacked his slightly older post-modernist contemporaries, of whom a number were his friends, or had been—John Barth, Robert Coover, Stanley Elkin; I never understood the bitterness of some of these rivalries, which hurt John more than they hurt others, and

132

made enemies of individuals who should have been friends and supporters at a time when John badly needed support.

But then, I don't really understand the messianic personality—the hectoring Tolstoy, the righteous Martin Luther. I never understood why so exceptional a personality as John Gardner wanted so badly to influence others. During our often noisy evenings together, when John lectured in one of his lengthy lurching eloquently drunken monologues, or argued with someone who dared to challenge him, the calm still sane words of Henry David Thoreau came to me: *I never found the companion so companionable as solitude.* Why this compulsion to enjoin others to think as you believe they should? It seemed futile to me, foolish.

Years of proselytizing, preaching, and sniping at other writers provoked a considerable backlash against John in the late 1970s and early 1980s, as he might have anticipated. I have no doubt that some of the negative publicity John drew helped to account for his moods of depression, which in turn provoked drinking, and driving-while-drinking—recklessly, on the motorcycle that would eventually kill him, in an accident on a graveled country road in upstate New York outside Susquehannah, in 1982.

At the time of his death, John had been divorced from two wives, and about to marry another, much younger woman writer, a former student at SUNY-Binghamton.

I remember first hearing of John's death. I'd been invited to give a reading at the Princeton Public Library and my librarian-hostess told me the shocking news: "John Gardner is dead." Not for a moment did I think that this "John Gardner" might be the other Gardner, a writer of popular mysteries; I'd known immediately that this Gardner was my western New York friend. And I'd known, or seemed to know, that John's death (at the age of forty-nine) would turn out to be both accidental and—perhaps— to a degree—self-willed.

What would John Gardner's life be now, if he hadn't drunk so heavily? So compulsively, like a fated character out of Dostoyevsky or Eugene O'Neill? If he hadn't succumbed to an alcoholic's wildly inflated vision of himself—in which he saw his destiny loom large in the writing of the "great American novel" that would "alter the consciousness" of his time? My most vivid memories are of John hugging me, hard. This was John's customary greeting, as it was John's customary farewell. I remember John kissing my cheek, smelling of whiskey—his silvery hair falling disheveled to his broad, slightly rounded shoulders, his gesturing hands edged with grime, like fingerless gloves. I remember the glisten of his eyes, and the sharp smell of his smoldering pipe: "Joyce, you know that we're as good as—maybe better than—Lawrence, don't you? Lawrence, Joyce, Faulkner—we are their equals, or will be. You know that, don't you? Come on!"

Early Influences. Often it's said that the only influences that matter greatly to us come early in our lives, and I think that this must be so. Of the thousands—tens of thousands?—of books I've probably read, in part or entirely, many of which have surely exerted some very real influence in my writing life, only a few shimmer with a sort of supernatural significance, like the brightest stars in the firmament: Lewis Carroll's *Alice's Adventures in Wonderland* and *Through the Looking-Glass*; Frances Hodgson Burnett's *The Secret Garden*; *The Gold Bug and Other Stories* by Edgar Allan Poe—the great books of my childhood.

Add to which, in early adolescence, at a time when I borrowed books from the Lockport Public Library each Saturday when my mother drove into town to shop for groceries, such thrilling titles as Henry David Thoreau's *Walden*, Emily Brontë's *Wuthering Heights*, Ernest Hemingway's *In Our Time*, William Faulkner's *The Sound and the Fury*—the great books of a more self-consciously "literary" era in my life.

Of course as a student I had influential teachers—a succession of wonderfully encouraging, inspiring, and insightful teachers at both Williamsville High School, in Williamsville, New York, and Syracuse University, from which I graduated in 1960. As a child, I attended a one-room schoolhouse in rural Niagara County, north of Buffalo, of which I've written elsewhere—a hardscrabble "education experience" which has provided useful memories of the kind we all retrieve and hone for nostalgic purposes but not an education of which one might reasonably boast, still less present as ideal or "influential" in any significant way. (My memory of our Amazonian teacher Mrs. Dietz, confronted with the rebelliousness and general obtusiveness of six-foot-tall farmboys with no love of book learning nor even of sitting still for more than a few minutes at a time, approaches the succinctness of Faulkner's terse encomium for the black housekeeper Dilsey: *They endured.*)

If I had a single "mentor" who guided me into my writing life—or at any rate encouraged me—it wasn't any of my teachers, wonderful though they were, nor any of my university colleagues in the years to come, but my grandmother Blanche Woodside, my father's mother. (Oates was the name of my grandmother's first husband.) In our not-very-prosperous farmhouse in Millersport, New York, at the northern edge of Erie County near the Erie Barge Canal, there were no books at all—*not even a Bible.* (How curious this was wouldn't occur to me until I was much older. Though eventually my parents converted to Catholicism after the sudden, premature death of my mother's father, when I was in junior high school, the household of my early, formative years was utterly without "religion" of any kind—the prevailing tone of secular skepticism was set by both my mother's father, a Hungarian immigrant who worked in a steel foundry in Tonawanda and as a "village blacksmith" at home in Millersport, and by my father Fred Oates, who'd had to drop out of grade school to help support his mother after his father Carleton Oates abandoned them in or about 1917.) Along with articles of clothing she'd sewed or knitted for me, my grandmother gave me books for Christmas and my birthday, year after year; when I was fourteen, inspired by my predilection for filling tablet after tablet with my schoolgirl handwriting and drawings, in the way of a budding serial novelist, my grandmother stunned my parents and me by giving me a Remington portable typewriter for my birthday!—an astonishing gift considering that my grandmother had very little money, and typewriters were virtually unheard of in rural households like ours.

Most of the children's storybooks and young-adult novels my grandmother gave me have faded from my memory, like the festive holiday occasions themselves. The great single—singular—book of my childhood, if not of my entire life, is *Alice's Adventures in Wonderland* and *Through the Looking-Glass*, which my grandmother gave me when I was eight years old, and which, with full-page illustrations by John Tenniel, in a slightly oversized edition with a transparent plastic cover, exerted a powerful influence upon my susceptible child's imagination   a kind of hypnotic spell that lasted for years.

Here is my springboard into the imagination! Here is my model of what a "storybook" can be.

I was too young for such exalted thoughts, of course. Far too young even to grasp that the name stamped on the spine of the book—*Lewis Carroll*—was the author's name, still less that it was the author's "penname." (Many years would pass before I became aware that the author of the *Alice* books was an Oxford mathematician named Charles Dodgson, an eccentric bachelor with a predilection for telling fantastical stories to the young daughters of his Oxford colleagues and photographing them in suggestive and seductive poses evocative of Humbert Humbert's nymphets of a later, less innocent era.) My enchantment with this gift began with the book itself as a physical/ aesthetic object, quite unlike anything else in our household: both *Alice* books were published in a single volume under the imprint Illustrated Junior Library, Grosset & Dunlap (1946). Immediately, the striking illustrations by John Tenniel entered my imagination, ranged across the field of the book's cover—back and front—in a dreamlike assemblage of phantasmagoric figures as in a somewhat less malevolent landscape by Hieronymus Bosch. (I still have this book. It is one of the precious possessions in my library. What a surprise to discover that the book that loomed so large in my childhood imagination is only slightly larger than an ordinary book.)

The appeal of *Alice* and her bizarre adventures to an eight-year-old girl in a farming community in upstate New York is obvious. Initially, the little-girl reader is likely to be struck by the fact that the story's heroine is a girl of her own approximate age who confronts extraordinary adventures with an admirable equanimity, common sense, and courage. (We know that Alice isn't much more than eight years old because Humpty Dumpty says slyly to her that she might have "left off" at seven—meaning, Alice might have died at seven.) Like most children Alice talks to herself—but not in the silly prattling way of most children: "'Come, there's no use in crying like that!' said Alice to herself rather sharply; 'I advise you to leave off this minute!'" (Obviously, Alice is echoing adult admonitions—she has interiorized the stoicism of her elders.) Instead of being alarmed or terrified, as a normal child would be, Alice marvels, "Curiouser and curiouser!"— as if the world so fraught with shape-changing and threats of dissolution and even, frequently, cannibalism were nothing more than a puzzle to be solved or a game to be played like croquet, cards, or chess. (Alice discovers that the Looking-Glass world is a continual game of chess in which, by pressing forward, and not backing down in her confrontations with Looking-Glass inhabitants, she will become Queen Alice—though it isn't a very comfortable state pinioned between two elderly snoring queens.) The *Alice* books are gold mines of aphoristic instruction: "Who cares for you? You're nothing but a pack of cards!" Alice cries fearlessly, nullifying the authority of malevolent adults as, at the harrowing conclusion of

Looking-Glass, she confronts the taboo fact of "cannibalism" at the heart of civilization:

> [The Pudding] was so large that [Alice] couldn't help feeling a *little* shy with it, as she had been with the mutton; however, she conquered her shyness by a great effort, and cut a slice and handed it to the Red Queen.
>
> "What impertinence!" said the Pudding. "I wonder how you'd like it, if I were to cut a slice out of *you*, you creature!"
>
> It spoke in a thick, suety sort of voice, and Alice hadn't a word to say in reply; she could only sit and look at it and gasp.

The banquet dissolves into nightmare as the White Queen seizes Alice's hair in both hands and screams, "Take care of yourself! . . . Something's going to happen! . . ."

> There was not a moment to be lost. Already several of the guests were lying down in the dishes, and the soup-ladle was walking up the table towards Alice's chair . . . "I can't stand this any longer!" Alice cries, as she jumped up and seized the tablecloth with both hands: one good pull, and plates, dishes, guests, and candles came crashing down together in a heap on the floor.

Both *Alice's Adventures in Wonderland* and *Alice Through the Looking-Glass* are brilliantly imagined fantasies that shade by degrees into nightmare—only to be routed by Alice's impetuousness and quick thinking. The child reader is meant to take solace in the possibility that, like Alice, she can exorcise adult vanity and cruelty; she may be very young, and very small, but she can assert herself if she knows how. Both *Alice* nightmares end with Alice simply waking up—returned to a comfortable domestic world of kittens and tea-things, and no adults in sight.

In essence, I think I am, still, this child-self so like an American cousin of Lewis Carroll's Alice: my deepest, most yearning and most (naively) hopeful self. I think that I am still waiting to be "influenced"—by a loving mentor, or even a monster. By someone.

Who?

THE SCHOLARS AND THE
PORNOGRAPHER

Carolyn See

Dame Helen Gardner and George Newton Bowlin Laws—it seems funny, but very good to me to see them in the same sentence.

I first saw Helen Gardner, brilliant scholar, denizen of Oxford University, later to be made a Dame on her learning alone, at UCLA. She was so smart and so dazzling in the way she taught that she made your eyes water. You left the huge class at UCLA, when she was a visiting professor and still hadn't quite achieved her "international reputation," and there you were in bright, glaring sunlight, staggering about as if you'd seen *For Whom the Bell Tolls* at an afternoon matinée; Gary Cooper had just sent away the beautiful, bewildered Ingrid Bergman so that he could "blow the bridge" in Civil War Spain, but he's told her their love was so strong that they would always be together. . . . And so she fled and Cooper faced an honorable death that meant something, and there you were, in an iffy neighborhood in West Hollywood facing a long walk home as a little kid, but it was okay because the walk would give you time to dash away your unseemly, twelve-year-old tears, and try in some way to measure the highest meanings of love and death and art and sorrow, and the regular, usual glaring world we mostly have to live in. (And, yes, I know, it was a corny movie, but I was only twelve!)

At UCLA, coming out of Helen Gardner's Modern Poetry class, after an hour of "God's Grandeur," I was twenty, still plagued with watery eyes, and only had ten minutes in the harsh California sun to get over my damn self before my next class, to get over the secret, occult, glimmering meanings of "The world is charged with the grandeur of God/It will flame out, like shining from shook foil; / It gathers to a greatness, like the ooze of oil / Crushed . . ." I would have died of embarrassment if the students all around me—sniffling, dabbing their eyes, forgetting to talk—hadn't been in much the same condition. Helen Gardner was a stunner, a class act; she held the keys to the kingdom, and she was offering them to us Monday, Wednesday, and Friday from eleven o'clock to noon.

Outside of having much the same build as Dame Helen, a little bit short, a little bit stumpy, a wide pleasing face with a constant smile, sometimes attentive, sometimes absent, George Laws had nothing to do with her. He was born in the early part of the twentieth century to a hard-luck family who made their home in Oak Cliff, a suburb of Dallas, Texas. They had fled Virginia after the War Between the States. Word was, they were descendants of Pocahontas, and they lived about as poorly as she had. George's brother died at seventeen, after he cut his finger on his first day at work in the Dallas sewers. His sister would die soon after and his father (after reportedly killing someone in a gunfight) drank himself to death with some dispatch. But George's defining loss had come much earlier when he discovered the body of his mother, who had blown off her head with a shotgun when George was fourteen. He managed to graduate from high school, stuck around to watch his sister die, then headed west to flee the past.

His mother had left a vindictive suicide note about preferring to die rather than put up with her husband's "dreadful perversions," so George took that knowledge with him to California. You could say it colored his attitude toward women, men, sexuality, life. His only solace—outside of screwing every living female he could get to lie still—was the world of books, of art, and the abiding sense that he could have been a novelist—a good one—if life hadn't fucked him over in such a definitive way.

I should have asked him about all that—he was my father, after all—but he had a coping mechanism that was foolproof. You can't ask questions when you're laughing, and he kept everybody laughing, all the time, except for that Christmas when I was three when he tried to kill himself too and spent some time in the hospital, where, needless to say, he kept all those nurses laughing. George left one, two, three of his wives—when, to my knowledge, they loved him the most. My mother was his second. But he was a good, even faithful dad, calling me every week or so, taking me out, delivering lectures on Melville and Twain, and telling me not to turn up my nose at C. S. Forester. His own favorite novel was *Jurgen*, by James Branch Cabell; he hated Joseph Hergesheimer, whom he dismissed contemptuously as "the darling of the intellectuals." That's how I found out there were intellectuals. But something in him kept him from writing.

I ended up only taking three weeks of Helen Gardner's class. I'd been living on my own since I was barely seventeen; I was so tired. I married a boy from high school, a soldier who was stationed up in Newfoundland. I took a few talismanic things with me—among them a six-by-twelve-inch cardboard poster, an announcement for a public lecture on the UCLA campus that I had attended: Helen Gardner, speaking on "Comedy and T. S. Eliot." Just a couple of weeks ago, my first husband found it in some papers and gave it back to me. Yellowed with age, in an antique type, dated April 19, 1954. She spoke that day on whether or not you should do what you love even if you aren't very good at it. She was a little nervous because the audience was mainly faculty, rather than the undergraduates who loved her so much, doted on her every word.

Flash-forward to me in Newfoundland, pregnant, throwing up all day, peeing in a bucket in the corner of our bedroom, and not thinking much about the consolations of art. At twenty, justifiably perhaps, my first husband and I felt our lives were over. We went to Paris, I had the baby, came home, finished school over my in-laws' strenuous objections. I wrote an (unpublished) novel before I got my PhD. I don't know how else to say this: My life was *here*, my wished-for life was *there*, where the writers were. My father was by now married to his fourth and last wife; we were in the same predicament. I married again, had another daughter, divorced. We had some good times, but my second husband liked to tell me that "wives and children killed more artists than cholera."

At one time when my own life was killing me, I called my dad and begged him to let me visit. He was ensconced in a town in the South with his then fiancée, more than thirty years his junior, and one of her girlfriends. His fiancée would become his last and favorite wife. They'd all come down with a case of crabs and my dad found a movie poster—*The Attack of the Crab Monsters*—and hung it in the bathroom. That more or less set the tone. They were flat, flat broke; my dad sold reducing machines to farm wives. He was quite chubby, and when I went with him one day to sell those machines out among the kudzu vines, a wife somewhat sourly reminded him of this fact. "Ah, Madame, you should have seen me *before* I began to use this marvelous machine!"

My dad, his fiancée Lynda, and I used to spend the long Southern evenings watching triple features at the drive-in. They saved the worst for last, and once at about one in the morning we watched a jungle movie, made in somebody's backyard, with white explorers in pith helmets and a lot of very reluctant African-Americans dressed up like savages and speaking in broad Southern accents. The two main savages were Maga and Futu. The dialogue consisted mostly of sentences like: "Quick, Maga! Send for Futu!" Or, "Quickly Futu! Maga must be found at once!"

We went back to the apartment, forgot about it for a couple of days. Then one night as Daddy was cutting up lettuce for a salad, he said, just chatting along, "I wonder what Maga and Futu are doing tonight?" I can't express the impression this made on me. Here was another person who knew another world was out there! If you couldn't get to it, maybe you could make it come to you. And you conjured it up out of words.

Just as Gerard Manley Hopkins had evoked infinity by "shining from shook foil." "Don't you see," Helen Gardner had said, pleased beyond words, "how if you took a great handful of foil, scrunched it up and *shook* it, light would fly out from it as far as the eye can see? Or if you have just a tablespoon of oil and you put the heel of your hand down and *crushed* it, it would spread and spread, you really couldn't get rid of it then — it would just get greater and greater?"

It gathers to a greatness, like the ooze of oil/Crushed.

This isn't going to be an essay about monsters. I've been double-crossed a few times and lied to more than once but I find editors and writers and scholars to be, on balance, extremely kind, and almost everyone I've known in these contexts has been extremely kind to me. I'm going to flash forward from Maga and Futu ten more years, past my PhD and the beginning and end of my second marriage. I'm a divorcée, "a woman alone with two children." I live by that phrase for over a decade, and collect some fairly miscellaneous boyfriends. My adored PhD adviser, John Espey, was widowed. I was doing magazine assignments and working on my first novel, which somehow got published. My dad wasn't all that crazy about this development—his feeling, never before explicitly spoken, was that if you'd suffered enough, you really didn't *have* to write. But he yearned. He yearned to write.

Then a cultural development happened: the underground literature in England and America came out above ground like vast fields of rice sprouts, all green and fresh. A rash of trials spread throughout the land. I went downtown to see my idol, my icon, John Espey, explain the central image in *Tropic of Cancer*—a flashlight turned full blast on someone's vagina by the ever enthusiastic Henry Miller. "He was simply trying to shed some light on the subject," Espey said. "I can't say that I see anything prurient about *that*."

Soon enough—and not related to Mr. Espey's testimony—some desperate attorneys called me as a newly minted, unemployed PhD to defend a pathetic little volume called *Lust Thy Friends and Neighbors*. I was so wonderful as an expert witness on the stand that day that they tore up my check (for fifty dollars) and made it out for a hundred. For the next two years I made a very nice living defending pornography, and got a book out of it as well, *Blue Money*, which dirty old men still read to this day.

Soon there came an afternoon, during a biblical Southern California flood, that I went down to my dad's house in Cardiff-by-the-Sea, a suburb of San Diego, to help out after Daddy's fourth wife, Lynda, had her first son. I was thirty-five years old; my dad was sixty-nine and out of work, as usual. In a moment of quiet, I was working in their kitchen, with a stack of novels, taking notes. "What are you doing there, Squirt?"

"I'm taking notes, Daddy. I'm an expert witness in pornography trials!" (As in, "I'm making a living over here. You ought to try it sometime!") He picked up a volume by Akbar del Piombo and began to peruse it with care. Men tend to get hypnotized by pornography—I saw it for myself a few years later in the U.S. Supreme Court, when Justice Renquist reached down for some from the bench and didn't resurface again for the rest of the trial. But my dad was another story. He read critically, and said, as James Fenimore Cooper famously had when he first picked up a "wilderness" novel, "I could do better than this."

The very next morning he went into the guest bedroom and began to type. And type. And type. He would publish seventy-three hard-core pornographic novels before he died, and if we lived in a different culture, there'd be statues of him in public parks. I only read four of the novels (there's a certain unseemliness in reading your dad's sex fantasies), but his first—and my all-time favorite—is written in the "moonlight and magnolias" literary style George grew up with in the Texan South. An intrepid but beautifully brought up heroine, Carrie Hunt ("Transpose those letters!"), sets off on a train ride in the nineteenth century, complete with the requisite picnic basket of cold fried chicken. The train is robbed; she meets plenty of gallant outlaws and very quickly loses her virtue. She meets men who say things like, "I have no vocation for hard work. These hands just don't fit a hoe." There's sex on every page, of course, and Carrie loves every minute of it. Toward the end, after six strapping young men have taken their pleasure of her, she considers: "For a girl my age I had had a lot of fun, but honestly I had never had all the sex I wanted, even when I had all I needed. Maybe, maybe six men would really leave me wanting no more." Daddy wrote a porn western called *The Secret of Hidden Gap*, a porn spy thriller for a friend of mine named Marina called *Marina Blows Her Cover*, as well as a porn treatise on saving the earth, *Olivia's Ecology Lesson*, and many more.

It's the curse of the pornographer—even more than the ordinary writer—that his work is not perceived as work; it's as if "Since you can fuck, you can write porn," which, of course, is not the case. During the late sixties, when my dad began his career, we gave a lot of parties. Because he'd grown up in the Depression, he'd learned to roll his own cigarettes and was the only one among us who could effortlessly roll big, fat, firm joints. He'd be engaged in this occupation at parties, mainly standing at the kitchen sink, and handing them off to crowds of young hipsters, when he'd be approached by some callow youth or other. "I . . . uh . . . I've read some of your work. I've thought of doing that someday, just to make some extra money."

The man who'd endowed Maga and Futu with lives of their own would answer crisply, "If you do, be sure to be specific. Nobody likes generalities. That juice that exudes from an excited cunt, for instance. Most men automatically think of it as clear. But in actuality, it has a certain custard quality . . ." He'd go on like this for a few more minutes until the brash boy slunk away, and then he'd smile, give me a wink, go on rolling joints.

Time went on. Both my dad and I published. Then my life, quite wild at the time, took another turn. John Espey waited the requisite year after his wife died, and paid me a serious social call, in which he brought along a photo album that showed him mountain climbing, to prove he was in good physical shape. (He was twenty-one years older than I.) He was the son of Presbyterian missionaries to China and had been a Rhodes Scholar. He knew the Coffins of Maine were a prominent family; I thought they might be pine boxes. When Helen Gardner had come to UCLA maybe twenty years before, the rest of the faculty had shunned her—she was a woman in her fifties, in *the* fifties. It was a miracle she'd been invited at all. But John sought her out. They had mutual Oxford memories, and, as I think I've already said, each one was about as learned as the other. Her specialty was Eliot; his was Ezra Pound.

Mr. Espey was many a social class away from me, but we tried it anyway, and stayed together twenty-eight years, until he died in 2000. Many years before that, Helen Gardner—by this time Dame Helen Gardner— came back to Los Angeles, to study for a year at the Clark Library. John was thrilled to see his old friend, and took the opportunity almost every day to go off to the Clark to do some research. He was absurdly proud of her, proud to know her. They would elude the other scholars swotting away under basement fluorescent lights. They lunched together on the lawn, making fun of the others. She told him, one Monday, how on the Sunday before, she'd attended church and became so incensed at the minister's inanities that she'd declined to take communion; she hadn't felt herself to be in a state of grace. She was getting testy in her old age, but her obsession with words, and the fun and pleasure they could bring, never abated.

After finishing his seventy-third novel, my father stopped. He developed lung cancer, and worse, a severe clinical depression. His jollity, his joviality ceased to kick in. He took to his bed and wept for a little over a year. Even then he kept a goofy streak that surfaced in unexpected ways. He and his wife and young son drove up to visit us for some holiday or other.

144

When he got out of the car, he looked awful; he'd lost maybe forty pounds and his face was gray. He clutched a little brown paper bag. I took it from him, looked in it. A half-eaten apple, and a quarter of a gnawed-on sandwich. "It was all we were able to take with us, over the border," he said glumly.

Helen Gardner went home, glowing with academic praise and delight in her Damehood. My father died. Then Oxford decided to throw a fiftieth anniversary bash of the Rhodes Scholars Reunion. By that time, John Espey had traveled to Europe and China and Japan and Indonesia and Alaska, but he fretted like a teenager asked to the prom. We would stay at the Randolph instead of rooms in Merton, his old college. We received — and studied — the protocol and dress and behavior for each event we chose to participate in. I was to wear a different evening gown (full length!) for every night. I would need a hat and elbow-length gloves for the Queen's tea. John fretted over his tuxedo and repeatedly told me it was *not* to be called a tuxedo. He bought extra black ties, and white. We spent several evenings at home before we left, training me to eat pudding with a fork and tablespoon, lessons I would appreciate while watching a lanky blond American woman in Merton's hallowed halls take a heaping tablespoon of blancmange and pitch it straight onto her ice-blue sequined chest.

John and I had never married, but the Rhodes Scholar committee took care of that for us. I was Mrs. John Espey for the duration of the stay. I never saw such a bunch of nervous scholars. They felt about that school the way I felt about Dame Helen — they revered, they venerated the place. By and large, they were ashamed that they hadn't lived up to the amazing gift that had been given them.

We drove out one day to see Dame Helen, in a flower-covered cottage out of a fairy tale. She'd never had much use for me. I couldn't begin to match her learning or her repartee, but she knew — from John — how much she meant to me, and she was thrilled, in a stubby, British way, to see us. The house was both cozy and luxurious, everything on a very small scale. The walls were lined with books and she offhandedly showed us the medal and sash she had received, making her a Dame. It resided in a little niche in the wall, propped up on blue velvet. We ate smoked trout off pewter plates and drank very strong martinis.

Then Dame Helen asked me outside to see her garden. Not John, just me. "Here are my cabbages," she said. "Here are my runner beans.

I always plant too much squash, but I think everybody does, don't you?" The sun shone brightly, directly into her eyes. She looked exhausted, an old lady, stubby, her green dress robbed of its luster. It was like coming out of a matinée into the harsh sun. (It wasn't "like" that; it *was* that.) The look in her eyes was the same that I had seen on my father's face in the nursing home weeks before he died. Undefended despair, and all the invocations of Gerard Manley Hopkins, all the goofiness of a brand of pornography that relied on words to suggest, just suggest, that sex might be fun, all the Magas and the Futus in the world couldn't stop that condition, that terrible turn of events.

All of them used the best weapons they had—words and wit—and my father, the knowledge that every minute you were laughing meant you'd cheated death and the knowledge of death.

They're dead now. George Laws, a.k.a. Hardy Peters; Dame Helen Gardner, who hypnotized young men and women into the reckless love of poetry; and John Espey, who was less my mentor than my saviour. They saved me from the monsters. And writing is the best way I can pay them back.

"But What I *Really* Love About This Is This Amazing Game That You've Invented"

AN APPRECIATION OF JOHN HAWKES

Jim Shepard

There are a lot of writers out there who I'm sure pride themselves on not having needed a mentor—fiercely independent types, self-taught at everything from the possibilities of figurative language to the rudiments of crossbow construction—but as for me, when I was starting out, in literary matters I couldn't have found my ass with both hands and a banjo. The first fiction writer with whom I worked, Stephen Minot, did the best he could with me, but he was starting a few floors below the lobby. One of his colleagues in the English Department at Trinity College, Milla Riggio, who taught things like Anglo-Saxon poetry and medieval and Renaissance drama, had, with a marvelous charismatic seriousness of purpose, taken my hand and led me into an appreciation of the joys of close reading. But they had *so* much ground to cover: I'd gone to a pit of a high school and had grown up reading almost exclusively nonfiction, so the only canon of which *I* had any knowledge had two n's and was the kind that was built into the side of a man of war.

In keeping with a life that up until that point had been constructed from a desultory combination of inadequate planning and no planning at all, I lucked into graduate study with John Hawkes at Brown University by having decided at the last minute to *not* try to write in my parents' basement, and to take advantage instead of the two years in which I'd be left alone to get an MFA.

With what feels in retrospect like a touching pathos, I spent the summer trying to prepare, as much as I prepared for anything, by reading John Hawkes's work, or, more accurately, those of his novels that I could find in the Stratford Public Library. I read *The Blood Oranges, The Cannibal,* and *Death, Sleep and the Traveler.* The charitable way to characterize my response might be to say that I groped around in the murk of my understanding. I did, to my credit, realize that I had much to gain by studying with someone whose imagination worked in these ways.

The speed with which I went from solely intimidated to pleased and comfortable and just plain delighted to be in the guy's presence had everything to do with the amused and slightly teasing way in which he negotiated his public roles as teacher and literary lion. Jack Hawkes ("It's *Jack,*" he'd correct you when you first addressed him, as though amiably exasperated at having to tell you for the fifteenth time) was the first writer I ever got to know who was self-consciously playful when it came to his public persona. (Back then in America it was still possible for an esoteric writer to *have* a public persona.) Much was written about him then, especially by academics and Frenchmen, and he loved to quote it and then play off it. These were all Jacks who were in some ways authentic and all of them allowed him to access those values he held most dear. As well as those that he pretended to hold most dear. So that an audience at one of his readings might glimpse four or five of those figures in his opening patter. Like Jack the fanatical Francophile: "Are any of you able to *drink* American wine?" he might ask the assembled, with an anxious curiosity, as though he were asking about antifreeze. Or Jack the outrageously unapologetic hedonist. Or Jack the logistically helpless: I remember him enraging Michael Harper, the poet who ran the program at that point, after one reading by complaining innocently but with a childlike repetitive intensity, "Why is it that the *food* we have at these readings is so consistently uninteresting? Who is it that's in charge of the *food?*"

One of the Jacks that he liked to trot out a lot around me was Jack the deaf, dumb, and blind hermit when it came to popular culture. Though we were never sure to what extent he was exaggerating, he prided himself on his nearly pristine lack of involvement with the sort of stuff you'd find in *People* magazine or *Entertainment Weekly.* Mickey Mouse he conceded that he'd heard of. Movie stars of the day? No chance. Popular music? Sure, if you count Scriabin.

148

That Jack was the Jack about which I liked to tease him most, and whenever Jack was teased he became more like the figure you'd been teasing. It seemed to be, for him, a lovely and subtle form of play. Halfway through my second year in the program, we had a tutorial about a story that featured a narrator who found himself quarterbacking the Minnesota Vikings with his mother as the fullback and his father as the coach. He told me that I'd really hit on something, here. He praised the story's psychodynamics and brutal comedy, and then added, "But what I *really* love about this is this amazing *game* that you've invented, with its own lunatic *logic*: I mean, these great masses of people all helmeted and uniformed and *pushing* at one another. And if you score by crossing your line, you get to *kick* an *extra point*. And no one even questions *why* you get to kick an extra point."

And there I was, thinking, he's kidding, right? And in the meantime he continued marveling at the feat of imagination I'd pulled off, especially in terms of the offhanded intricacy of this game and the power of its surrealism. I ended up saying something like, "Jack, you've heard of football," and his response was something like, "*This* is football? This is the same game?"

It's a measure of how good he was at ambiguities of tone that about half of our workshop, having heard that story, believed he was putting me on, and the other half was fiercely convinced of the opposite.

But probably the most valuable Jack that Jack modeled for us was Jack the rigorously well-read. He was encyclopedic and passionate about the kind of literature that we all knew we should have encountered, but almost none of us had, in any quantity: the Eastern Europeans, the South Americans, the French. Really, almost anybody that Americans would consider esoteric. And not just non-Americans, as well: I remember him rhapsodizing about Nathanael West's *Dream Life of Balso Snell,* and going around the room twice to make sure that he wasn't mistaken; that, in fact, *no one* in his workshop had read the thing. I bought *The Complete Works of Nathanael West,* shamefacedly, at the used-book store on campus later that same afternoon.

He'd draw his examples, when discussing our work, from that sort of literature. This or that gesture in someone's story might remind him of a moment in a work of Svevo's, or Borges's, or Gide's, or Tournier's, or Cortázar's, and when we'd looked back at him blankly, he'd say, "Wait. You haven't *read* that book?" the way you might ask the Pope if it was really true that he hadn't read the Bible.

He'd be equally appalled, and pained, to hear that you'd read some of his favorite more canonized authors, but only a very small amount of them. You've read *some* Nabokov? Well, why'd you *stop*? You've read two Flannery O'Connor stories? Well, do you know how many she *wrote*?

And when you did come back to him, having engaged and enjoyed a work you hadn't known existed, he was so beside himself with pleasure, and with an eagerness to catalog its virtues, that you resolved then and there to please him, and yourself, that way again.

In other words: like just about any good teacher, he made abundantly clear what a *gift* high literary culture really was.

What he did for me as a reader is of course indivisible from what he did for me as a writer. But like any MFA student, what I had been most hoping was that as a reader and an editor he'd transform my own fiction. And boy, did *those* hopes work out.

I remember finishing *Death, Sleep and the Traveler* that summer before I began at Brown and wondering if there'd been some kind of mistake, in terms of my admission. I mean, up to that point I'd been writing what I hoped were lucid, naturalist stories about suburban kids negotiating your run-of-the-mill family dysfunctions. What was he going to make of stuff like that?

As was characteristic of me, once I was faced with a challenge, I gave up. Confronted with such an intimidating mentor—I mean, who was going to compete with one of the premier Fabulists when it came to imagination?—I somehow decided that I might as well hunker down and go even smaller when it came to ambition: maybe even more obsessively attempt to write about *only* what I knew. *Oh yeah, Mr. Bigshot-I-seem-to-have-read-everything? Well, let's see if you know more about Catholic schoolteachers in Bridgeport, Connecticut, than I do.* I cranked out, in accordance with that plan, any number of stories about bookish and sensitive and wry and troubled but covertly adorable young boys saddled with Italian Catholic backgrounds on the suburban Connecticut shore. Jack waded through each with his version of a weary patience, which might more accurately be described as a kind of civil *im*patience: when vehement about something (which was nearly always, when it came to literature; he spent, I'd estimate, about 10 percent of his time diffident, about

30 percent either bemused or amused, and the other 60 percent vehement), his voice would take on a self-consciously hectoring and wheedling nasal lament which was uncannily channeled by Gilda Radner and Bill Murray on *Saturday Night Live* in their skit "The Whiners."

He sighed a lot when fiction didn't excite him. He'd sigh, and begin to praise the story in minor ways, and my heart would sink right through the floor. He'd walk me through the story—this was fine, that was fine, this was certainly a well-turned phrase, he supposed—but nothing would get him *excited* until he finally ran across something bizarre, something unexpected. The boy's being scolded, and for no apparent reason he puts his finger in the ashtray and *licks* it? Jack would seize on such moments the way you'd seize on water in the desert, and explain through them how much more arresting they made my otherwise bland protagonists.

I caught on, slowly. You want *weird*? I remember thinking, not entirely discouraged. Well, that won't be hard for *me*. Hence that story about the boy who found himself quarterbacking the Minnesota Vikings with his mother as the fullback and his father as the coach. Or another, soon after, about a doting father and husband who spent his covert hours lying on runways near the touchdown points of incoming aircraft.

As our teacher, Jack modeled for us so many things. He reminded us of the ways in which fiction so often was willing to confront ugliness in the service of its opposite. He taught us to value obsessive focus. He insisted that when writing we not forget our allegiance to the body. He demanded we stay willing to be educated about our emotions.

But most of all, he taught us to leap at the astonishingly idiosyncratic wherever it appeared in our work. To value the expressive potential of the unexpectedly strange.

Celebrating such stories as they came across his desk, Jack exulted in the excess, the unruliness, the energy that resulted in our having turned ourselves over to our intuition. What he was teaching me, when he taught me always to look for the strangeness and to value the weird, was to understand that those moments that I *hadn't* fully planned were reliably the ones in which I electrified my inert little narrative, and most likely, most fully revealed myself. Or at least: revealed what was potentially my most interesting self.

Which, I realized years later, was also where Jack's playfulness with his public persona came in. In and out of the classroom, he was tirelessly showing us all, with a kind of gleeful and sly definitiveness, how foolish it was to fret that we only had ourselves to write about, as though there wasn't something unutterably—and savingly—strange and multifarious about the self anyway. As William Gass later wrote in an essay on Katherine Anne Porter: "Our ignorance [of who we are] is reassuring to Porter because the self she fears she is she hopes will remain unknowable to others, while the self she wishes she were takes its public place. Yet the self she regretted and the self she desired are actually states of that populous nation that a self is: cowgirl, coquette, cook, queen, artist, the disillusioned well-used lady, and the girl with the dream—a roaring, riotous, shrewd, and foolish community of loving and quarreling equals."

Or maybe here's another way of putting it, a formulation from the poet Michael Ryan that Jack would have loved: "You can *do* anything. But it all counts."

152

Munro Country

Cheryl Strayed

One afternoon when I was twenty-five, I opened the lid of the black metal mailbox that was bolted to the front of the house where I lived and found a plain white envelope addressed to me in a grandmotherly scrawl from an address in British Columbia. It was January in Minneapolis and cold—*really cold*—but I pulled my gloves off anyway and tore the envelope open and stood on the frozen wooden stairs to read the letter inside. *Dear Cheryl*, it began in the same hand that had addressed the envelope:

> *Your letter and story were forwarded to me here in B. C. where I am staying until April—near to 2 of my daughters and my one grandchild. I want to say that I was moved and delighted by the Horse and Blue Canoe. It's a wonderful, unexpected kind of story and I wouldn't change a hair on its head. (That's what my favorite editor always says to me before he proposes about 50 changes.) You are quite right to stay out of academic life if you can. Are you eligible for any grants? If you were in Canada I'd certainly urge you to apply for one from the Canada Council. You must continue writing but you do have lots of time. You're two years younger than my youngest daughter. I wasn't writing nearly so well at your age.*
> *With great good wishes—Alice Munro*

A shaky, sickening glee washed through me and then drained away almost immediately, replaced by a daffy disbelief: Alice Munro had written to me. *Alice Munro!* Those two words were a kind of Holy Grail to me then: the lilting rise and fall of *Alice*, the double-barreled thunk of *Munro*.

Together they seemed less like a name than an object I could hold in my hands—a stoneware bowl, perhaps, or a pewter platter, equal parts generous and unforgiving. They bore the weight of everything I loved, admired, and understood about the art and craft of fiction, everything I ached to master myself.

She wasn't the only writer I loved, of course. Raymond Carver, Edna O'Brien, William Faulkner, Mary Gaitskill, and Flannery O'Connor had each been profoundly important to me. From them and many others, I learned how to write. I studied their stories and novels, their sentences and scenes, excavated their plots and characters and descriptions, and then attempted to do what they did all by myself on the page. From a purely craft standpoint, Alice Munro was at the lead of that pack in my mind, a virtuoso among virtuosos, but it wasn't her virtuosity that made her different from the others to me. Not her dazzling narrative authority or her gorgeously unvarnished prose, not her telescopic density or her breathtakingly intricate descriptions of the way her characters thought and lived and behaved. What made her different to me was another thing entirely, and it wasn't about style, but subject, and even more precisely, it was about Alice Munro herself. It didn't matter that she was Canadian and thirty-seven years older than me and that her life was, in dozens of particular ways, *not* like my own; when I read her stories, I felt like she'd lived my life.

The fictional world that she has spun in a fair portion of these stories has a name: Munro Country. It's the real-life Huron County, in southwestern Ontario, where Munro spent her girlhood and returned to live in middle age. In stories she's written for what's approaching fifty years, Munro evokes this hardscrabble place with searing specificity: its ramshackle farms and rutted roads, its small towns and social institutions and the complicated and contradictory, proud and humiliated, vain and self-effacing people who populate it.

I got my first taste of Munro Country when I read *Dance of the Happy Shades*, her first book, which was published in 1968, the year I was born. I'd found it on a sale table at a used-book store near the University of Minnesota in Minneapolis, where I was a student. I bought it because it looked interesting enough and it was marked down to something like two dollars and because I was twenty and consumed at that age by a kind of roving, voracious hunger to shuck off the sunny small-town beauty queen that I seemed to be and to become instead the earnest writer that I knew lived inside me, and I felt instinctively that reading just about any work of serious fiction that I could get my hands on would help me make that transformation. I didn't know anything about Alice Munro when I paid my two dollars and shoved her book into my bag. Didn't know that by then she'd published six books and was well on her way to being celebrated as "our Chekhov"—a comparison made first by the writer Cynthia Ozick, but immediately embraced by her peers. Didn't know she'd won numerous major awards and appeared regularly in *The New Yorker* because I didn't, at that time, read *The New Yorker*. Didn't even know that *The New Yorker* was a publication that anyone beyond the city limits of New York City would have an interest in reading. I only knew this, once I sat down to read the stories in *Dance of the Happy Shades*: that those stories *knew me*.

They knew my mother, too. And my stepfather and sister and brother. They even knew our two dogs and our one-horned goat named Katrina and the hens and the horses that lived in our yard. They knew the odd, picked-on boy who drowned one summer evening in a lake outside the town where I grew up and the flamboyantly feminist counselor who came from the Twin Cities to work at my school and only lasted one year. They knew the fundamentalist Christians who lived in falling-down houses and rusted-out trailers who wouldn't let their kids listen to music and the friendly old veteran who owned a rock shop and pushed himself around in a wheelchair after he lost both of his legs in the war. They knew, it seemed, the whole of Aitkin County, Minnesota, where I came of age. Its three tiny towns and dozens of far-flung townships, its long lonesome roads and endless swamps and bogs and woods and lakes, its bars and businesses and wild and domesticated beasts, its farms and fishing holes, its corn feeds and county fairs and city councils, its deer hunters and demolition derbies, its tractor pulls and taciturn old-timers, its Finns and Ojibwes and back-to-the-land hippies, its hot mosquito-ridden summers and its brutally cold winters. But most of all, those stories knew me, the eager, curious, grandiose girl who grew up in the midst of this and wanted out as fiercely as she wanted to hold on to it forever.

I'd never felt known in quite that way by fiction. By anything, perhaps. I'd identified with characters and situations, of course; had plenty of moments, as a reader, of revelation and understanding and connection.

But what I felt about Alice Munro after reading her stories went far beyond those things: I recognized her. Felt pinned and pierced by her, burned and branded by the truth and beauty of her words. *I love Alice Munro,* I took to saying, the way I did about any number of people I didn't know whose writing I admired, meaning, of course, that I loved her books. And I did. I devoured each of them after my chance discovery of *Dance of the Happy Shades,* my love intensifying with each volume. But I loved *her,* too, in a way that felt slightly ridiculous even to me. It wasn't an obsessive stalker's love, though it did make me ache a little when I thought about it too much. It wasn't that I wanted anything from Alice Munro. I didn't expect her to love me back. It was that I longed to express my love for her. To explain, somehow, all the layers of things we had in common: the small towns and the corduroy roads, the experience of being the prodigal daughter in a place where daughters were not raised to be prodigal—and make her understand what her work had meant to me.

Still, I'd never been much of a fan. As a girl, I didn't cover my walls with posters or pictures of anyone in particular, the way most of my friends did. I'd never written a letter to a stranger I admired. And writing to Alice Munro seemed impossible anyway. Where would I send the letter? How could I find the words to express myself in full? Time passed, she published another book, and I went on silently loving her, studying her stories, trying to write my own in imitation of her. She was scheduled to read at a museum in Minneapolis and I bought a ticket, but she canceled at the last minute. And then, when I was twenty-two, my mother died and everything I felt for Alice Munro darkened, deepened.

Her mother had died young, too, and she haunts the pages of Munro's stories the way my own mother began to haunt mine. I read Munro through my sorrow, rereading certain stories and scenes over and over again, memorizing particular sentences. Class and culture and cold country climates had bound me to Munro, but they had nothing on dead mothers. Ours had died differently—hers around sixty, after a long struggle with Parkinson's disease, mine at forty-five, of lung cancer, only seven weeks after she was diagnosed—but I sensed viscerally that the losses Munro and I had suffered had gouged us in the same way. The fictional motherless daughters in her stories told me so. The sad, subtle ways they turned their heads, the glitteringly sharp laughter that tamped down the memories of the mothers they didn't have, the way they could never be free, never released, never shucked clean of the mothers that were loved or unloved, that had been wrong or almost always right, that lived on and on no matter how many years passed without them. And I understood more deeply the living mothers in Munro's fictions, too. So often they seemed to be the same one, in story after story. The same enterprising, intellectually striving, socially thwarted, subtly unconventional, and mildly whimsical woman, who, in spite of everything, had no choice but to get dinner on the table or the cows milked at dawn and, always, there'd be wash to do.

Which was, to put it plainly, the story of my own mother's life.

I tried to write that story, the one of my mother's life and my own, mimicking Munro. Of course I failed, so I wrote whatever I could get down on the page. I wrote and wrote and read some more. I read and I wrote. At twenty-four, I finished a story that I thought was perhaps good enough to be published, so I sent it to a contest in England and, months later, I got a phone call from a man in London, telling me that it had won. The prize, the man explained, was a Parker pen, a check that amounted to twenty-two hundred U.S. dollars, and two copies of the book in which my story would be published. "One for you," he said with his British accent, "and one for your mum."

I hung up the phone and cried my heart out. I was happy about the prize. I was grateful for the money. I wasn't crying because of those things. I was crying because I didn't have a mother, or a father, for that matter. Because I didn't know what to do with the second copy of the book that contained my first published story.

"She writes about me!" my mother had once proudly proclaimed to her own mother about my first efforts as a writer—stories I'd written in college and had let her read. The three of us were riding in the car, driving to Duluth, where my mother would die in a month.

"I do not," I'd scoffed bitterly. I was twenty-two, past the stage where it seemed that every cell in my body longed to push my mother away, but her giddy insistence that my budding literary career bore any relation to her riled the old teenager in me back to life. I was furious and humiliated, regardless of her cancer. "I write about all kinds of things, not just you," I hissed, though it wasn't true. Each of the stories I'd written had, in fact, thinly fictionalized versions of my mother at its center.

"Okay, honey," she said soothingly, unperturbed.

That exchange played itself out horribly in my mind for years—one of the few regrets I have about what happened between the two of us in my mother's last days—and it played itself out again as I wept in my living room on the afternoon I heard my story had won a prize.

The story is called "The House with the Horse and the Blue Canoe," a barely fictionalized account of a hard and beautiful time in my girlhood, when my family lived in a dilapidated farmhouse that adjoined a pasture that enclosed our horse, Lady, and her makeshift water trough. The trough was a blue canoe my family had smashed up one winter using it as a tobog-gan on the big hill nearby that went down to a lake named Grace. The house was on the side of a well-traveled highway, so when people asked where we lived, all we had to say was "the house with the horse and the blue canoe" and everyone knew where we were talking about. In the story I write about the things that happened the year I was eleven: how my step-father fell from a roof and broke his back and how this led to us eventually having to move out of the farmhouse because we couldn't afford the rent. How in his months-long convalescence my stepfather carved and then painted an entire village of wooden figurines to populate the miniature log cabin that my mother put out each Christmas and how my mother sang "O Tannenbaum" to us as she lit the Christmas lights. It's not so much a story as a gathering of reminiscences, an elegy for the family I used to have, the one that died with my mother.

And there was only one person on earth I wanted to read it: Alice Munro.

When I received my two copies of the book several months later, I drafted the letter. It's lost to time, but I remember sitting at my computer for hours, composing each sentence, questioning each word, crafting the letter as painstakingly as I did my stories, trying to tell her everything but also rein myself in; to express my fervor without scaring her off. I included the copy of the book that was meant for my mother. I told her that I knew it was highly unlikely she had time to waste on reading my story, which, by the way, began on page 121, but if she was interested—*she might be inter-ested*—well, then, she should just go ahead and read it. I did not expect her to write me back. I knew she was far too busy to write me back. I was sure she received a deluge of letters from the likes of me and how could she possibly write us all back, what with the demands of her actual writing, but if she would *like* to write me back, well, then, she should feel free to do so.

On the envelope I wrote her name above only the words "Clinton, Ontario, Canada." Having grown up in the country, where letters are sometimes addressed with the confidence of an absurd insularity—*Joe, who lives just past the dump*, say—I gambled that anyone who worked at the post office in Clinton would know where to find the now world-famous author. I mailed my letter and story to her on December 20. On January 18, her reply appeared in my mailbox.

I stood on the porch reading it and then I went inside and read it some more. I was leaving the next day for a writing residency at the Ucross Foundation in Wyoming and I took the letter with me, neatly folded and in the envelope it had come in. I propped it on my desk in my studio and gazed at it for long stretches. It never occurred to me to write her back, to keep in touch, to attempt to parlay our exchange into something more. To do so seemed to me a violation of the gift she'd given me in her reply, to take a mile when all I really needed was an inch. Her letter traveled with me, in me, for years, as I wrote and tried to write, the best lines from it—*I wouldn't change a hair on its head* and *It's a wonderful, unexpected kind of story* and *I wasn't writing nearly so well at your age*—humming inside of me like an ancient gong.

By the time I turned thirty I'd begun publishing stories and essays, but I still hadn't managed to finish the novel I'd claimed to be writing for years. So I did what I'd told Alice Munro in my letter that I would not do—I applied to graduate school to get my MFA in fiction writing, despite her agreement that I was *quite right to stay out of academic life* if I could. I couldn't. I'd been working mostly as a waitress for more than a decade, writing on the side. I'd won grants and gone to writing residencies every chance I got, but those things hadn't allowed me the shelter I needed to complete a book.

I went to Syracuse University and was mentored by a string of stunning writers and good souls—George Saunders, Mary Caponegro, Arthur Flowers, and, in my final semester, Mary Gaitskill, who'd been a shining star in my constellation of literary influence dating back to the days before I knew *The New Yorker* magazine wasn't just a local city rag. Each of them, along with my talented classmates, helped me further down the path, told me things that I needed to know; and yet, still, there was always Alice Munro, teaching me by the frank force of her fiction—how she moved her characters in and out of a room, how she conveyed an emotion or a moment just so. She was my most important mentor, though I'd never even laid eyes on her, until finally, at the end of my first year of graduate school, I got my chance.

She was participating in the New Yorker Festival in Manhattan, appearing in a doubleheader with Richard Ford. I took the train to see her on an uncharacteristically hot day in early May, traveling five and half hours from Syracuse to Penn Station and then the subway to the Lower East Side and a short painful walk to the Angel Orensanz Foundation, the sandals I hadn't worn since the summer before rubbing blisters into my tender heels. The Angel Orensanz Foundation is a stylishly dilapidated former synagogue that dates back to the nineteenth century. I handed over my ticket just inside its gaping neo-Gothic doors and walked inside feeling silent and solemn amid the din of a hundred conversations all around me and found a seat to the side of the stage, a few rows back. The room was cavernous and packed. Tickets had sold out months before. "Sarah Jessica Parker married Matthew Broderick here," the woman next to me said as I scanned the faces near the low stage, trying to spot Munro. And then the lights dimmed and the crowd hushed.

Richard Ford came on first. I watched him in profile, handsome and lean in a purple blazer and white shirt. He read "Reunion" by John Cheever and then his own story called "Reunion." I listened raptly, almost forgetting Alice Munro. I'd always admired Richard Ford, too, his book *Rock Springs* among those I'd read again and again. When he finished, Alice Munro walked elegantly onto the stage, her smile shy and bright, her hair soft and white. She wore dangling black stone earrings and a matching black stone necklace that sat close to her throat. Her cream-colored dress flowed bridelike to the floor, topped by an equally long black vest that closed with one button at her chest.

The sight of her knocked me sideways, the way so many of her stories had. At the sound of her voice, I wept. I'd not expected this. Futilely, I searched my purse for a tissue as unobtrusively as I could, mortified by my tiny gasps and copious tears. I gave up and wiped my face with my bare hands and tried to concentrate on her words. She was reading a story called "Nettles," the crowd breathing with one breath. I weaved in and out of listening and quietly weeping, the tears seeping ridiculously out of me, despite my inner pleadings that I get a grip. Later, I'd laugh when I told this story. I'd say that when I saw Alice Munro, I understood for the first time all those screaming, inconsolable girls in old footage of the Beatles in the sixties. And yet that wasn't what was happening at all. I wasn't crying for joy or excitement, or because I was overcome with emotion to see someone I loved from afar. I was crying because something had come to an end. I knew it only in glimmers — it would take years until I fully understood — that a spell cast long before had been broken the moment Alice Munro walked onto the stage.

Of all the lines she'd written in her letter to me, of all the phrases that had repeated and hummed like a gong in my head, there was one that hummed more persistently than the rest: *You're two years younger than my youngest daughter.* Such a neutral statement, and yet I couldn't keep myself from coloring in the lines. In the country called Munro, I'd subconsciously staked a fantastical claim. *I could be her daughter*, I'd sometimes think, remembering those words she'd written, about how close I was in age to her youngest. I'd have been the final one, kindred and kept and adored.

I didn't *really* think I was Alice Munro's daughter, of course. I'm not talking about delusion. I'm talking about longing and instinct and the eternal ache of a girl who lost her mom. About the way life, like a Munro story, unfurls and then turns back on itself in the most unpredictable, inexplicable ways, ambiguous and overlapping, perpetually at odds with itself. About how I loved Alice Munro more excruciatingly than I ever had in that moment she walked onto the stage and also how, in that very same moment, I began, finally, to let her go. Not Munro the great writer, whom I continue to learn from and admire, but Munro the maternal mentor, from whom I simply had to move on. Munro Country had been my motherland for years and yet by then, at thirty-two, hip-deep at last in my own novel, I was beginning to understand that in order to write my book, I had no choice but to set out into territory that was all my own.

These realizations didn't come to me in great, lucid waves as I cried while listening to "Nettles." They were not an epiphany. Instead, they were ephemeral and shadowy, as if a bird had darted in and then disappeared into a dark corner of that cavernous room. At the sight of her, I only knew that I knew things I could not yet say. If you'd asked me why I was crying, I'd have told you the story about the girls and the Beatles in the sixties.

When she finished reading, she sat in a chair on the stage to receive her admirers. I hung back, dry-eyed and chastened, lingering toward the end of a long line. As I waited, I rehearsed what I would say when it was my turn. *I love your work! Your books have meant so much to me—to my development as a writer. Actually, you probably don't remember, but you wrote me a letter. You read a story of mine. You said you wouldn't change a hair on its head!* I swapped the words and phrases around in my mind, the same way I do when I'm writing—expanding and deleting, trying to craft an opening sentence that would draw her in and make her want to stay. But as the line inched forward, I could feel the words crumbling inside of me, becoming more inane with each step in her direction. Should I even mention the letter? I wondered. Surely she wouldn't remember the letter. And doesn't *everyone* say they love her work? I tried to think of a single thing to say that she hadn't likely heard a thousand times before and came up with nothing. No matter what I said, I believed, my words wouldn't stick. I could feel them falling already, leaden and clichéd, straight from my mouth to the floor.

One person approached her and then stepped away and another and another until at last the person who stood in front of me stepped forward to talk to her. It was my turn next, I realized, with a fluttering in my gut, and a minute or two later, Alice Munro's eyes met mine. She gazed at me with the same bland, agreeable, and guardedly receptive expression as she had all the others, and in the flash of a second, I knew I wouldn't speak to her. There had been so many words between us already. Entire sentences she'd written that I'd etched into my brain. Gestures conveyed just so on the page. Those girls who laughed glitteringly. Women who turned their heads in sad and subtle ways. They were hers. They were mine. About the savage love I felt for them, there was both too much and nothing to say.

I gave her a small wave and then shifted my eyes and walked away.

MOTHER COUNTRY

Evelyn Toynton

Ilived in two places as a child, one I was directed to call home, another that *was* home, though I didn't know it at the time. For twelve days out of every fourteen, my older sister and I lived with our father and stepmother and half brother in a commodious split-level house in the suburbs, where I had a spotless room to myself, with built-in shelves adorned with china parrots and shepherdesses and a built-in desk of shiny white Formica flecked with gold. For the other two days—every other weekend—we stayed with my mother in a tiny apartment in upper Manhattan, with a pullout couch that we slept on together. My mother's narrow bed, covered in lumpy pink chenille, was squashed into the alcove between the front door and the single room that comprised the living area. Sitting at her rickety table, we ate TV dinners or boiled eggs and toast and told each other stories. Being there did not count as real life, any more than daydreaming counted. And like daydreaming, it was pure happiness.

As a young woman my mother had been high-spirited, graceful, almost beautiful—I knew that from the snapshots she kept in a scalloped envelope in her little pine desk. But by the time I knew her, there were veins bulging in her forehead; her gait was clumsy and lopsided; her left arm hung, stiff and useless, by her side. When she was pregnant with me, she'd started having blinding headaches; a tumor—benign, removable was discovered in her brain. A month after I was born, my father went deeply into debt to hire an eminent surgeon to remove it.

Eminent though he was, he botched the operation, severing certain vital nerves. My mother spent several years in a makeshift rehabilitation center on Long Island, really a sort of lodging house where people recovering from strokes and drunks who were drying out were sent by their families until they were deemed fit to enter the world again. When she returned to Manhattan, she moved, alone, into the dark apartment, close to where she had lived with my father, and where my sister and I still lived with him: his remarriage would take place the following year, the move to the suburbs a few years later. Apart from our twice-monthly visits—and the monthly checks my father sent—the only things in my mother's life were books.

I have just been looking at a novel called *Brief Gaudy Hour,* one of my mother's favorites, and probably the first adult book I ever read. "Nan! Nan!" it begins. "Come and be fitted for your new dresses to go to court!" Nan is Anne Boleyn; the book tells the story of her ascension to the throne of England as Henry VIII's queen and her subsequent downfall and beheading. Much of my mother's reading consisted of such novels, with titles like *Within the Hollow Crown* and *Isabel the Fair,* about the Tudors and Stuarts and Plantagenets, the scheming and intrigue at the royal court.

When she had fled Nazi Germany in the thirties, she had lived for six years in England, and was on her way back to London when she met my father, also a German Jewish refugee, during a visit to her cousin in New York. After her banishment, English history, not of the serious academic kind but the sort akin to romance—the sort known as "the rich pageant of history"—became her chief source of entertainment. It was also her chief means of entertaining us on our twice-monthly visits.

She told us about proud, wicked John of Gaunt and poor, clever, murdered Lady Jane Grey, and Mary Queen of Scots's reckless passion for Bothwell. She told us how Anne of Cleves, a sensible woman, had made eel pie for Henry VIII after their divorce, and that Richard III had been not a monster but a wise and gentle king, traduced first by the Tudors and then by Tudor historians: the first thing I remember learning about Shakespeare was that he had been unfair to Richard.

But there was another kind of history, too, hidden in the scalloped envelope in the desk. Sometimes my sister and I would fetch it after supper and make my mother tell us, once again, the stories behind the black-and-white photographs. Many of the snapshots of my mother were a little blurred, as though she had been captured in motion: turning to smile at the camera, holding her glass aloft, gesturing with her hand. The woman in the cape she was laughing with on a London street was her friend Charlotte, with whom she'd just returned from Paris; they had run out of money while they were there and had to choose between eating and buying their tickets home (they chose the tickets). The little boy on the pony was her pupil; she had finagled a job as a governess in Kent and had to study mathematics secretly, at night, to keep up with him. The picture of her walking down a path between two hedges had been taken by Charlotte in the Scilly Isles, when my mother had ducked into a maze to escape from a too-ardent suitor acquired on the train.

All her stories were in a comic vein, including the ones about my father, whose extreme gravity, even sternness, she had evidently felt free to tease him about. Someone had once said to her that before she married him he had seemed like everybody's grandfather; now, thanks to her, he only seemed like everybody's father. There was no hint of bitterness, no allusions to his perfidy—he had asked for a divorce three years after her operation, and been granted custody of the children; no judge in those days would have awarded custody to a brain-damaged woman. When she spoke of him, she only sounded fond and amused, as though he were still her husband, who might walk in the door, home from the office, at any minute.

And I tried to amuse her in turn, telling her about ridiculous goings-on at my school, most of which I exaggerated to make them more interesting. Together we engaged in what I took at the time for witty repartee, or held tea parties at which we pretended to be different characters from English history, even trying to imitate their speech. She seemed to take such pleasure in it all that I honestly believed she wanted nothing more from life than to act out the part of Margaret Tudor every other weekend. It was years before I realized what a gallant fraud she had been.

But then I too refrained from referring to anything unpleasant, such as the situation in the split-level house. I did not tell her about my Catholic stepmother's hatred of dirt in all its forms, as though it were the outward manifestation of sin; or her seeming belief that any mud we tracked into the house, any food stains she detected on our clothing, were by way of being malicious personal attacks on herself. I did not tell her that we were all—even my brother, my stepmother's son—forbidden to enter the living room or use the telephone or remove an apple from the refrigerator or even talk to each other when my stepmother was not present; that failure to comply, or failure to express sufficient gratitude for those unceasing efforts to banish uncleanliness from our lives, would result in explosions of curses, long days of furious sulking, retributive assaults with dishtowels and pointy red nails. Compliance and expressions of gratitude, however, were no guarantee that such things could be avoided.

My sister impressed on me that certain things were never to be mentioned in my mother's hearing: how I had been locked in a closet, for example, for some minor act of disobedience, and had to beg and cry for hours before I was released; how my sister had sawed away at her wrists with a razor blade one night and then, frantically, had to scrub the bloodstains from her blouse in secret; how she had found my magisterial father, who seemed to us children very much like the God of the Old Testament, weeping in his study after a particularly vicious diatribe from my stepmother. "She's God's judgment on me," he had said, "for what I did to your mother."

If my stepmother's power seemed absolute, my mother never exercised the most ordinary maternal prerogative: she never told us what to do. My sister and I were the bossy ones, telling her she must have her hair cut or her coat cleaned, telling her she ought to go out, it was such a nice day. Then we would bustle around, helping her into her shoes and her coat, fetching her purse, and take her to the little park near her house, to sit on a bench looking out at the Palisades. After a few minutes, when her nose started running, one of us would fetch a crumpled Kleenex from her bag and hand it to her.

In my rageful adolescence, when I was as nasty to her as I did not dare to be to my father or stepmother, I sent her to the park alone, embarrassed to be seen with her in public, though I never went as far as to say so. And I became bossier than ever, in a scornful, withering sort of way; I marched her fuzzy old coat directly to the incinerator instead of telling her to replace it, declaring that it made her look like a bag lady. Then I might rummage in her closet until I found some piece of finery left over from her old life—a pair of black satin sandals, a green silk blouse with silver buttons running diagonally along the front—and lock myself into her bathroom to try it on in front of the mirror, turning this way and that, tossing my hair into my face and back again. I rummaged in her battered jewelry box, too, and festooned myself with gold clips from the thirties and square Art Deco rings. If she knocked at the door, asking timidly to be let in, I would tell her to leave me alone, I was busy.

She only ever gave me two pieces of advice. One was that if a drunk asked for my telephone number on the streets of New York—something I don't believe ever happened—I should give him the number of the weather line. The other, offered in a mild, musing voice, as though she were talking to herself, during my period of greatest surliness, was that I really wasn't suited to having a boss or a nine-to-five job; I would have to find some kind of work that did not entail either. Maybe, she said shyly, I could be a writer. At the time, I suspected she only meant I was unfit to be around other humans: people could not *decide* to be writers, the way they decided to be teachers or airline pilots or nurses. She might as well have told me to be a duchess when I grew up. It did not occur to me that the idea had any connection to herself.

Yet shortly before she died, she told me that she had taken a writing course at the New School years before; her teacher, she added, had complimented her on her powers of description. How nice, I said, trying to sound pleased; what I really felt was such a confusion of pity that I could not even ask what it was she'd been describing. A sudden, painful image had flooded into my head: my mother, in her shapeless brown coat, shambling uncertainly into the room, sitting at the table without meeting anyone's eyes while all the hip young people in the class chattered or flirted across and around her (I knew what the atmosphere in those classes was like; I had chattered and flirted there myself once, when I was first trying to write.) I should have asked her, at least, who her teacher had been; I should have asked her a lot of things, but I was afraid of what she might tell me.

Both my parents died painful deaths, my father of bone cancer, my mother, twenty years later, of slow suicide. The day I told her that my father was dying was the only time I ever saw her cry. But after his death she seemed to become more acerbic, less humble; her humor was laced with a certain defiant cynicism. The planet would be such a lovely, peaceful place, she said, once we humans had finally killed each other off completely: imagine how happy the animals would be. Religion was a particular bugbear: mostly just an excuse, according to her, for people to hate each other. "How much better off we would be if nobody had ever invented God."

Her death itself was an act of defiance. Blind and crippled, living in a nursing home, she was not permitted to close her door; the other patients on her floor, all of them demented, wandered in and out of her room, rant ing and crooning, trying to get into her bed, or trying to steal her blanket, or accusing her of stealing theirs. She had had enough, she told me, and besides, if she didn't do something soon, there would be no money left for us. "I wouldn't mind robbing you of your inheritance if I were enjoying myself. But there's not much enjoyment around this place." Because we could find no other legal way for her to die, she starved herself to death, a long and agonizing process.

My older sister, to all appearances more conventional than I am, was more of a rebel when it came to my mother's influence. She majored in Irish history in college—that long litany of shameful deeds by the English—and became what my mother sorrowfully referred to as a religious fanatic, that is, a practicing Jew. I, on the other hand, not only became a writer but wound up living on a semifeudal estate in England, a country I came to associate with love at such an early age that even after being here for eight years, I can hardly see it objectively. I did not deliberately set out to return to the scene of my mother's stories, or the scene of those photographs in which she was whole and happy, but when circumstances brought me here, it felt oddly like coming home. Some years ago, I scattered my mother's ashes in the ancient walled orchard next to my crumbling cottage and started a novel based on her life.

My stepmother began to turn benevolent—sentimental, even—when she reached eighty-five. At ninety-four, she lives alone in split-level house, which she cleans herself, unable to find a cleaning woman who comes up to her exacting standards. After my father's death, she became active in all the good causes he had sponsored, and is now an esteemed member of the community, much in demand, as she takes pride in telling us, at charity luncheons and raffle drives. She accounts for her continuing good health by claiming, with a trace of the old belligerence, that God must be taking special care of her. I always want to ask her about the less fortunate ones: why did God decide not to take care of them? How does she explain His choosing her instead? But as with so many other questions about the why of things, there would not seem to be any good answer to that one.

THE SEDUCER

Lily Tuck

Nineteen eighty-eight is the year I quit smoking and the year I begin studying with Gordon Lish. A slender, handsome, white-haired man, Gordon bears more than a passing resemblance to Steve McQueen, if only Steve McQueen had lived a little longer. Gordon favors khaki. He wears a combination of cowboy—the hat—and hunting outfits—canvas trousers with reinforced knee padding. Instead of a briefcase, he carries a brown LLBean duffel bag stuffed with books and papers. A writer of two novels and many short stories, he is presently an editor at Alfred A. Knopf and the editor of a literary magazine, *The Quarterly*. He has taught at Yale, Columbia, New York University, and his private workshops have become legendary. When I first call to enquire about them, Gordon tells me, "No, no," the class is already full, but then, hearing the disappointment in my voice, he relents. For me and for once, he says, he will make an exception.

There are twenty-two of us—seventeen women and five men, of varying age and ethnicity—taking his creative writing class. (One student travels to class from as far away as New Mexico, another from Cleveland, still another from Washington, D.C.; several commute in from New Jersey, Connecticut, and the suburbs; most of us, however, are from New York City.) We will convene once a week, for twelve weeks, from six o'clock to midnight. We meet in a student's apartment on the Upper East Side. The cost of the class is twenty-four hundred dollars.

I

February 25

"Writing," Gordon begins, "is a way of behaving and we must learn to behave importantly."

His legs crossed, Gordon sits in a straight-back chair at one end of the small, cramped living room; his jacket, hat, and duffel bag lie in a pile on the floor next to him. All twenty-two of us gather around him. Since there are not enough sofas and chairs for everyone, some of us have to sit on the floor. Already, in a note mailed to us before the beginning of the first class, Gordon has warned that there will be no eating or drinking and no breaks during the six hours of class (the only acceptable excuse to leave is to use the toilet). From where I sit, close up, afraid that I might attract his attention, I avoid looking at him directly and instead, I examine his shoes—old-fashioned highly polished brown lace-up boots that look custom-made and like ones Denys Finch Hatton might have worn riding around Karen Blixen's farm in Africa.

The sad and embarrassing truth is that before enrolling in Gordon's class, I had spent ten years writing, rewriting and rewriting a novel. I also wrote short stories, dozens of them. My novel and my stories were read and reread by my family and my friends. All offered advice, some a bit of encouragement. To no avail. My work remained unpublished. Stubborn, proud, I refused to give up, but if someone happened to ask me what I did, I answered, "I type."

"A writer must have authority. The effect of authority is created by many means but none more crucial than the appearance of conviction," Gordon says. "Your speech issues from your heart because you have no choice. Authority is not just possessing what you speak of but being possessed by it. You do not have to prove anything but your authority to say it. Never explain, never complain. You have the right to speak. You must speak. Great writing is logical discourse, logically rendered.

"Discover your voice," Gordon also tells us. "Determine how it is different from all other voices. Make it hot for yourself. Get in trouble. Go where the jeopardy is."

The woman who travels to class from Cleveland raises her hand.

Gordon ignores her.

"How do you get at your initial utterance?" he asks—no doubt anticipating her question. "How far you go de-constructing that statement is a measure of how brave you are. The best writers are those who put themselves at risk—first destabilize yourself, then restore yourself. Dig a hole for yourself," he says. "Write to convict yourself," he says, "that's where the conflict is."

Gordon talks and talks and talks. He talks seamlessly for six hours as if he is unraveling a long silk thread from his throat, through his mouth. No one else has said a word. I look at my watch. It is past midnight.

"Most people," Gordon says, "are conditioned for failure—except, for instance, astronauts. Astronauts are used to success. They come from small, homogeneous towns where they were the captains of the football teams. Start feeling successful," he tells us by way of parting, "and if you are, don't think it is an accident."

"I write," I say to myself on my way home.

II

March 3

I arrive a few minutes early and manage to secure a seat on the sofa. The woman from New Mexico sits down next to me.

"Cold out," she complains.

I agree. Earlier, after the first class, we had exchanged phone numbers, then met for coffee, shared a bit of personal information. Her name is Tina (names and place names have been changed). A pretty redhead with delicate features, Tina has taken Gordon's class once before and has published a story in *The Quarterly*.

"What's the story about?" I asked.

"Language," she answered.

"English," Gordon tells us tonight, "derives its true power from nouns. English," he says, "is a naming language. Use active and transitive verbs, avoid intransitive verbs. Watch out for adjectives. Most adjectives are unnecessary."

Then we start to go around the room. During a typical class, each student reads his or her work for the first time. The fortunate and talented student gets to read his or her entire work, the unfortunate and less talented one does not.

I read a story that begins: *The back of my mother's head was like the prow of a ship—*

Gordon lets out a snort. "Stop," he yells.

I stop, mortified.

Next to me, on the sofa, Tina shifts her weight away from me.

"Tuck, Tuck"—for some reason, Gordon calls us all by our last names, he also is in the habit of repeating it—"don't strain for a trope. Keep the object term as close to the subject term as you can manage without producing a tautology. Listen to this," he says, giving an example from a story he likes, "'Quiet as a church.'"

I, too, am quiet.

III

March 10

"Your first sentence ordains your world; do not be trivial or petty. Nothing is worse than being trivial," Gordon warns us at our third meeting. "As Joy Williams once said, 'The world makes everything taste like chicken.' Own your first sentence, make it yours," Gordon continues. "Each sentence gives rise to the next sentence, each sentence owes everything to its predecessor. Reveal how elastic a sentence can be. Get into the habit of recasting sentences. Learn how to open up a sentence. Think of yourself as a language-making machine."

Tentative friendships have formed in the class. People gravitate to the same seats. Peter, a lawyer, sits in the only comfortable armchair and takes off his jacket and loosens his tie; Marcia, a tall blonde, sits on the floor, her back against the wall; she smiles often at the dark-haired young man sitting next to her, who is working on a novel and has a part-time job as a waiter.

Every day and it is my husband burning, is how Janet, who has two small children and commutes from New Jersey, begins her story.

Gordon approves. "Listen up," he tells us, and he asks Janet to read her first sentence again.

"Porter, Porter," he tells Janet, "you did it, you finally did it. A great beginning."

Janet beams.

"You see," Gordon explains, "there's a cross-indexing in her sentence. Disparate elements are brought together by a third element which lifts the sentence into significance and gives the appearance of something profound being said. Think of two circles somewhat merged and the area created by their overlap. Therein lies the meaning, that's where the story is."

It is the turn of the woman who travels from Cleveland. *Alone, I went to the doctor's office*, she begins to read.

"No, no," Gordon shouts at her. "Self-pity—Murray, Murray—is not going to get you past that first sentence."

I breathe a secret sigh of relief—at least I am not the only one.

IV

March 17

"Writing has to be just," Gordon says. Although the weather has turned warm all of a sudden, he wears a long-sleeved T-shirt under his khaki shirt. The reason, he tells us, is that he suffers from psoriasis. Gordon is not afraid to describe the intimate details of his life or his family's: his stint in the loony bin, his wife ill with Lou Gehrig's disease, his youngest son a genius, his mother so old and frail she needs help going to the toilet. "The writer has to seek to know the object and honor its unknowability when reporting on it," he says.

Gordon mentions the names of writers who, he believes, do this well: Flannery O'Connor, Grace Paley, Cormac McCarthy, John Barth, and a writer I have never heard of, Walter van Tilburg Clark. (Later, when I look up Walter van Tilburg Clark, I learn that he wrote *The Ox-Bow Incident*, and several short story collections. I also learn that he taught creative writing and was noted for his eccentric dress.)

"The writer," Gordon continues, "is there to celebrate human mystery. He does not have an agenda. You must come to the page without pettiness, without holding a grudge," he exhorts us.

It is Tina's turn to read from her story. As far as I can make out, the story is about silverware—knives, spoons, forks.

Gordon listens attentively. When she is finished, he tells her, "Well done, Rathbone. You managed to fully occupy your terrain."

Tina looks pleased. I look away.

"Do not proclaim," Gordon says. "Instead, show the world being made." He gives us an example: "'His feet are together' is bad. 'His feet pressed together,' is better. The more you feel the object you are rendering, the less you have to explain."

In spite of myself, I glance at Gordon's elegant shoes.

173

V

March 24

There have been some defections in the class. The woman from Washington, a young Asian American poet who only read once, and the lawyer. Gordon mentions them briefly—mentioning their lack of courage, their lack of stamina, their lack of doggedness, qualities that make a writer.

Gordon calls on tall, blond Marcia.

"Morse, Morse. You look great, sweetheart," he says. "And what a great name for a writer. Marcia Morse," he repeats.

Marcia looks pleased and begins to read. *She felt the world was waking up that first day of spring . . .*

"Morse, Morse, you should know better by now," Gordon says, stopping her. "The arrogance, the ghastly pride—Morse, Morse—of equating yourself with spring. With nature. It's swinish," Gordon also says.

Marcia bursts into tears.

"It's important for the speaker voice," Gordon continues, unfazed, "to remain either on par with the world that it is reporting on or inferior to it."

"Bastard," Marcia shouts, as she gathers up her coat and papers and leaves. She slams shut the apartment door. The dark-haired young man who sits next to her and who is writing a novel and is also a waiter looks down at his hands. Nobody speaks.

Gordon motions to the young man to start reading. "You're next, Rothberg, Rothberg."

"I'm not sure my—" Rothberg mumbles. "I'd rather wait, Gordon," he says.

"Read, Rothberg. Read," Gordon commands.

VI

March 31

It is Easter week and instead of being in class I am on a beach in the Caribbean. Lying in the sun next to my husband, I try to describe Gordon to him.

"Is he gay?" he asks.

"Let's go for a swim," I answer.

VII

April 7
  "You missed an interesting class," Tina informs me.
  I shrug—does she not notice my tan?
  Gordon notices. "Where were you, Tuck?" he asks.
  I tell him.
  "You look good, Tuck," he says, smiling.
  "Writing is an act of seduction," Gordon tells us in this class.

VIII

April 14
  Gordon is friendly with Harold Bloom, Harold Brodkey, Don DeLillo, Cynthia Ozick, and James Watson, one of the co-discoverers of the structure of DNA. He regales the class with stories about them, he tells us how he often has dinner with them. He even mentions a favorite Italian restaurant in the Village. (I determine to go often to the Italian restaurant to try and catch a glimpse of Don DeLillo eating pasta.)
  This time I read a story about an unhappy woman who cleans her house and when the house is clean, a leaf from the outside blows into the house through the open door and since everything is put away and clean—even the wastepaper baskets—she does not know what to do with the leaf and so she eats it.
  Gordon has his head in his hands. Without looking at me, he says, "Tuck, Tuck, the story has no moral center. You should never make claims of feelings in the first person if there is no irony."
  I am tempted to protest but I know better. I want a cigarette.
  "There is no tension, no drama. The story has become an essay, a monologue," Gordon also declares.
  When will I learn?
  When will Gordon like one of my stories?
  "Fiction," Gordon tells the class, "must create an argument, if not it will be facile. Nothing is earned. Engage in an activity that is difficult for yourself and not merely an I reporting on itself."

IX

April 21

Before class, I meet Tina for an early dinner. Tina tells me she has a contract for a short story collection. She tells me how she has visited Gordon at his office. She met other editors, she was given books, she was fêted, she says.

"That's wonderful," I say. I try to sound genuinely pleased for her but I am not.

Melissa is another woman in class who has a contract for a short story collection. She is slender and blond and wears elegant red high heels (apparently I focus on people's shoes). She reads a story about a family who owns a house on a lake in Wisconsin.

Those were staggering, broken days, is how her story begins.

End-of-summer days when the sky was so wildly blue and the clouds came always in the shape of the bison of the Great Plains, one after another, immense, shaggy, humpbacked animals with heads bent to the flatness of the land . . . she reads on.

Gordon approves mightily. "Well done, Johnson," he tells her.

"How do you make magical utterances?" Gordon, à propos of Melissa's story, asks, and answers: "By expressing desire. Don't think in terms of communication but in terms of what enchants. You, the writer, are the visionary, the witness of your own desire.

"Dare to be different. Stand up to that difference. Be brave," he tells us as we leave.

On the way out, I pluck up my courage and I tell Melissa, "I loved your story."

It turns out we live not far from each other and we walk home together. We will become friends.

X

April 28

"The way to be an exception is to take the contrary view. Turn the question around. Adopt an adversarial point of view. Go against good sense. Do not succumb to convention, find your own solution. What defines a contemporary writer is that he realizes that he is writing fiction. Characters are not real people, they are words. Writers know this.

"There is a kind of shared lunacy," Gordon continues, "among second-rate writers who think their characters are real. That the characters control the narrative. All a writer does is create an effect. If there is a correspondence between the effect and the real, then that is the pleasure of the text.

"The writer is a maker not a scorekeeper—it is the effect not the substance that counts. Think of a scientist," Gordon says. "A scientist is in control of his experiment at the same time that he hopes to discover something new.

"Great works are achieved out of excess, out of imbalance, out of madness."

Gordon quotes his friend Cynthia Ozick, who he claims writes "obsessively, torrentially, comically, for life. Cynthia Ozick," Gordon tells us, "rarely gets up before noon but she writes all night.

"The writer makes the world," Gordon continues. "Fiction is like a dream. Another part of your mind is shaping it. Everything is invented— including your father, your mother. The sooner you understand that as a writer, the sooner you will be free. It is not the way it is but the way you make it.

"The world is harmonious because you, the writer, are looking. You must understand that everything you perceive is yours. You make your world, and when you comprehend that deeply, you will accept it. A true intelligence processes all the information and lives with it. At the same time, you must examine everything, see everything—always be an interrogating intelligence—not how or why but *what* it is. Become a more contemplative human being and see how everything you ever see fits because you are seeing it.

"As writers, you must try to keep yourselves alive, vibrant. Act as if you have never tasted the spinach," Gordon tells us. "Be alert, be mindful."

Gordon exhausts, exhilarates, annoys, instructs, angers, teases, prompts, and finally—most important—inspires.

XI

May 5

I have started to work on a novel: a conversation between two women on the telephone — a sort of modem (at the time) epistolary novel. In class, I read from it:

Molly said, 'She died standing up.'

I said, 'What?'

Molly said, 'Hello, Molly. Who? Inez?'

Molly said, 'They found her propped up — propped up like a broom.'

I said, 'Inez? Like a what? A broom? God, Molly. What time is it?'

Molly said, 'In the corner of the room. Inez was dressed in only her underwear. She was wearing boots.'

"Torque, don't forget torque, Tuck," Gordon stops me and says. "Show the flip side of each event. Show that each event has the same value. And, Tuck, Tuck, stay on the surface of the object. Keep going, do not stop to explain. You want inevitability not predictability. Read some more," he also says.

I said, 'Boots? Wait. Let me turn on the light, Molly. God, Molly, it's one o'clock in the morning. It's quarter past one in the morning, Molly.'

Molly said, 'Old fleece-lined boots. Do you know the kind I am talking about, Lily? The old-fashioned kind. Galoshes.'

I said, 'Galoshes? You woke me up, Molly. Hello?'

"Chitchat in the face of death," Gordon says by way of a compliment.

XII

May 12

"Be Grace Paley," Gordon tells us in the last class. "Scream from the rooftops. Burn down churches. Be a revolutionary. Every good writer was shocking in his day and said things no one else dared to say. Find a way to argue with yourself on the page. Destabilize your sense of yourself.

"Exploit your own quirkiness, your difference, your flaws.

"Think of a chess player who has to be able to look at all the possibilities at once.

"Think of the writer as a rider on a horse, the story is the horse, and the ground is the terrain covered. What is relevant is the structure of the terrain, how the horse moves and how the rider accommodates himself to the motion to achieve a smooth ride.

"The grand achievement is going forward. Position yourself morally before you start to write," Gordon also tells us, "so that you engage something worth engaging."

The last class feels like a victory. We, eighteen aspiring writers, have survived, more or less. We have listened to Gordon speak for nearly seventy-two hours and during that time we sat hardly moving or speaking. Will that make us better writers? I tend to think so. We have learned to be more precise, more attentive; we have learned to be more truthful, perhaps more daring. Will any of us become famous? Rich? And will it matter?

"Being a writer," Gordon says in farewell, "is a sanctuary, a haven in a heartless world."

I believe him. Absolutely.

HAROLD BRODKEY

Edmund White

A tall, blond biologist named Doug Gruenau, four years younger than me but like me a graduate of the University of Michigan, was living in the late 1970s with the novelist Harold Brodkey on West 88th Street. Harold had—which sounds like a contradiction in terms—an immense underground reputation. Everyone in New York was curious about him, but few people outside the city had ever heard of him. Long ago, in 1958, he'd published *First Love and Other Sorrows*, a book of stories that had been well reviewed, but they weren't what all the buzz was about.

Now he'd bring out a story occasionally in *The New Yorker* or *New American Review* or even *Esquire*. The one in *New American Review* (a quarterly, edited by Ted Solotaroff) was sexual but not dirty—a 50-page chapter, published in 1973, about a Radcliffe girl's first orgasm. The prose in "Innocence" could be strained if striking: "To see her in sunlight was to see Marxism die." It seemed the longest sex scene in history, rivaled only by the gay sex scene in David Plante's *The Catholic*—and reminiscent of the sex scene "The Time of Her Time," included in Norman Mailer's *Advertisements for Myself* (except that one had been anal!).

Then there had been troubled, labyrinthine stories about Brodkey's mother in *The New Yorker* of a length and complexity no one else would have gotten away with. This was obviously a writer, we thought, who must be, above all, extremely convincing. The mother stories nagged and tore at their subject matter with a Lawrentian exasperation, a relentless drive to get it right, repeatedly correcting the small assertions just made in previous lines. Everyone was used to confessional writing of some sort (though the heyday for that would come later) and everyone knew all about the family drama, but no one had ever gone this far with sex, with mother, and with childhood. We were stunned by this new kind of realism that made slides of every millimeter of the past and put them under the writer's microscope. In *Esquire* in 1975, Brodkey published a short, extremely lyrical story. "His Son, in His Arms, in Light, Aloft," about a baby boy being carried in his father's arms. Mother might get the niggling, Freudian treatment, but Daddy deserved only light-drenched, William Blake–like mysticism.

All these "stories," apparently, were only furtive glimpses of the massive novel that Brodkey had been working on for years and that would be the American answer to Marcel Proust. Brodkey's fans (and there were many of them) Xeroxed and stapled into little booklets every story he'd published so far in recent years and circulated them among their friends, a sort of New York samizdat press. His supporters made wide, fervent claims for him. Harold was our Mann, our James Joyce. That no one outside New York knew who he was only vouchsafed his seriousness, his cult stature, too serious for the unwashed (or rather the washed, a more appropriate synecdoche for Midwesterners like me).

He and Doug lived in a big, rambling West Side apartment with a third man, named Charlie Yordy, whom I met just once but who reeked of a hoofed and hairy-shanked sexuality that managed to put the Pan back in panic. He was a friendly, smiling man but seemed burdened, as all people possessed by a powerful sexuality are.

Harold was as bearded and hooded-eyed as Nebuchadnezzar but tall and slim and athletic as well. He must have been in his forties. His constant swimming and exercising at the 63rd Street Y (the one I'd lived in when I first came to New York) kept him as fit as a much younger man. His moods and thoughts were restless, rolling about like ship passengers in a storm. Sometimes he looked as if a migraine had just drawn its gray, heavy wing across his eyes. The next moment he'd be calculating something silently, feverishly to himself—then he'd say out loud, "Forget it." He seldom paid attention to what the people around him were saying because he was concocting his next outrage—for most of his remarks were outrageous, and he could not be cajoled out of them.

Harold had lived with Doug for some eight or nine years. Doug was so polite and respectful that even whenever Harold would say something absurdly far-fetched, Doug would cock his head to one side and up a bit, as if he were a bird trying to make sense of a new, higher, quicker call.

Doug was a big man with a bass laugh but around Harold he didn't take up much space. I think he'd decided that Harold was both cracked and a genius and that even his insults were, ultimately, harmless, but Doug taught biology in a private school and had endless hours of grading and preparation and counseling and teaching to do, whereas Harold appeared to have enough money to be idle—and to meddle.

I wasn't quite sure what Charlie did, though I must have been told. (Americans are never reluctant to ask strangers what they do.) I think he was a math teacher and then he manufactured clothes in the Adirondacks. He wasn't around often, and in any event he seemed to be more Harold's boyfriend than Doug's, though I'm sure Harold told me they were all three lovers. The apartment was big enough to accommodate them all and even give each one of them privacy. Harold was on the prowl. Not all the considerable amount of time he spent at the Y was devoted to swimming. People who knew who he was said he was a tireless, overt cruiser.

Harold seldom talked about his own work but he loved to deliver pronouncements about literature and how to make it. He particularly enjoyed giving other writers—even older, more successful writers—advice. As the years went by I kept hearing strange and then stranger stories about him. One of his great defenders was Gordon Lish, a top editor at Knopf and the man who had virtually invented minimalism. Gordon apparently walked into the office of his boss, Bob Gottlieb (who'd started his own career as the editor of *Catch-22*, and had even been the one to persuade Joseph Heller to change the title from *Catch-18*), and said something like, "You've published a few good books, Bob, but nothing that will make people remember you after you're gone. Now you have the chance to publish Proust—but you must write a check for a million dollars and not ask to see even a single page."

At that point Harold had been signed up with Farrar, Straus for years, but they'd paid him a considerably smaller sum—and they weren't willing to give him the full attention he demanded. Harold needed not one editor but several to go over with him the thousands of pages he'd already written. As far as anyone could tell, he was years away from delivering. But their reluctance to put the full resources of their staff at his disposal ate away at Harold. Responding to the challenge, Gottlieb wrote the check.

In a slow groundswell of media attention leading up to (the announced but not the actual) publication, various magazine articles appeared about

Harold, all wildly laudatory. I remember one in *Esquire* in 1977 by the religious novelist D. Keith Mano ("Harold Brodkey: The First Rave"), who confessed he'd set out to debunk Harold and his myth but who'd stayed to be conquered. Mano even told Brodkey about some of his personal problems—a minor betrayal by a friend. The passage is worth quoting because it reveals one of Harold's seduction techniques:

> . . . In passing I mention a personal misfortune, a betrayal—none of your business what—that had shocked and demoralized me the day before. Harold listens, advises; he parses it out. I hang up feeling both presumptuous and stupid. What am I to Harold Brodkey, he to me, that I should lay my tsuris on him? Yet, one hour later, Harold calls back. My distress, a stranger's distress, has alarmed him. We talk for thirty minutes on Harold's long-distance dime. The man cares. I am moved: such concern is unlooked-for. Subsequently, we talk several times. In fact I became, well, jealous; his stamina, his integrity, his grasp of circumstances is better than mine and these, dammit, are my circumstances. After a while I'd prefer to forget; it's human enough. But Harold won't sanction that; his moral enthusiasm is dynamic; he knows I'm copping out. And I feel understood, seen through, swept into the rational and oceanic meter of his fiction. A Brodkey character. Me. Imagine.

Denis Donaghue and Harold Bloom had both compared Harold to Proust. Bloom added that he was "unparalleled in American prose fiction since the death of William Faulkner." Cynthia Ozick declared him to be a true artist. Harold concurred: "I'm not sure that I'm not a coward. If some of the people who talk to me are right, well, to be possibly not only the best living writer in English, but someone who could be the rough equivalent of a Wordsworth or a Milton, is not a role that a halfway educated Jew from St. Louis with two sets of parents and a junkman father is prepared to play."

The press response (always by straight men) to Brodkey as a man (there still wasn't a book) was so extreme that I developed a theory about what was behind it. I figured that gay men were not competitive in the way straights were; it was no accident that gays played individual not group sports. Nor were gay men awed and half in love with their fathers. Most gays I knew had rejected their fathers and despised them (though there were always exceptions, such as Harold himself). Finally, gays were thoroughly disabused and especially suspicious of flattery—more likely to hand it out than to take it in. As a result, Harold's methods didn't work on them (on me), but they instantly seduced straights. Harold would suddenly announce to a straight admirer (or adversary), "You know, Tom, you could be the greatest writer of your generation. There's no doubt about it. And by the way I'm not the only one to think that." Long pause. "But you won't be—wanna know why?" Strong eye contact. "Because you're too damn lazy. And too damn modest. You don't work hard enough or aim high enough."

His interlocutor, after having his rank raised as high as it was in his most secret dreams, suddenly saw his hopes dashed, unless . . . unless . . .

He suddenly needed Harold to help him, to inspire him, finally to judge him. Harold was his father/coach, while the challenger was the son/ rookie. With any luck he might yet emerge as the world-class genius he dreamed of being.

Bitchy and disagreeable as gays are sometimes thought to be, they don't usually play lethal games like these. They don't try to mold behavior—perhaps they (we) aren't confident enough to challenge another man in his heart of hearts, the private interior place where he lives. We gays don't want to belong, we don't want to play ball—we're not team players, so how could we bow before someone evaluating us? We'd rather lose, quit the playing field—be a quitter. How can our father or father's brother bully us when we're all too ready to cry uncle? That sort of ducking out is our way of winning.

Of course it probably helped that Harold went to almost every literary party and spent hours on the phone every day with Don DeLillo, Harold Bloom, Denis Donoghue. DeLillo told him the way to stop worrying about death was to watch a lot of television.

The funny thing is that no one ever mentioned that Harold lived with not one but two men and that he was notorious in the YMCA steamroom. Harold was not known to be gay—and he was far from a cool, impersonal writer. His whole life's work was based on his childhood and adolescent experiences. He had turned himself into a tall, complicated, handsome, athletic, brilliant Jewish lad, and that's how everyone who didn't know him personally perceived him.

Harold had raised expectations so high—after all, he wasn't just trying to "get a second book out," he was writing the great American novel—that of course he had to introduce roadblocks in his own path. He bought a computer. But this was still the era when a computer filled a whole room, when only industries and spies owned them, when one had to master a whole new method of writing, of programming. Harold invited me to see the machines humming and buzzing in one room, which someone from IBM was teaching him, day after day, week after week, how to operate. The entire long, sprawling manuscript would have to be transferred to the computer. Only then could it be properly analyzed for content, repetitions, inner consistency, and flow.

My heart sank, I who still scribble in notebooks with a ballpoint. I rewrote, but quickly, only once; it was the least demanding part of composition and by far the most pleasant.

What was hard for me was composing, writing. I had so little confidence or stamina that a single paragraph could send me into a paroxysm of self-doubt. Sometimes I felt I was blasting my way through a sheer wall of granite, forcing a small path through vast thick ramparts of low self-esteem and resistance. At other times I felt I was racing through the woods but that the trail had given out, was overgrown—or had broken into two paths or three. I had no idea where to go, no momentum, no sense of direction.

Harold appeared to have none of these doubts. He sometimes spoke of writing in a way that reminded me of the methods discussed by French writers. A French author might say that he'd worked the whole book out in his mind, done his research, constructed the whole intrigue—and now all he had to do was the "redaction," by which he would mean the actual writing, as if that were a detail, the way some composers refer to the "orchestration." I was never shown any of the manuscript in all its voluminousness, but I would get vague, haggard battle reports about how the organization was going.

I think you could have called Harold a phenomenologist. He once said to me (à propos of some of my own writing), "When someone writes, 'She went down on him,' it's always a lie." His idea was that shorthand expressions (going down on someone) were smug and false because the real experience (of sucking or being sucked) is so profound, so unrepeatable, so thick with emotions and half-thoughts and fears and tremblings that the only expression adequate to it is minute, precise, original, and exhaustive. In print Harold wrote: "I distrust summaries, any kind of gliding through time, any too great a claim that one is in control of what one recounts."

Perhaps because it suited my own temperament, I learned from Harold to "defamiliarize" the world and to render it in the freshest, most Martian way possible. Where I disagreed with him was that I thought not everything could be treated so thoroughly. There had to be background and foreground, and what was in the background necessarily should be sketched in—not with clichés but with some familiarity, even facility.

If his ideas about "defamiliarization" were the most sensible part of Harold's advice (even if I didn't always follow it), he was also capable of strange little obsessions. In reading a description of mine of a skylight above a library (one that happened to be installed in a nineteenth-century opera house), Harold insisted that I describe the overhead windows as an eye. I didn't think it made much difference in a book of 220 pages whether I used that metaphor or not, but I quickly acceded to his demand to humor him and to show him that I was flattered that he had had a concrete suggestion of any sort. Presumably he had read the rest of the book (it was A Boy's Own Story) but he made no comment on the other 219 pages.

When my book was in the proof stages he called my editor, Bill Whitehead, and said, "Stop the presses! White has stolen my style." Bill, who could be very firm, said, "That's nonsense—he wouldn't want your style and anyway a style can't be patented," and hung up on him. Harold kept calling back, threatening legal action, but he seldom contacted me and Bill never again took his calls. Harold also accused John Updike of stealing his personality. "I am the Devil in The Witches of Eastwick," Harold announced.

The years went by and Harold promised to publish his book. Sometimes it was said to be 2,000 pages long and sometimes it was said he'd written between 3,000 and 6,000 pages. The most famous fashion photographer in the world, Richard Avedon, told me that he was collaborating with Harold since he was convinced he was America's greatest author. Harold wrote the introduction to a book of Avedon's photos taken between 1947 and 1977, an essay that had the distinction of being both laborious and stylish. The title of his novel changed from *Party of Animals* to *The Runaway Soul*, i.e., from a striking title to a forgettable one. It was reported he'd gone back from Knopf to Farrar, Straus. As the new high priest of heterosexuality and the female orgasm, he had no need of the embarrassing evidence to the contrary that Doug Gruenau and Charlie represented.

Charlie had already moved out with a new lover in 1975 and Doug left the apartment in 1980. Harold moved a woman in—Ellen Schwamm, a writer he'd met jogging in the park. (There are other versions of how they'd met. In one, Ellen asked Gordon Lish who was the greatest living writer and when she found out it was Harold she set her cap for him. In another they met at a bookstore, the then fashionable Books & Co. next to the Whitney). Ellen and Harold cut their hair so that they would resemble each other, like the couple in Hemingway's posthumously published and thrillingly good *The Garden of Eden*. She had left her rich husband for Harold. Charlie became an early victim of AIDS and died. Doug found a new lover and remained friendly with Harold and Ellen, though he was never to be mentioned in the press. I tried to date Doug but he was too sweet, too genuine for me—and besides he didn't smoke, he took long hikes in the desert to photograph bison, and got up every morning at six to go jogging around the reservoir. With any luck I was just rolling into bed at that hour, putting out my seventy-second cigarette of the day. I felt sooty and superficial next to Doug—and soon he found a serious lover he's still with after these many years.

I kept hearing nutty reports about Harold. He'd accepted a job teaching the occasional semester at Cornell. Alison Lurie, who taught there, told me that Harold had accused a sweet elderly novelist, James McConkey, of climbing across several roofs and slipping like a cat burglar into Harold's room in Ithaca in order to copy out long passages of Harold's novel and publish them as his own. There was a tremendous row that in a more sensible century would have ended in a simplifying duel instead of the mess that went on for years.

Susan Sontag told me about her evening with Harold. He had said to her, "You and I, Susan, are the greatest writers of the twentieth century." She had replied, "Oh really, Harold? Aren't there a few others? What about Nabokov, for instance?"

"Oh, he's nothing," Harold said, "but at least he had the decency to acknowledge his debt to me."

"Really, Harold? Where did he do that?"

As though slowing down and simplifying things for a child, Harold took a breath and smiled and said, "You remember at the beginning of *Lolita* that Lolita has a father who's already died?"

"Yes . . ."

"And do you remember his first name?"

"Yes, his name is Harold."

Harold shrugged—case closed. Harold seemed seriously to believe that his stories in *First Love and Other Sorrows* had inspired Nabokov—another instance of his style being stolen.

The writer Sheila Kohler told me that when she had dinner with Harold, she told him that she was happy to meet him since Gordon Lish had said he was the greatest living writer. "Why, he compares you to Shakespeare," she told Harold.

Harold looked at her balefully and said, "I bet he wouldn't put Shakespeare on hold." Harold suggested that for this grievous insult he was considering changing publishers yet again.

C. K. Williams, the Pulitzer Prize–winning poet, the sweetest and one of the most talented men of Harold's generation, was introduced to him by Avedon, but rather quickly Harold fought with him. Harold accused Williams of pilfering some of his pages to put into a poem—though later Harold realized that Williams could never have seen those pages since they hadn't yet been published. For once in his life Harold apologized.

And then *The Runaway Soul* came out and it was a terrible flop. James Wood, even though he was defending it, called it "microscopically narcissistic." Pages we'd once admired In *The New Yorker* were now so bent out of shape through rewriting as to be incomprehensible. No one could follow the action. Hundreds of pages went by and we were still mired in earliest childhood—and Harold's insights and observations seemed utterly implausible. No one had that kind of detailed recall about what happened when he was two or three. Piaget had demonstrated that even if we were given complete access to our infant memories they would make no sense to us since they were inscribed in a different, earlier language than the one we think in now. And, anyway, who cared? It was all the fault,

I thought, of that infernal computer and Harold's infinitely expanded opportunities to rewrite. The book was no longer a performance but a smudged palimpsest.

Once his masterpiece went belly-up in such a conspicuous and unresounding way, Harold filled his days more usefully by writing bits and pieces for "The Talk of the Town." He was a good journalist, good at getting the story and willing to curb his eccentric style enough to communicate to the average educated reader. Apparently he also wrote TV pilots for money as well.

Then one day Harold wrote a short piece in *The New Yorker* announcing he had AIDS and was dying. Harold claimed he'd been infected in the 1960s, since that was the last time he'd fooled around with a man. I wondered how Doug reacted to this denial of all their many years together. I thought, only Harold could write a page and a half about his imminent death from AIDS and manage to irritate the reader. Before long, Harold had fought with his two best friends, Renata Adler (*Speedboat*) and Richard Avedon.

He wrote a strangely homophobic book about his AIDS, *This Wild Darkness: The Story of My Death*. He claimed that the book was born of a decision to be honest, not to lie, but in fact he obscured many of the facts. He never mentioned Doug Gruenau or his countless tricks. He acted as if his major contact with Charlie Yordy was based on the fact that they were both orphans (Harold's parents died when he was very young). He claimed that his affair with Charlie (which in the book sounds like his only gay relationship) was a way of reliving the childhood trauma of being sexually abused by his stepfather. As an adult, he said, he had "experimented with homosexuality to break my pride, to open myself to the story" of being abused as a child. This experience may have helped Harold to come to terms with being repeatedly raped, but Harold goes on to say, "I think he was the one who gave it to me." In the gay community it had been decided early on that it wasn't kosher to try to pinpoint the one who'd infected us. Hurling accusations of that sort was a waste of breath—especially since Harold, like the rest of us, had had not one but hundreds of male partners.

When Harold died, it felt anticlimactic. He was obviously a brilliant if underemployed and meddling man. He had great natural gifts and more than a touch of madness. His own wife (Ellen was his second wife—he'd been married to a magazine editor when he was young and had an adult daughter from that union) had written a novel (the ironically titled *How He Saved Her*) in which Harold appeared as the devil, destroying everyone around him. He died nearly the same day as the more famous Russian poet Joseph Brodsky and had the misfortune of being confused with him in many people's minds. Now he's been practically forgotten—and the loss of this large, ambitious talent seems tragic. We all wanted him to be a success. It's more fun to have a genius in our midst.

PART II

BOOKS WE READ

COMPANY

Michael Cunningham

I grew up in a suburb of Los Angeles, where the schools looked more like strip malls than temples of learning and where, as part of an effort to make education "relevant" (it was the 1960s), we students were frequently asked to write papers on our political views, our feelings, or rock lyrics, which made us at least intermittently less surly and relieved the faculty of doing much of anything at all. By my sophomore year I'd written in-depth analyses of the work of Simon and Garfunkel, Joni Mitchell, and the Doors, but would, if asked, have been baffled by the names Spenser, Gogol, or Stendhal. I did read actual books, but my tastes ran to Hesse, Heinlein, and Stone—Irving Stone, that is, author of *The Agony and the Ecstasy*. Certainly not Robert Stone.

I can't lay the blame entirely on lax schooling. A more determined and precocious child could, easily enough, have extended his range by himself. Susan Sontag, or so rumor has it, grew up outside of Phoenix, Arizona, compared to which the suburbs of Los Angeles were *fin-de-siècle* Vienna, and, as soon as she was allowed to leave the house on her own, found a library and read every book in it. She later moved to Los Angeles, and graduated—at fifteen—from North Hollywood High. I was, I'm sorry to report, not especially determined or precocious. Like so many of the undereducated, I believed I knew all I needed to know.

My composure was shaken when, one day in the spring of my sopho-more year, I found myself briefly alone with a girl I've come to call, pri-vately, the pirate queen of my high school. I suspect every school offers some variation on girls like this. She was beautiful in a fierce, chiseled way; she was smart and tough and self-possessed; and she vanished, every day after school, into the VW van of a mysterious older boy from another town. She wore heavy eye makeup and white lipstick and dressed, as I recall, in the skins of animals she had slain.

She and I had, by chance, gone at the same time to sneak a quick cigarette in the dusty little nowhere zone behind the gym, where we all went to smoke. I was doing my best to look as sexily dangerous as it's possible to look when you're fifteen and smoking a Newport you've stolen from your mother's purse. She was smoking a Marlboro from a pack she had clearly not needed to steal. We said hello to each other—we were acquainted—but she was not the sort of girl who'd feel compelled to start meaningless conversations, certainly not with the likes of me, who brought nothing of value to the table. She did not, as far as I could tell, dislike me. It was worse than that. She thought nothing of me at all.

It was probably the fear of invisibility that got me started talking. Although, like any novelist, I have always maintained a generous and, all right, even hyperbolic relationship to what I might accomplish, whom I might defeat in battle, and who is and is not in my league, I don't think, even at fifteen, I actually imagined this girl would consider leaving a sinewy, van-owning, nineteen-year-old semiprofessional criminal for me. I did, however, want to make some sort of impression on her. I lived then, and to some degree still do, in a state I've come to call the morbidly romantic. We morbid romantics are of the opinion that something is always better than nothing, and that although it may be horrifically painful at the time, any encounter, however disastrous or humiliating, will reveal itself, over time, to have been preferable to just slipping unnoticed out of the room.

I won't subject you, or myself, to too many details about my fifteen-year-old's idea of what constituted a stimulating discussion. I asked her if she'd heard the new Leonard Cohen album, to which she did not commit one way or the other. Undaunted—the only thing worse than going on would have been stopping after a single question—I asked if she liked Bob Dylan, to which she nodded affirmatively. It was 1968. Everyone liked Bob Dylan. It wasn't exactly optional.

I'm not sure why I thought it would be a good next move to insist that Leonard Cohen was superior to Bob Dylan. I can only cite, once again, morbid romanticism. For some of us an argument, even one we know we can't possibly win, an argument that may in fact involve the assertion of an opinion we don't actually hold, is better than saying, Hey, well, I guess we both like Bob Dylan, then, and waiting out the silence until she'd finished her cigarette and moved on.

As promised, I'll spare us both the details. I've pretty much repressed them anyway. I believe I quoted lines by both musicians, and scoffed at Dylan's tiny talent. I may have sung a snatch. I prefer not to remember.

I do remember, am doomed to remember, this. She listened, or at least did not ostentatiously not listen, until she'd smoked her cigarette down to the filter and flicked away the butt. She looked at me with a leveling expression. While I know I was sitting relatively still, I picture myself cavorting for her in a hat and a little vest. I suspect I had started to sweat.

She said, in a tone more incredulous than harsh, "Have you ever thought of being less stupid?"

It would have required more desperation and delusion than I possessed to take this as encouragement. I was, however, for the sake of my own survival, by way of an instantaneous rerouting of certain neural connections, able to interpret it as a form of noirish, tough-girl flirtation, something Bacall might have said to Bogart in a smoky, crepuscular bar. Which was not, I suspect, the case. But I do think she was briefly fascinated by what I'd just demonstrated by way of adolescent boyness: our naked, unconcealable needs; our willingness to do or say just about anything in the hope that someone—someone like her—might toss us a scrap from the banquet table. She was asking, in essence, or so I choose to believe, What's wrong with you boys, why are you *like* this?

I distinctly recall having answered, *Actually, I have thought about it, and I've decided I'm pretty happy with the stupid that I am.* I cannot, of course, possibly have said anything like that, and the fact that I remember it as clearly as I remember my sixth birthday party (Lone Ranger theme) is a testament, if we're willing to call it that, to a certain human capacity to live in the world by inventing a history that pleases us more than the genuine article ever could.

Whatever my response, or lack of same, a conversation ensued. A conversation of sorts. A lecture, really, delivered in the way smart, bossy girls have, throughout history, undertaken the instruction of their dimmer, less assertive cohorts. She asked what book I'd read last, and when I told her (not without a note of pride) *The Martian Chronicles*, she asked if I'd read T. S. Eliot and Virginia Woolf. She did in fact speak their full names, slowly and at slightly increased volume, as if talking to a foreigner. I was about to say, *Sure, who hasn't read them,* but some instinct, which (obviously) worked for me intermittently at best, told me I was sure to be found out. "No," I said. "I haven't."

I should mention the fact that neither Eliot nor Woolf appeared on any reading list at our school. The accelerated English class was reading *Great Expectations* in its unabridged form. This girl was going outside the curriculum. I should also mention that I wasn't so ignorant as to be unaware of the names Eliot and Woolf, and, further, that I knew them to be authors and not rock bands. I had just never imagined myself reading them. They were so entirely deceased. The girl of my dreams informed me that Eliot and Woolf were the foundations of contemporary thought, and were probably the greatest artists who had ever lived. I lacked the ammunition I'd have needed to contradict her. I wasn't prepared to argue that Leonard Cohen, much as I loved him, was the greatest artist who'd ever lived.

The exchange pretty much ended there, and the girl and I did not part enemies. She clearly felt she had done good work—shone a beam of light into a corner of the local darkness—and I, like so many of the hopelessly besotted, only loved her more for having taken the time and trouble to make me feel ridiculous.

And, yes, I did in fact endeavor to read Eliot and Woolf. I went the next day to the school library, which was housed in a prefabricated trailer that stood on cinder blocks, the actual library having been under construction since most of the faculty were children. There was no Eliot on the shelves. There was one book by Woolf: *Mrs. Dalloway.* I was the first student to check it out.

I took it home and read it. I took it home and *tried* to read it. It was, I'm sorry to say, incomprehensible to me. I couldn't tell what was going on, who was who, or why we were in one place at one moment and another the next. I wasn't ready for *Mrs. Dalloway.*

I was ready, however—or maybe I should say I was ready to be ready—for Woolf's sentences. I had not only never seen language like that; nothing I'd read had prepared me for the fact that a human being could do what she had done, line by line, using the same ink and paper available to anybody. I had neither read nor conceived of sentences that complex and muscular and precise and beautiful. It may, perversely, have helped that I didn't quite understand what the sentences actually meant. It may have helped free me to better appreciate their tones and variations, the sheer

196

virtuosity of their structures and sounds. I remember thinking, Hey, she was doing with language something like what Jimi Hendrix does with a guitar. Riffing, that is, as only a genius can; finding over and over again an exquisite balance between recklessness and control, between chaos and pattern.

Although I didn't understand *Mrs. Dalloway*, Woolf's language did turn on a small, dim lightbulb over my foolish fifteen-year-old head. I could see for the first time that language was a living medium, that it could soar and swoop, and that the simple declarative sentence, much as we all may love it, was no more indicative of the full range than a single apple is of the natural world. Sentences were malleable and voluptuous and infinitely various; they could in the proper hands be luscious, surprising, and almost unbearably graceful. Each sentence—its weight and density, its duration, its rhythms—determined the weight and density and duration of the next sentence, just as a note of music implies the next note and the next and the next.

The experience altered me. Subtly, of course. I didn't suddenly become erudite, or even particularly studious. I remained a kid to whom the term "goombah" could be all too readily applied. And by the time I managed to talk to the girl again, and tell her I agreed about Woolf's greatness, she not only didn't remember our previous conversation but had moved on to Joyce. I do not, by the way, I'm sorry to report, have any idea what happened to her after we graduated from high school, beyond a single rumor, now more than two decades old, that she had changed her name to Sunshine and gone to live in the Rocky Mountains. I assume it goes without saying that I hope she's happy and well.

My experience with Woolf and *Mrs. Dalloway* did, over time, turn me into a reader, and ultimately, much later, into a writer. Although Woolf did not transform me into a smarter, more serious kid overnight—there's probably no such potent magic anywhere in the world, in any form—I could not go back to Irving Stone afterward. Nor could I return to Hesse or Heinlein, at least not with the same ardor. I had, in a sense, seen Paris, and could never quite go home again.

When, years later, it began to be clear to me that I was going to spend my life trying to write fiction, I wanted to do something for, or about, or with the work of Virginia Woolf. I had no idea what form that desire might take but I felt, even early on, that reading *Mrs. Dalloway* at a relatively

197

young age had been such a transforming experience for me, had mattered so much, that it was literally part of my autobiographical material, every bit as much so as a tragic (or fabulous) love affair, the death of a parent, or other such events that inform what and how novelists write.

I kept putting it off, though, in part because an impulse, however strong, needs to be more than that if it's going to become a novel, and in part because I thought it would be best to wait until I was more skilled, more fluent, and, okay, smarter and more talented before I wandered any-where near Virginia W. By the time I reached my early forties I realized I was never going to feel smart or talented enough, and so might as well just go ahead anyway. I knew almost immediately that whatever I wrote would be called *The Hours*, which had been Woolf's original title for *Mrs. Dalloway*. It seemed an improbable stroke of good fortune, and an uncon-scious, posthumous act of generosity on Woolf's part, to have left that title lying around for over eighty years, waiting for someone to pick it up and attach a book to it.

The Hours started out as a reimagining of *Mrs. Dalloway*, faithful in its particulars, set among gay men in New York City. As a gay man who lives in New York City, I can tell you that certain aspects of gay society—wealthy white gay society, at any rate—bear a rather upsetting resem-blance to the aristocratic, money-and-status-obsessed London of the early twenties, in which Clarissa Dalloway lived. My version was going to center on a fifty-two-year-old gay man, Clarissa's age in Woolf's novel, an age that has much to recommend it but at which, no matter how well you've held up, you can't plausibly think of yourself as young. Aging is of course an enormous concern for everyone, but women and gay men are particularly severely punished for showing signs of it. My no-longer-young gay man was going to throw a party at his apartment in Chelsea, at which he would have a Dallowayesque epiphany.

It took about a year for that book to turn, by slow degrees, into a trip-tych involving a day in the life of a contemporary, and female, Clarissa Dalloway; a day in the life of a woman reading *Mrs. Dalloway* in Los Angeles in the 1950s; and an invented day in the life of Virginia Woolf, in the early 1920s, when she began writing *Mrs. Dalloway*. It took another two years for me to write it.

By that time, however, I'd lived almost another three decades, and had been inspired by uncountable writers, artists, musicians, literary theorists, philosophers, physicists—it's a long list. But there's been nothing and no one as singular as Woolf, not only because she was a significant writer but because she was the first significant writer to tumble open in front of me. Great art helps keep us mindful of the fact that the world is both local and universal, and that time is largely an illusion. At one moment, it seems, we have Virginia Woolf, in her basement room in a suburb of London, beginning to write *Mrs. Dalloway*, half convinced that she's more a hysteric than she is an artist, and that the book upon which she's embarked will be just a tinselly little experiment, to be stored away with all the other crackpot gestures, the dreadfully earnest paintings and the useless inventions and the manifestos that changed nothing. And then, fifty years later, a moment later, we have a kid in an American suburb, sitting on the narrow bed in his disorderly room and reading Woolf's prose in hope of impressing a girl, just barely aware that that act is going to change everything for him, and that he'll return to the book again and again, will in a sense grow up with it, and feel accompanied by it as he tries, with faltering conviction, to write books of his own. It was, in a true sense, companionship, a devastating if one-way friendship, delivered across a half century, and like any properly vital relationship, it was an experience from which I've never fully recovered.

FIVE MILLION HEAD OF CATTLE

Samantha Hunt

He drove me out to the Highway Department's sand pile. There was a machine gun on the seat between us. I thought that he was going to kill me and bury me in the sand. The wind turned the top edge of the pile into dust.

"Ever shot anything?" he asked. I had touched one gun before in my life.

Each blast made a small shower of sand, reminding me of M*A*S*H's opening credits. The sound drowned out anything else. No talking just explosions and I enjoyed that, like we were standing by a waterfall. If I was about to die I didn't want to have to talk to some guy from my English class I barely knew. He screamed when he pulled the trigger but I couldn't hear him under the blast of the gun. I was deaf, waiting for him to turn with a strange look in his eye, aim the barrel at me, kill me just a little bit.

There are two versions of my life, fiction and nonfiction. He never turned. He left me freezing, bleeding, dead.

Later, alive, back in the car, I had a sense of satisfaction, each bullet having carried off something bad and left us both calmer, purer, reborn after slaughter.

"You know Breece D'J Pancake?" he asked.

"Sure." I had no idea what he was talking about. I didn't even recognize the words he said as a man's name at first. I didn't know what a Breece Pancake was but I had some sense that this anciently odd handle was a thing I wanted so I lied. The boy from my English class should have been more careful in front of me, brandishing that name as if it were a badge he'd earned. I took it. A liar *and* a thief, I plucked the name from him and made it mine.

By midnight, the college library closed and I was halfway through the only book Pancake ever published. I went home and got into bed for three days, poisoned. *The Stories of Breece D'J Pancake* were beside me under the covers like a fresh cut I couldn't stop touching. I'd read some more. I'd stare at Pancake's black-and-white author photo where he hid his face in his neck. I'd play Rick Danko's heartache, "It Makes No Difference," one more time.

On first read, Pancake seemed my opposite: muted, male, and mysterious; certain, dangerous, and dead. I fell in love with him the way I'd fallen for Michael Furey and Montgomery Clift before. Ruined beauties departed too soon.

The depths Pancake's stories reached were new lows. Plummeting past the gas wells and coal mines of his native West Virginia, Pancake's stories dive into alcoholism, incest, adultery, dead dogs, murder, war, suicide, and prostitution, mapping the landscape of the underworld.

"A Room Forever" tells the jolly tale of an Ohio riverboat worker in town for a rainy New Year's Eve. He purchases a prostitute and takes her back to his dingy room. "It's nice here," she says of the room. "Yeah. They spray regular," he answers. After the deed is done, he realizes that she's only fourteen years old and so he makes some effort to look after her. "Why don't you just shut-the-fuck-up. Just pay me off, okay?" He pays. She leaves. Later that night when she's found bleeding in an alley having "cut both wrists down to the leaders," the sailor, filled with disgust, can't quite bring himself to care. A real nice holiday tale.

In "The Mark," Reva has had an old-fashioned pregnancy test, a rabbit's been injected with her blood and then cut open in order to see whether its ovaries swelled. Waiting to hear the results, Reva heads off to a local agricultural fair with her husband, a man who breeds bulls. Reva is not pregnant and she knows it. "She was sorry the rabbit had died for nothing." Over in the sideshows she watches a man swallow a snake and some monkeys lining up to rut a female. All the while she is thinking of her brother. Pancake, through some alchemy, leads us to believe that Reva, like the animal husbandry surrounding her, is wholly unnatural. She can't conceive because she lusts after Clinton, her own brother.

By the moss-softened locks, Reva stared at two moons, one hanging quietly above Ohio, the other broken by the slow current

201

of the river. Mosquitoes buzzed about her ears, taking blood from beneath her tender scalp, but she did not move. Upstream, a deer's hoof sucked in the soft mud, but Reva kept watching the swimming moon—the same moon she knew Clinton watched with his Cincinnati whore. She felt her belly for the child that had never been.

Pancake's best known story, "Trilobites," tells the story of Colly, a young man whose father has died. Colly is now losing their farm as he's too young to care for it. The story is wrapped up in geology. Colly and the other characters become the land. "All the water from the old mountains flowed west. But the land lifted. I have only the bottoms and stone animals I collect. I blink and breathe. My father is a khaki cloud in the canebrakes and Ginny is no more to me than the bitter smell in the blackberry briers on the ridge." Colly loses the land that he has become.

For three days I lay in bed. It wasn't just the misery that had me sunk. Pancake's language made such a beautiful knife I was slow to realize how badly I'd been cut up. Pancake warns off sensitive readers before they enter these stories. He makes a fence of regional language that is at times so dense it's hard to penetrate meaning:

> I take up my sack and gaff for a turkle. Some quick chubs flash under the bank. In the moss-dapples, I see rings spread where a turkle ducked under. The sucker is mine. The pool smells like rot, and the sun is a hardish brown. I wade in. He goes for the roots of a log. I shove around, and feel my gaff twitch. This is a smart turkle, but still a sucker.

I've always read his localisms as some sort of DANGER, NO TRESPASSING sign. Which, of course, only makes me want to enter them more.

In bed, feeling bruised, staring at my navel, I modeled myself after this tragic American. I writhed, certain of some link between writing and sorrow. In Pancake, I'd found the entrance to an underground passage. I tumbled down after him.

Back to school on the third day, I wore Pancake's story collection as a shield clutched before my heart, title facing out. I displayed him like a woman who tattoo tears on her cheeks, one for every year her man has been in prison. I was frolicking in misery the way only a young person without much real sorrow can.

An upperclassman had once pinched my cheek and told me, "You're so pink." The insult made me burn. The only just response, "You're so shit brown," would have gotten me assigned to a Saturday morning cultural sensitivity training session. She was claiming less guilt for the world's ills because her hair was black, her skin olive. She was from Greenwich, Connecticut. I wanted to strike her across the face with Pancake's stories.

At nineteen, no one could see the dark night of my soul. No one would have even guessed that it existed no matter how desperately I wanted one. Breece became my visible scar. The book got tattered. The library fines I owed on it could have purchased two or three copies but I carried it still, waiting for something essential in its pages to get transferred into my chest, branded on my brain.

No one ever noticed. Months passed. And then finally, one day:

"Why, Samantha Hunt. What are you doing with that nasty man Breece Pancake?"

It was my writing professor, David Huddle. Huddle was famous on campus because of his beautiful accent, hailing, as he did, from Ivanhoe, Virginia. He'd recently written an article for *Playboy* about ogling his female students, raising the ire of many a campus woman. It made David seem furtively sexy. I couldn't come up with a good answer. I smiled and kept walking.

What *was* I doing with Pancake? I asked myself this question all that day and night so that I'd have something to tell Huddle next time I saw him. Just making myself miserable? No. I liked the way Pancake's stories hurt but it was more than that. Pancake was teaching me how to lie better.

When Breece got to the University of Virginia in 1977, women and minorities had only gained entrance approximately a decade earlier. An insecure West Virginian down in Virginia, Pancake decided to become the one thing he imagined they were already thinking about him: hillbilly. He shot squirrels and ate them for dinner. He harvested roadkill and kept it in the freezer. He drank oceans of liquor and swaggered about in dusty boots. Pancake lied about who he was. The truth is he'd grown up solidly middle class. His father Bud had worked at Union Carbide for thirty-five years but when Pancake showed up at UVA he didn't want to be Bud's sol-idly middle-class son so he created a character named Breece D'J Pancake and then he started writing stories.

I have to imagine his lying angered people. But to me Pancake's lies seem noble as they insist that all identity is a creation. Pancake proves that knowing the Other is my direst responsibility as a writer. Why write what I know when I can imagine anything? When I want to know the whole world?

As a girl, I told a stranger in a diner that my father was a cattle farmer. He asked how many head and I answered quickly, five million. I had no idea what size herds come in but quickly realized I'd gone a bit overboard. The stranger walked away laughing. Waiting alone on park benches, rid-ing the bus, I'd make up stories: I grew up in Chile. I worked in a sardine factory. I was married. I was a runaway. I was unrepentant. I never thought of these lies as deceit. They were always obviously lies. I was entertaining people, doing a song and tap dance to make the day more colorful.

Pancake was dead years before I'd even heard his name. Following his created identity all the way to the end, he shot himself at UVA when he was only twenty-six. I don't think much anymore about a link between sorrow and writing.

Pancake is my anti-mentor. He's never asked me, "What are you doing with your life?" That suits me fine. It's not that he doesn't speak. He just would never say anything so plain and well adjusted. His words are closer to "Fuck 'em," or "Shit for brains," or "Tell me the one about how your dad was once the greatest cattle farmer who ever lived."

On *Fat City*

Denis Johnson

Exactly which year of the 1960s the book came out, I can't remember, but I remember well which year of my lifetime it was—I was discovering that it wasn't a joke anymore, I was actually going to have to become a writer, I was too emotionally crippled for real work, there wasn't anything else I could do—I was eighteen or nineteen. *Newsweek* reviewed *Fat City*, a first novel by Leonard Gardner, in a tone that seemed to drop the usual hype—"It's good. It really is." I wanted to get a review like that.

I got the book and read about two Stockton, California, boxers who live far outside the boxing myth and deep in the sorrow and beauty of human life, a book so precisely written and giving such value to its words that I felt I could almost read it with my fingers, like Braille.

The stories of Ernie Munger, a young fighter with frail but nevertheless burning hopes, and Billy Tully, an older pug with bad luck in and out of the ring, parallel one another through the book. Though the two men hardly meet, the tale blends the perspective on them until they seem to chart a single life of missteps and baffled love, Ernie its youth and Tully its future. I wanted to write a book like that.

But how? What, exactly, had Gardner done? I sensed some mystical connection between what I found in the style itself and its ability to draw my sympathy for a type of character whom I'd surely never meet. Its measured tone, its attitude of respect for all, its keen eye and appreciation for passing details, from its opening—

> He lived in the Hotel Coma—named perhaps for some founder of the town, some California explorer or pioneer, or for some long-deceased Italian immigrant who founded only the hotel itself. Whoever it commemorated, the hotel was a poor monument, and Billy Tully had no intention of staying on.

—to its finish, the nighttime landscape Ernie Munger watches from the windows of a Greyhound bus, riding back to Stockton after winning one by a knockout,

> riding through the night coolness of low delta fields, past dark vineyards, orchards and walnut groves, isolated lights of farmhouses, irrigation ditches full of moonlit water, then on the outskirts a gigantic Technicolor face speaking silently on the screen of a drive-in movie.

Phil, my neighbor across the road, also a young literary hopeful, felt the same way I did about *Fat City*. We talked about passages from the book one by one and over and over, the way couples sometimes reminisce about each moment of their falling in love.

And like most youngsters in the throes, I assumed I was among the very few humans who'd ever felt this way. In the next few years, studying at the Writers' Workshop in Iowa City, I was astonished every time I met a fellow writer who could quote ecstatically line after line of dialogue from the down-and-out souls of *Fat City*, the men and women seeking love, a bit of comfort, even glory—but never forgiveness—in the heat and dust of central California. Admirers were everywhere.

I recall sitting in my grad-school office with young Tracy Kidder—at that time himself already the author of a nonfiction book about central California, later to win a Pulitzer for another book—while he quoted the opening of chapter 4—

> Days were like long twilights in the house under the black walnut trees . . .

—and recited the hoarse remarks of an old trainer reminiscing in the gym:

> "Manny Chavez," he whispered, "had the clearest piss of any man I ever seen. He'd take a specimen and the piss in that bottle would be just as clean and pure as fresh drinking water."

Phil, my neighbor across the road, was the poet Philip Schultz, another eventual Pulitzer winner. He told me he'd come across Gardner in a drugstore in California once, recognized him from his jacket photo. He was looking at a boxing magazine. "Are you Leonard Gardner?" Phil asked. "You must be a writer," Gardner said, and went back to the magazine. I made him tell the story a thousand times.

Though a student at the major school for creative writing, in that era of my youth I was terrified and arrogant and not directly "teachable." Leonard Gardner's book, and the writers who talked about it with me, were my mentors in fiction. Between the ages of nineteen and twenty-five I studied *Fat City* so closely that I began to fear I'd never be able to write anything but imitations of it, so I swore it off.

When I was about thirty-four (the same age Gardner was when he published his), my first novel came out. About a year later I borrowed *Fat City* from the library and read it. I could see immediately that ten years' exile hadn't saved me from the influence of its perfection—I'd taught myself to write in Gardner's style, though not as well.

Now, many years later, I've looked through the book again, and I find it's still true: Leonard Gardner has something to say in every word I write. I turned first to a five-page passage late in the book—an argument between Billy Tully and his girlfriend Oma, the first bit of dialogue I'd ever scrutinized for its ups and downs, the turns and turns-about, the strategies of the combatants; and I suspect that considerations of this kind, beginning here with this book, led me eventually to try writing dialogue for the stage. I could nearly recite the lines along with the characters, yet they sounded new. I looked back at the novel's opening paragraph, and before long I read the whole thing again and found myself just as moved as I'd been the first time.

And just as mystified: How does Gardner do it? My experience with *Fat City* shaped my philosophy as an artist, and somewhat, too, as a person: That in the world's grays and sepias, in its shadows and lonely nights, a fine beauty is visible to the eye that stays open. But how does he create that experience? How does Gardner's measured speech and clear seeing produce in me a sense that in the meanest-looking lump of humanity the heart still beats? I don't know. I will read the book again.

MAD HOPE AND MAVERICKS

ZZ Packer

I'm ashamed to say that I came across James Alan McPherson's fiction much later than I should have. He was on sabbatical during my first year studying at the Iowa Writers' Workshop, and I wanted to make sure I'd read his stories by the time he returned. So I bought a used copy of his Pulitzer Prize–winning collection *Elbow Room* and began reading "Why I Like Country Music," "The Story of a Dead Man," and then "The Silver Bullet." As I read each story I experienced what is best described in terms familiar to addicts of any stripe—the rush as the drug gets started, the pure, free-floating euphoria of riding the high, the ultimate disappointment when all the goods are gone. McPherson, more than any other contemporary writer I've read, understands the pure addictive quality of a story well told—story not as cleverly crafted gem full of ironic phrasing and hip posturing, but Story, the kind we tell around campfires to comfort ourselves, the kind we tell as parables to warn each other, the kind we tell to save ourselves.

Inevitably, with any short story collection, one expects a few not so stellar pieces, and after having read the first three excellent stories in *Elbow Room*, I was prepared for the fourth to lag; but after reading it—after reading all of *Elbow Room* in a single night—I found myself outside, needing a strong dose of the Iowa winter air to keep myself from reeling. I'd had a similar feeling after reading Toni Morrison's *The Bluest Eye*, then *Song of Solomon*, then—heart attack—*Beloved*. I'd also had a similar feeling reading the famed "Grand Inquisitor" passage of Doestoevsky's *The Brothers Karamazov*, reading Halldór Laxness's Icelandic epic *Independent People*, and *Invisible Man*, written by McPherson's mentor Ralph Ellison. The difference in reading *Elbow Room* was that here was a writer whose ear was so finely tuned to the rhythms and cadences of speech in general—and transplanted black Southerners' in particular—that I felt as though I were riding the Greyhound bus with the lot of them as each unfurled his tale. The beauty of a McPherson story lies in its dead-on characterization, keen sociological observation, high psychological drama, and earnest, folksy conviction that the art of storytelling deserves its proper reliquary in the cathedral of Literature.

Perhaps more than anything, I was ecstatic that someone had finally got it right: captured the hoots and hollers of my great-uncles, the superciliousness of certain "uppity" cousins, the unconscious steadfastness of aunts who love and love again despite it all. Here was someone, finally, who wrote black characters whose happiness came from the same fount as their misery, whose problems were real, not lifted from Hollywood scripts.

Before reading McPherson's work, I hadn't realized how much I tensed up at reading any depictions of blacks, whether by white or black authors. In the canon, blacks were evil, shifty, lazy, dumb, and the liberal white writers of the sixties didn't do much better. Black women became "sassy" or "wise" or "matriarchs" or "natural women." Black men became sidekicks, cool daddies, or "angry black men." Black authors, in an attempt to right so many wrongs, tended to overstate black strength, pride, and perseverance to such a degree that their "corrections" were quick recipes for character death. McPherson, on the other hand, shows us characters most black writers would be uncomfortable creating for fear of airing dirty laundry; McPherson shows us complex characters most white writers simply wouldn't dare create.

In "The Story of a Dead Man," McPherson invites the reader to reconcile the lives of two cousins, both christened William, who've taken divergent paths. Whereas the narrator has achieved a modicum of comfort and middle-class security, William's cousin Billy has landed a job as a henchman for a collection agency, shortly after a stint in jail. Though the story works on the doppelgänger model in which the "good narrator" lives vicariously through the adventures of the evil twin, McPherson subverts this convention: William's patent unreliability and annoying lack of self-awareness compel the reader to search for an alternative good character in the "evil twin," Billy. In contrast to William's pretense, Billy's refusal to be disingenuous is his ultimate strength, for without Billy's maverick sense of how life should be lived, William's own story slinks into insignificance.

Though Billy is revealed to be the criminal he is, he is the one to unveil himself; and his insistence on laying claim to the horrible truths of his life accords him a respectability we cannot grant William. McPherson suggests that such is the struggle for black America: gaining socioeconomic freedom without losing authenticity.

Having read the stories in *Elbow Room*, and later, the stories in McPherson's debut collection, *Hue and Cry*, I'm struck by how the world seems divided into two periods: before reading McPherson and afterward. While traveling from Oakland to Michigan by Amtrak, I observed the relationship between the black dining car waiters and the mostly white passengers and found myself recalling "Solo Song: For Doc," McPherson's much-anthologized story from *Hue and Cry*. The narrator of the story is a railroad waiter who tries to convince the summer "youngblood" that the official waiters' manual he's poring over is not the all-important text the railroad executives would have him believe. In assembling the "big, black book," as the manual is referred to, the upper echelons of the railroad have stripped away the beauty, grace, flash, and style of the waiters that "built the railroad," and filled the void with an instruction manual that, if heeded, can only bring about a loss of manhood and freedom. The true "book" from which the youngblood should learn, our narrator suggests, is the oral testimony of past waiters, the styles and "pretty moves" and waiters' craft that the über-waiter Doc Craft embodies.

Instead of openly rebelling or refusing to rebel, Doc Craft is "crafty" and sly, the precursor to the street hustler.

> [He took] over his station and collected fat tips from his tables by telling the passenger that the Sheik had had to get off back along the line because of a heart attack. The Sheik liked that because he saw that Doc understood crackers and how they liked nothing better than knowing that a nigger had died on the job, giving them service.

The narrator values Doc above all because he is a "waiter's waiter" who follows his own code of excellence, rather than the one established by those in power. If the railroad world is a microcosm of American society in which the waiters represent blacks, the youngblood to whom the story is addressed is, like so many other McPherson characters, a black for

whom the process of assimilation is the beginning of the end. The youngblood cannot cling to the "big black bible of the instruction manual"
and at the same time be a waiter's waiter because, as the critic Herman
Beavers writes, "to be a waiter's waiter is to be the creator of the text, not
the recipient."

Another abiding interest of mine that McPherson explores in his fiction
is how society—especially the close-knit community that is black society—
accepts or rejects its members. McPherson wrestles with this concept in
nearly every story. In "The Story of a Scar," a woman chooses to converse
with and date a college-bound man while her former mailroom friends are
content to play cards during lunch hour. In upsetting the order of things,
she gets a taste of how a community can punish those who don't conform
to it:

> Red squared with me when I asked her what was goin' down. She
> told me, "People sayin' you been wearin' a high hat since you start-
> ed goin' with the professor. The talk is you been throwin' around
> big words and developin' a strut just like his. Now I don't believe
> these reports, being your friend and sister, but I do think you ough-
> ta watch your step. I remember what my grandma used to tell me:
> 'it don't make no difference how well you fox-trot if everybody else
> is dancing the two-step.'"

It was while reading McPherson's memoir, *Crabcakes*, that I saw how
closely his life and mine tracked, though mine more resembled the hap-
less youngblood than McPherson's skillful Doc Craft. He entered Harvard
Law School during the sea change of the mid-1960s, when racial politics
seemed to open up new possibilities; I entered Yale during another sea
change, when the shantytowns on Beinecke Plaza were just being demol-
ished as Yale divested itself of its holdings in South Africa, and I graduated
when the witch hunt against affirmative action seemed to be at its peak.
He had rented out a house in Baltimore just two blocks from where I later
lived when I taught high school. He had been to Japan, having long been
in thrall to its code of honor, and I had lived there as well, searching for I
know not what. And finally, a love for writing and a relationship upheaval
had brought each of us to Iowa, a place hardly known for its burgeoning
black communities.

And yet to say our lives have been similar is impossible. Here is a man who's logged in enough jobs, hours, and learning to fill several people's lives, and in his own unassuming way he is a legend around the Workshop, if not in Iowa City itself. In addition to winning the Pulitzer Prize in 1978, he has worked as a reporter, research assistant, community organizer, dining car waiter, and janitor, and has served as a member of several think tanks. But above all, McPherson is a public intellectual who in the course of a conversation might offer theories on anyone, from Richard Pryor to Tacitus, Bill Clinton to Malraux. As any Iowa workshopper can tell you, to mention a subject to McPherson is to find yourself laden with books he has handpicked as recommended reading. He is expert in all media, and to visit his home is to find not only thousands of books, but thousands of old records, collectibles, videos, and time-worn documents. He is always on the lookout for the human, the real, the authentic.

At a time when literary fiction ebbs and flows with the currents of popular culture, McPherson has been unwavering in the humanist bent of his writings, his insistence that principles and ethics are as much the warp and woof of fiction as they are of life. McPherson's continual search for the authentic is what imbues his stories and essays with both a tragic and a comic sensibility, both freshness and timelessness. Perhaps most illustrative of his work and its cumulative effect is one of his favorite quotes, from the Spanish philosopher Unamuno: "It is despair, and despair alone, that begets heroic hope, absurd hope, mad hope."

Getting it. Deeply immersed. In awe. Learning. Reading Ms. McDermott. Appreciating beginnings. Still appreciating beginnings. Nailing it.

Anita Shreve

Getting it

I was sixteen, a junior in high school. I'd been assigned *Ethan Frome* to read over the weekend. I lived in Dedham, Massachusetts, and we must have had a recent snowstorm of significant proportions. The tree limbs held three inches of snow, and the world outside my house was silent. I recall sitting in a chair in a corner of my room reading *Ethan Frome* and occasionally looking out the window at the winter scene with grim clouds as a backdrop. Though the house was warm, I felt cold. The prose was stark, the name of Wharton's New England town was Starkfield, and I felt stark inside. Though I was moved by Ethan's plight, I was more intrigued by the theme of passion within a framework of restraint. Never before had exterior scenery matched the words in front of me so well, and never before had the words in front of me matched my interior thoughts so well, and never before had my interior thoughts matched so well the outside world. And so on, and so on. It was as though I had inadvertently found a kind of holy grail without even knowing I'd been searching for it. The two hours I spent in my room reading Edith Wharton's *Ethan Frome* and spinning in that metaphorical circle marked the beginning of my life as a writer.

DEEPLY IMMERSED

By the time I was a senior in high school, I was a voracious reader. With a small library and little guidance, I found myself reading all of Eugene O'Neill's plays. I read them like children read *Harry Potter* today, late into the night and in one sitting. When I had completed them, I set to reading them again. I thought then that I would be a playwright. As it happened, I didn't become a playwright, and when I recently went to see *Long Day's Journey into Night* (which when read doesn't necessarily advertise its length), I couldn't wait to get out of the theater. My favorite play of all time now felt clunky, awkward, and intolerably long. My affair with Eugene came to an abrupt end.

O'Neill, however, had been a tremendous influence. As in one of those chicken and egg conundrums, I have never known if I was enraptured by this bleak playwright because I tended toward the bleak, or if the words of the celebrated playwright had stamped themselves upon my literary unconscious. I still don't know the answer to that, but I do know this: I have never been accused of a happy ending.

IN AWE

In 1975, I was included in a volume called *O. Henry Prize Stories*. My very short story had been a modest offering among names that would shortly become stellar: Rosellen Brown and Tim O'Brien, just to name two. One among us was already stellar: John Updike. I had read Updike before and had even been lucky enough in college to have attended a talk given by him. But when I read his story, "Separating," in that 1975 volume, I was awestruck. I still maintain it is the best short story I've ever read with the possible exception of Rose Tremain's "The Stack" and Ian McEwan's "On Chesil Beach" as it appeared in *The New Yorker*. Updike's is the story of a suburban couple who have decided to separate and now face the task of telling their children at dinner. Whenever I get to the point in the story at which Updike writes, "Yet it was the thought of telling Judith, the image of her, their first baby, walking between them arm in arm to the bridge that broke him," I begin to tear up. By the time I reach the scene in which John, their younger boy, wads a paper napkin into the leaves of his salad and fashions a ball of paper and lettuce and pops it into his mouth as his way of trying to erase the moment of being told about the separation, I am sobbing. The story is full of raw emotional power and scintillating sentences like this one:

> Yet, a summer ago, as canary-yellow bulldozers churned a grassy, daisy-dotted knoll into a muddy plateau, and a crew of pigtailed young men raked and tamped clay into a plane, this transformation did not strike them as ominous, but festive in its impudence; their marriage could rend the earth for fun.

The early Updike works represent to me the pinnacle of literary achievement, and I took it personally every year he was passed over for the Nobel. He was an author whose words I admired above all, whose sentences I could never hope to emulate. Though I will mourn his passing the rest of my literary life, I am reminded that magnificent role models never die.

LEARNING

I was a journalist for fifteen years. By that, I mean that I wrote feature articles for magazines. I wrote for anyone who would give me an assignment: *Motor Boating and Sailing, Town and Country*, and *The New York Times Magazine*. I almost always had a deadline and a word count. I learned how to *see* the shape of a story as well as the importance of knowing one's lead and one's ending. I also learned how to research a story and what salient details to use. Most of all, I absorbed the valuable lesson that writing is not precious. It is work. Though I yearned to be a writer of short stories and possibly even a novel (instead of writing the silly pieces I was sometimes assigned—a *Cosmo* article on the sex appeal of men's white shirts comes to mind), I owe those years in journalism a great deal. Without them, I wouldn't know how to shape a novel or how to use a body of research or know that writing is simply work—the last being the most important lesson any young writer can learn.

Reading Ms. McDermott

Alice McDermott doesn't know this, but I owe an enormous debt to her words. (It's usually not the author but the words on the page to whom a new writer is indebted.) I'd have to work back to figure out what year this was, but let's say it was midsummer of 1985 or 1986. I'm at a summer rental in New Hampshire, and my five-year-old daughter is at my feet in the dining room of the rental setting up an imaginary business with various dolls filling in the needed parts: secretary, best friend, boyfriend, food guy. No boss. She's the boss. I have just read the last page of Alice McDermott's stunning novel *That Night*. I turn right back to the first page and begin reading again. I'm struck by the cadences and the rhythm of the prose, by the repetition of the phrase *that night*, by the seemingly simple yet complex way of telling the story, and by the sheer power of that first scene. I grab a pad of lined paper and begin making notes for what will become my first novel, *Eden Close*. I write ten pages, single-spaced. I tell my daughter I am being a boss, too, and we have a short discussion about how there can be only one boss, and thus I am demoted to secretary. In the middle of the ten pages, I do something I'm now convinced allowed me to write the book. I change the gender of the protagonist from a female to a male, thus giving me distance from the main character and igniting the imagination, both essential, as it happened, to my life as a novelist.

There is no doubt in my mind—none whatsoever—that had I not read *That Night* at that particular moment in time, I would not be a novelist today.

Appreciating beginnings

The beginning of a novel is, alas, its most important part. (The same is true of a TV drama. For example, I'm in front of the TV while my husband is changing the channel: "Hurry up, we'll miss the beginning, which is always the best part.") When teaching a creative writing class, I hold my thumb and forefinger apart to illustrate a length of perhaps six inches. This is how long you have to capture the reader's interest in a short story. I pick up a book and hold open its first page (which includes its back). This is how long you have to capture the would-be reader of your first novel. It's a sad story, I tell them, but it's true. We are readers of little patience. No longer can the author slowly make his way into a novel and develop its themes without giving even a hint of plot. Today, the novel must immediately have promise. This is why a disproportionate emphasis is put on the first chapter of a novel. (Try this at home. Open a novel. Is the writing in chapter six as good as in chapter one?) Personally, I spend 50 percent of the time allotted to the novel on the first 50 pages and the second half of the time allotted on the second 250 pages. It might take me a year to write those first 50 pages. Why? To answer all the questions that need to be answered when writing the novel (who's telling the story? present tense or past? first person or third? tone? and so on), and, perhaps most essential, to hook the reader.

Ian McEwan is the master of beginnings—*The Child in Time* and *On Chesil Beach* being sterling examples. I can't convey their power and beauty in so short a space, so you'll just have to read them. When I read the first chapter of *The Child in Time*, I wept. When I read the first chapter of *On Chesil Beach* in short story form in *The New Yorker*, I ran down the stairs of my house, shouting to my (now grown) children, "This is the best short story I have ever read!" The care and beauty and extraordinary attention to detail of the opener is simply dazzling. Unfortunately for McEwan, he failed to get the car in the garage in each of these two novels (more about the car-in-the-garage phenomenon later). The books begin slowly to deflate after those exhilarating beginnings. Still, they are worth reading and remain as shining stars on the shelf of my bookcase reserved for special novels.

STILL APPRECIATING BEGINNINGS

Read the opening scenes of *Cal* by Bernard MacLaverty and *Transit of Venus* by Shirley Hazzard. I dare you to put the books down. I couldn't. I've read each at least a half dozen times. After the third time, I began to read for technique. Though the novels are very different, each has an astonishing beginning. *Cal* gets you in the gut. *Transit of Venus* seductively draws the reader in by setting up an unforgettable scene and by the sheer brilliance of the writing. Each sentence in *Transit of Venus* is a universe unto itself.

NAILING IT

You've just read what you think is a masterpiece—a big, rollicking, yet serious novel. You're near the end. Actually, you don't want the book to end because you've enjoyed it so much. But you do read the ending. You have to. And it's (how to say?) a huge, flipping disappointment. This author of dazzling gifts couldn't get the car in the garage? Did he run out of gas? Did the publisher snatch the barely completed novel from his computer? Did he grow sad toward the end of his opus and not want to end it? Or was he simply impatient *to be done*? Hence the rattling to a close.

Not being able to get the car in the garage is a more frequent phenomenon than we would like to think. How often have you read a novel and said to yourself, Huh?

Those who can accomplish the deft parking feat of bringing the novel to a satisfying close endear themselves to readers. We feel we got our money's worth. We want to linger at these endings. We want to read them again and again in case we missed something. A subtle message has been sent: this author cares as much about the ending as he did about the beginning. We close the covers feeling exhilarated, or breathless, or perhaps having experienced true catharsis. We want to call someone and tell her she has to read the book.

I can think of two marvelous endings to novels. The first is that of Brian Moore's *Lies of Silence*. A novel about a Belfast hotel owner who is forced to make a choice between allowing the IRA to bomb his hotel when a conference of important political foes will be there or having his wife shot in the head, its ending is a shocker. All the more so for the intricate way it is set up and for the manner in which our expectations are dashed. I promise you, you will not be able to imagine this ending. I have never met anyone who has read this spare and wonderful book and not commented on the last page. It's a short, sharp shock that leaves the reader breathless.

Another superb parking job is to be had at the ending of *Transit of*

218

Venus (mentioned before as having a captivating beginning, and hence my years-long selection as the best novel in the English language). An ending is a tricky subject to discuss for fear of giving too much away. Suffice it to say that rather than deliver the short, sharp shock (though there is that as well), Hazzard deftly brings together at the end a number of crucially important threads of the novel even as she is leading us to a brilliantly clever close that puts a bullet in the chest and leaves the reader, literally, speechless. I learn as much from lovingly constructed endings as I do from beguiling beginnings.

But, hey, no peeking.

Paper Mentors

Martha Southgate

I was a voracious reader as a child. When I was ten, I had one of those reading experiences that you never forget. I was lying on my stomach in bed, reading the longest book I'd ever read at that time, when I came to these words in a letter from an adult character to the eleven-year-old protagonist:

> Naturally, you put down the truth in your notebooks. What would be the point if you didn't? And naturally those notebooks should not be read by anyone else but if they are, then, Harriet, you are going to have to do two things and you don't like either one of them:
>
> 1) you have to apologize.
> 2) you have to lie.
>
> Otherwise you are going to lose a friend. Little lies that make people feel better are not bad, like thanking someone for a meal they made even if you hated it, or telling a sick person they look better when they don't, or someone with a hideous new hat that it's lovely. Remember that writing is to put love in the world, not to use against your friends. But to yourself, you must always tell the truth.

This paragraph contains the heart of *Harriet the Spy*. The heroine has been keeping honest but scathing notes on her friends, relations, and the world around her, and here she is told, in so many words, that sometimes it's best to keep one's private world private, even if it means lying—something ten-year-olds are routinely instructed against. My feet stopped dead still against each other. A gong went off in my head—"I knew it! I knew there was something those adults were keeping from me."

When I first read Louise Fitzhugh's novel, I had no interest in being a writer. I wanted to be a psychologist—or, failing that, Jermaine Jackson's wife. But now I know that there are only a few books that have influenced me as much as this one did, that have, in a sense, mentored me into being the writer I am. I haven't had a human mentor, not the way the term is usually used when talking about writers or lawyers or bankers. I haven't formed a lasting relationship with anyone who spotted a spark in my work and blew on it gently, and then a little bit harder, until it burst into a novel or a collection of stories. I've had teachers—good ones who guided and encouraged me. But they haven't become people I have dinner with occasionally or turn to for blurbs or for career advice. On the other hand, I have also never had a teacher or editor who tore up my early efforts with a few contemptuous remarks and stomped on the shreds—that experience, I'm happy to have missed out on.

I envy those who ended up with mentors. It could be that one of the reasons I didn't was because I didn't start writing fiction seriously until I was in my early thirties and earned my MFA at thirty-four, married and eight months pregnant. I finished my first substantial fiction just months before I plunged into the all-consuming world of first-time motherhood. Not much time for mentoring conversations and long lingering dinners then. Or maybe it was a temperamental thing, or a case of not meeting the right person. In any event, I'm working on my fourth novel now and it still hasn't happened.

My mentors have been the books I've obsessed over and had crushes on. One of the surest marks of a writer is his or her devotion to good books. There are good readers who aren't good writers—but there aren't any good writers who aren't good, enthusiastic readers. On my list of favorite books, there are few to none of the nineteenth- and twentieth-century greats. In fact, at literary gatherings, I am sometimes embarrassed by the sheer number of books I should have read that I haven't, or books that I feel I ought to love that I don't. And of course, the books I'm writing about here are not the only books that have inspired me. I picked these two because one influenced me long before I ever thought of telling a story of my own and the other drove me to reach farther as a writer than I thought I could at the time. What they have in common is that both novels encouraged me to look beyond my own circumstances and engage as best I could with life's ambiguities.

Harriet the Spy was the first book I ever really adored. Most of the people who read this beautifully written novel are brainy girls between ten and twelve years old, but I continue to think that boys (and, for that matter, grown-ups of both genders) could profit greatly by reading it. First published in 1964, it chronicles the adventures and misadventures of Harriet M. Welsch, the self-assured ten-year-old daughter of a television writer, attending private school and growing up monied on the Upper East Side. Harriet is a bold girl: she sneaks around eavesdropping to learn more about her neighbors, writes down acerbic, often unkind remarks about her friends in her journal, and lies about her writings in order to preserve those friendships.

What's more, though I didn't perceive it as such at the time, the novel offers an astute and gimlet-eyed view of social class and the ways it plays out in children's lives (Fitzhugh would later tackle race and class, more directly but less skillfully, in her last novel, *Nobody's Family Is Going to Change*). For a bookish, working-class, black girl like me in Cleveland, Harriet's milieu—of grown-ups having drinks before dinner and leaving their daughter with the nanny when they went out—might have been on Mars, but it was a planet worth learning about. Harriet's comfortable circumstances are presented neither as a virtue or a flaw—but her privilege is clearly acknowledged in a way that is not all that common in children's books today and was unheard of in 1964. Here's a bit from Harriet's journal about her friend Sport and his novelist father who, like a lot of writers, is always broke: "Sport's house smells like old laundry, and it's noisy and kind of poor-looking. My house doesn't smell and is quiet like Mrs. Plumber's. Does that mean we are rich? What makes people poor or rich? . . . Are rich people ever going to grow up to be writers or are writers all like Mr. Rocque with no money?"

But what got to me most about the book and what stays with me still—the way in which it is a mentor to me—is the degree to which it praises and heralds the idea that recording one's experiences and observations honestly and artfully is important. It may cost you dearly, but it's worth fighting for. That sank in.

The other great lesson of this novel for me is about gray areas—not something that most ten-year-olds have much tolerance for or are encouraged to consider much. This is the first book I ever read that stated so boldly (and to date, I still haven't read one that says it quite so nakedly) that it isn't always wrong to lie to protect a relationship. This was the first book I read as a child that invited me to engage in a degree of negotiation with the hard facts of the world. Even as a ten-year-old, I sensed this fundamental conflict somewhere in the marrow of my bones—that honesty is not always kind, that some things have to be kept to oneself. I sense it still—and I try to write about it honestly.

Despite the effect this book had on me, I never climbed into a dumbwaiter or spied on a neighbor or friend. I didn't start keeping a journal until I was eighteen. Though Harriet was a fond memory, when I graduated from college—and for some years afterward—fiction was something I read, not something I wrote. The reasons for this are complex. As an African-American woman, I think a lot of it had to do with the territory I felt entitled to. I also definitely bought into the cultural myth that if you haven't always wanted to be a writer, you can't be one. Furthermore, I wasn't so sure that I had a story worth telling. But I kept reading. *Looking for Mr. Goodbar* by Judith Rossner when I was sixteen, *Happy All the Time* by Laurie Colwin, *Shining Through* by Susan Isaacs, *The Postman Always Rings Twice* by James M. Cain, *Carrie* and *The Shining* and *Firestarter* by Stephen King (his disciplined early work shows his particular gifts to best advantage), *The Color Purple* by Alice Walker, *The Age of Grief* by Jane Smiley, *Black-Eyed Susans*, a seminal anthology of work by black women, edited by Mary Helen Washington, and *The Chaneysville Incident* by David Bradley (a one-off masterpiece).

The books I read when I was younger all run together now, years and pub dates and what I was doing at the time all a blur. But what I know for sure is that I always had a book in my hand. I remember lying in my narrow dormitory bed in college and being transformed by Toni Morrison's *The Bluest Eye*. I just stared at the cover for a while after I read it, dazzled that so much about all life, especially black life, could be contained in one book. Same thing happened when I read *Song of Solomon* a couple of years later. After college, back in Cleveland, while I worked as a community organizer (I read a lot of Laurie Colwin and Jane Austen then—I needed cheering up), as a magazine editor (Jane Smiley's *The Age of Grief*—I wasn't married yet but I read it over and over and over, mesmer ized by the way that she'd drawn the complexity of marriage long before I'd begun to live it), and then as a newspaper reporter (read *The Hours* then: I distinctly remember thinking, *what am I going to read that will top that?* It took awhile to find something). I slowly, slowly began to take an occasional fiction writing class to feel that I might want to add my voice to the chorus.

My list skews somewhat to the white and the contemporary. But though I wasn't always reading about the past or stories about people whose background I shared, I also know now that I learned a lot about how to tell the good from the bad in reading contemporary fiction. The immediacy of the concerns in these novels touched me in a way that I wasn't ready to be touched by "greater" works of fiction. Also, many of them were written at a level and in a way that I might aspire to. I've accepted that I'm never going to be Toni Morrison, James Joyce, or Jane Austen. It helped me, immensely, to read Gloria Naylor or Jane Smiley, who wrote in a way that I felt I had some hope of emulating.

As far as the mostly white thing . . . How can I say this without sounding defensive? I am deeply interested in telling stories of black life in this country and that's what I've done in all my published fiction thus far. At the same time, my goal as a writer (as I developed a sense of myself as such) was never to privilege race over character. To make whatever statements I wanted to make about being African-American in the United States through the vehicle of fully realized characters in fiction that was as rich and detailed as I could make it. Those were and are the kinds of books I loved, that influenced me, and I loved them without regard to the author's race or gender.

I kept reading and time went on. In my middle thirties, after a lot of effort self-questioning, and getting an MFA, I had published two novels, the second of which, *The Fall of Rome*, was hugely influenced by Kazuo Ishiguro's masterful *The Remains of the Day*.

In thinking about my experience with Harriet, I know now that that book was an enormous influence on me as an inchoate fiction writer. It pointed the way to something that I'm still walking toward, but it didn't lead me there. I didn't turn to it directly as a source or inspiration for writing and haven't reread it until recently (it's still great). But now, as I work through my fourth novel, I know precisely how one particular book, read at the right time in one's writing process, can have a direct and profound and inspiring effect on the work. It happened to me with Michael Chabon's *The Amazing Adventures of Kavalier and Clay*. And in this way he mentored me without ever having met me, without ever having read a word I'd written.

It wasn't unusual to read *Kavalier and Clay* in 2001, after it won the Pulitzer. I got the book for a Christmas gift and then didn't read it for nearly a year. I was not immediately drawn in, either. But somewhere around page 145, as Sammy Clay and Joe Kavalier labor to bring The Escapist to life, I fell into the book completely—after that, I was gone. I read morning, noon, and night. I laughed, I cried, I loved it. And after I finished it, I spent the next few months with Michael Chabon as my literary boyfriend.

In the years since then, I've been fortunate enough to meet and socialize with Michael and his wife Ayelet Waldman, but at the time of my great passion, I only knew this book. As soon as I finished it, I immediately read *Wonder Boys* (which moved me to call a friend on my cell phone as I rode on the bus where I'd finished it, shrieking about the great last paragraph), his other works, Ayelet's books, fan sites, whatever I could get a hold of. I gazed affectionately for long minutes at his author photo. I smiled fondly at people I saw reading *Kavalier and Clay* on the subway. I carried my own copy everywhere and read the paragraph below over and over, trying to parse out why it was so beautiful (I now think it's because of its skillful use of some of the musical tools of poetry and because of the way it neatly encapsulates one of the major themes of the novel):

> It was at these times that he began to understand, after all those years of study and performance, of feats and wonders and surprises, the nature of magic. The magician seemed to promise that something torn to bits might be mended without a seam, that what had vanished might reappear, that a scattered handful of doves or dust might be reunited by a word, that a paper rose consumed by fire could be made to bloom from a pile of ash. But everyone knew that it was only an illusion. The true magic of this broken world lay in the ability of the things it contained to vanish, to become so thoroughly lost, that they might never have existed in the first place.

But aside from the girlish, goofy aspects of my crush, Chabon's book urged me to step out more boldly with *Third Girl from the Left*, the novel

I was then working on. I was attempting to tell the story of black women who labored in the backgrounds of the blaxploitation films of the 1970s — and to report their fictional lives with meaning and dignity. To tell a story that hadn't been told. *Kavalier and Clay* does much the same. It takes something that is archetypally lightweight — the world of comic books and their creators — and through immense skill, craft, and love, creates a meditation on what it is to be Jewish, an immigrant, the meaning of art, the meaning of love, and a loving portrait of New York in the 1940s. All on a scaffolding that hardly seems able to support such weight.

But support it it does. It made me brave. *Third Girl* was set largely in a pop culture world too. It's the book of a movie geek (which I am), just as *Kavalier and Clay* is the book of a comic book geek (which Chabon is). *Kavalier and Clay* swings for the fences and hits them, freely mixing historical figures, places, and events with fictional ones and leavening its big statements with humor, love, and narrative drive. In my novel I strove, to the best of my abilities, to do the same. I can even point to paragraphs I wrote that were directly inspired by a stylistic challenge that Chabon took.

Every day that I worked on *Third Girl*, I did it with two things on the shelf overlooking my desk: a great picture of Wilt Chamberlain from the 1970s, and my paperback copy of *Kavalier and Clay*. On a difficult writing day, I'd look up at the cover, or look at that paragraph I love so much, and feel like I just had to keep going.

Louise Fitzhugh died suddenly in 1974 at the age of forty-six. And while I have been lucky enough to meet Michael, I've not told him in detail how much his book meant to me (sorry for the stalkerish aspects there, buddy — I'm a little obsessive). So this essay gives me a chance to thank the mentors who didn't know they were my mentors, who did it only through their work. At a time when novels are seeming more and more peripheral to the heart of the world, this is my salute to two of the writers (out of many) who have been anything but peripheral to my heart. Thanks, Louise. Thanks, Michael.

PART III

TIMES OF OUR LIVES

COMING OF AGE AT BREAD LOAF

Christopher Castellani

TURNING THE TABLES

In August of 2000, my so-called writing career takes a dramatic turn: I become a waiter. I'm already a waiter, a klutzy and distracted one, at an upscale Italian place in Boston, but this new gig—at the Bread Loaf Writers' Conference—has literary perks. In exchange for a couple hours a day serving meals in the dining hall, I get to take a workshop and attend two weeks of readings, lectures, craft classes, and parties. I'll be too busy to write, they tell me, which is both a surprise and a relief.

The waiters arrive a few days early. There are twenty-two of us, fiction and nonfiction writers and poets. The directors gather us on the porch of the Bread Loaf Inn to welcome us and tell us we're the true stars of the conference, that our potential inspires them, that we're an exceptionally strong group. It's a perfect summer day in Vermont, the sun on our faces, the air dry and still. We're at the top of a mountain surrounded by green fields, rocky creeks, tall heavy-breathing pines, and a scattering of yellow cottages that will be our home for the rest of the month.

It's the first time here for all of us. Our crew is jittery and companionably clueless. We range in age from mid-twenties to early forties, and most of us have other professions, some more legitimate than others. I'm twenty-eight, a recent grad of an MFA program that bludgeoned my spirit, taught me little about craft, and offered no direction. My instincts and confidence are shot. My hair is thinning and I have zero publications. For the past few years, I've been struggling through a novel and amassing rejections of what I consider my one decent story. I feel unmoored. And yet I've beaten out hundreds of other applicants for this spot on the porch.

229

Someone at Bread Loaf saw something in me, and I'm eager to find out what it might be.

We're housed on the same floor of the inn, trained and oriented by two of last year's waiters, and thrown keg parties in the laundry room. There's a bonfire and a meteor shower and drinking games and impromptu rehearsals of the public readings we'll be giving next week. Then the rest of the conference shows up: three hundred or so fellow writers, and soon there are bags of luggage in the hallways of the cottages; there are readings and workshops in the theater and library; the dining hall is packed; and we're on.

I don't admit this to my fellow waiters, but I've had a crush on Bread Loaf since high school. I came upon it while doing a research project on Anne Sexton, with whom I was obsessed. Anne had attended the conference, as had most of the twentieth-century American writers in our textbook, and so, too, would Christopher, one day. I sent away for brochures before I was eligible to apply. I wasn't sure how the place worked exactly, but it loomed in my imagination like a portal to another dimension, a gateway to the world of letters. Now here I am, in the heart of the literary world, my hand shaking as I hand a bowl of soup to M—, whose most recent book made my heart soar. I think, they're onto something with this writer-waiter idea. Serving meals turns out to be the perfect job for the socially anxious, the artistically insecure; it entails only brief bursts of superficial, mostly happy conversation and little eye contact, yet you feel you've connected with dozens of different people.

Connection is maybe what I've come to Bread Loaf for. By connection I mean a kind of acknowledgment. Permission. A sense of belonging. Sure, I want to learn to write a better novel; and I want an escape from my wobbly life; and I want to live deeply and separately and intensely in the company of brilliant artists. (In college, I longed to be a Romantic, or a Beat.) But what I want most is to be known, for someone to tell me who I am.

On the way to workshop, the day my novel chapter is to be critiqued, one of my classmates runs up to me. "You!" she says. She's been a grandmotherly presence in the class so far, kind but firm, a vigorous head-nodder. She tells me she loves my book, that it transported her to the Italian village in the 1940s I was trying to bring to life. I get a thrill, like a handsome gentleman has just bought me a drink at a bar, but I'm also kind of a snob; the opinion of G—, the seasoned author who's our workshop leader, is the one that matters most.

As it turns out, G— is not enchanted. He says the story's too Italian, yet not Italian enough. I don't understand until he points out how and where. The next day, we go over the pages one-on-one, scene by scene. It's two different voices, he says, two different styles and modes and tones, sometimes in the same sentence. Pick one and believe in it, he says.

I revise those pages for the three-minute waiter reading a few days later. It's held in the Little Theater, a white-shingled building with creaky wood chairs and a fireplace with an ivy-covered chimney. The ceiling is high, crossed with knotty wood slats, and the podium in front, where we will read, is the same podium from which the faculty and fellows have been speaking all week. The reading starts at ten o'clock at night, and we're told there won't be an empty seat. Beforehand, in the hallway of our dorm, we do shots and shaky run-throughs. One waiter, a trained soprano, sings an aria to calm us down; instead it surrealizes the night. The men wear ties and jackets; the women cocktail dresses and makeup; the opera singer's hair is unloosened and flowing; it's promlike; it's opening night. There are agents in the audience, we're told, scouting for new talent. This is our chance to impress, to debut, to come out.

The reading transforms me, not because an agent takes interest but because I fall in love. They're so beautiful up at the mic, my fellow waiters in their rumpled dress-up clothes, sweating and rubbing their brows. They've wrestled with every syllable. They believe it matters. They're not my competition; they're my brothers and sisters in art. And as I'm up there before the crowd with my fresh revision, I fall in love with . . . *myself*, with the world I've created, and the world I'm in. It's partly the shots, yes, but it's just as much the rapt and generous audience, the dozens of connections I've made over the week, the faculty and fellow readings that gave me shivers, and—though I won't fully understand this until next year—the ghosts of Bread Loaf hovering above.

My grad school had a sink-or-swim philosophy. You were a writer with innate talent, or you weren't. The program's goal was to anoint the real writers and spare the "nonreal" ones from years of heartbreak. By the end of my waiter stint at Bread Loaf, I don't feel "real" or "not real," and I begin to understand that such a distinction is meaningless, that the questions should be: Am I working hard? Am I learning? Am I digging deeper, embracing complications? Am I "failing better"? At Bread Loaf, these are the questions being asked in workshops and lectures, and at the salad bar, and around the keg. They seem like the most important questions in the world.

As the conference winds down, I'm filled with hope and desire. I want to carry the urgency of these questions and the intensity of the two weeks among artists into my everyday life. And, most selfishly, I want to be asked back—as a head waiter next year and then, eventually, after my novel gets published, a fellow (Anne Sexton's role), and, many years from now, after my third book at least, a faculty member with the vita of G—. For the first time, I see, however naively, a career path, a direction.

On the last night, Charles Baxter reads from *The Feast of Love*. In the scene, the character of Bradley realizes, through the tenor of his new wife's lovemaking, that they won't last as a couple, that she's in love with another man, that the passion between them is contrived. By the time Baxter, the second reader of the night, approaches this scene, it's quite late and we're all spent, but you can hear our hearts beating fast; we're spellbound, hanging on every syllable. I look over, and one of the fellows has tears on her cheeks. Illuminated at the podium, Baxter gently shuts the book, closes his eyes, and recites the final paragraphs from memory. It's an achingly human moment in the novel, a subtle revelation rendered with honesty and profound clarity.

As we clap, I remember thinking that Baxter's words have entered him, become him, and that *this*, ultimately, is what I want for myself: to be one with the text, to forget where I start and it begins.

WE GO TOGETHER

Riding a rare wave of confidence, I send the first fifty pages of my novel to an agent. The Bread Loaf scholarship made the query stand out, she says, and offers to represent me. A few months later, in early 2001, I'm invited to be on the social staff for the upcoming conference. I don't know what social staff does, but I say yes, absolutely, I'm in. I finish the novel and send it to New York.

Spring comes and I rollerblade a lot, singing with unabashed glee as I glide up and down the Esplanade, serenading myself, convinced of an imminent book deal and daydreaming of an August refuge in Vermont. Then my agent finishes the draft I sent her. Turns out she's fallen out of love with the characters, the story, the setting, and me. "I'm sure you'll be the one that got away," she says in an e-mail, and wishes me luck. I lie facedown on my bed, hands over my eyes, my days of arrogant foolish blading over.

Once more I turn to Bread Loaf for constancy and consolation. They've chosen only six of us for social staff, this time from a large pool of former waiters. Our job is to throw the all-campus receptions, work the dances, and befriend the lonely, lost, and dejected wherever we encounter them. We're given a van and a small budget for our theme parties. We room together in Treman, loud and grungy as a frat house. At night, after the readings, we're granted access to the faculty club downstairs, an equally grungy inner sanctum we never glimpsed as waiters. We sit on couches by the fire alongside major American writers—gossiping, drinking, flirting, reciting poems, dissecting the night's readings. This part's not easy for me, at first. It's obvious that whoever I'm talking to would rather be talking to somebody else. I cling to the other staffers—who all seem more confident and poised than I—nodding and smiling in their reflected light. But it's my job to talk small and approach strangers on my own and break the ice, so I learn how. It's liberating to have a designated function, a clear purpose. Despite the defined roles people play here—waiter, staff, scholar, fellow, faculty—we're all conscious that, in the real world, no such distinctions exist. In the real world, we're all squatters on the writing and publishing terrain. The Catholic in me loves the rituals and role play of Bread Loaf, and is comfortable in service, as eternal apprentice, humbling myself. I no longer daydream of being on faculty, but of returning year after year on social staff, my potential safe and unexposed.

Except the conference insists on exposure. This summer, my faculty leader loves the novel excerpt I submit. He also happens to be a client of the agent who kicked me to the curb and convinces me that her instincts are usually right. I should consider her suggestions, revise, swallow my pride, and resubmit to her in due time. After the staff reading, he comes up to me, congratulates me on the "fine prose," and says, "You're really an old-fashioned writer, aren't you?"

"I think so," I say. "Is that good?"

"It's not good or bad," he says. "It's who you are."

Old-fashioned sounds right, as though I'm part of a tradition, as though I fit in. I think of the Bread Loaf History slide show, held just a few nights before. I sat in the far back of the Little Theater, mesmerized by the black-and-white images of Eudora Welty and Carson McCullers and other writers from my high school textbook that appeared on the screen. They were smiling, or arm-in-arm, or in serious solo poses. They were on the steps of the little yellow houses, in the Adirondack chairs. They were drinking from — could it be? yes! — the same coffee cups we still drank from in the dining hall. Somehow, it hadn't sunk in until that moment that we'd walked the same paths, ate from the same plates, slept in the same rooms. If I'm old-fashioned, I tell myself, let it be in that way, as a standard bearer. I'm not one for reinvention; I trust that the tools of the ancestors will yield great works of original beauty.

In one of the slides, Anne Sexton sits on a rock in the middle of the field behind Treman. So one day, at dusk, I trek out to the rock, stand atop it, and recite "To a Friend Whose Work Has Come to Triumph" in a vain (in all senses of the word) effort to commune with the dead. That kind of geeking out is encouraged here. Even when we play poker, late at night in Treman, the faculty gone, our conversations are pretentiously allusive and self-referential, hilarious to no one but us.

For us staffers, the final dance is jubilant and bittersweet, like the carnival at the end of *Grease*. As we put our arms around each other and kick up our legs in a jaunty can-can, we're all wondering the same thing: Will we see each other again? How will we make our way in the big bad writing world alone? All week we've been whispering about who might be asked back next year, and in what capacity, though it's unseemly to speculate. I've only been here twice, but I'm already addicted to the fix of camaraderie and tough love, to the instant passionate friendships, to the communion and seclusion, and I'm not ready to give it up.

SUMMER AND SMOKED

Back in Boston, I trick myself into believing that if I tackle the deep revision of my novel, if I do my best work, I'll be rewarded with another invitation to Bread Loaf. The trick pays off. In February, my agent takes me back, sells the book, and, soon after, the e-mail comes: they want me on social staff again.

I arrive triumphant, those roller-blading songs on full blast in my head. The mountain is magic. I stride from parties to readings with the confidence of a maestro. But not for long. For my workshop, I've dusted off and submitted my one halfway-decent short story, written three years ago in grad school, and which now, in the light of my success, seems transcendent. Visionary, even! It's told in the voice of Tennessee Williams, a bold move I expect my instructor to admire. Instead, he methodically, and with apparent delight, dismantles its tone, its structure, its plot, the very *idea* of it. This bruises not only because I'm supposed to be legitimate now, a member of "the club," but because I heard the instructor read in the Little Theater the night before, and fell madly in love with his work. I wanted to *be* him, and now he's shaking his head in befuddled disappointment.

My classmates smell blood and pile on. There's a lot of laughter and the nodding of heads. "Who do you think you are?" someone says. "Tennessee Williams!"

Eventually, the instructor calls off the dogs, comes to my rescue. He's figured out the story's fatal flaw, and helps me address it. The frame narrative has to be as strong and compelling as the main story, and, later, over coffee, we brainstorm how to make it so.

This year, I leave the final dance with a plan. By next summer, my novel will be out, and I'll be eligible for a fellowship.

JOLLY GOOD FELLOWS

In early 2003, I submit the galley of my book for the fellowship. If I don't get it, it will confirm what I always feared: that I got by at Bread Loaf purely on charm and potential and three-minute sound bites, that once the Powers That Be read my novel cover to cover, the fraud will be exposed.

In the meantime, there are all the joys of a first novel: the miracle of my name on the cover; my first signing; my immigrant parents, whose histories inspired the book, holding it in their hands like an amulet. There are also a host of anxieties brought on by the realization that the book will never get the chance to be better, that it exists forever in a state of arrested development, that the ghosts I met at Bread Loaf are probably looking down and wrinkling their noses.

I win the fellowship—it doesn't cure the anxiety. Instead, the good news ushers in new worries. I'm no longer the kid with promise and potential, pouring drinks and herding people onto the hayride; I'm now an authority and expected to behave as such. No more flash readings late at night; I'm assigned a twenty-minute slot in prime time. I'm paired with a faculty member, and together we lead a workshop, meet with students,

and counsel them on structure and syntax. I teach a craft class on historical fiction and thirty students scribble notes.

The whole time I'm thinking, wait, wasn't that me, just a year ago, on
the other side of the room? What happened between then and now? I published, of course, and gave a bunch of readings and Q&As, but am I wiser?
Do I know how the hundred thousand words I picked fit together and
made a book, or why it worked better the second time around? Not quite.
The writing process remains mysterious. I don't feel qualified to explain it,
or suggest strategies for others, but I realize it's my job, and I have to figure
it out. I get advice from my fellow fellows, debate aesthetics with my faculty mentor, and reread student manuscripts until I get a handle on them.
I've led workshops on my own before, but the stakes here are higher; I owe
it to the tradition of the place to turn in a quality performance.

Despite all this, a fellow's schedule is luxurious and uncluttered.
There's time to steal away to restaurants in Middlebury or go antiquing
in the country. But I have no desire to escape. Instead, my friends and I
take frequent twenty-minute hikes down the Long Trail to Lake Pleiad,
where we sunbathe on the surrounding rocks, and swim in the murky
frigid water. Each time, we come upon the lake with surprise, as if we'd
dreamed it yesterday and the day before, as if it couldn't exist all by itself,
so purely, in the middle of the woods. It's enough for us city folk to pretend
we could give it all up for this.

At the end of my fellow year, I see no path back to the conference.
You can't be a fellow more than once, and the next rung up—faculty—
requires three books. Maybe I can visit, I think, as I drive off. I'm saying
good-bye for good, leaving behind what has been a happy childhood, but
unsure how it's prepared me for the rest of life.

No Joke

Two years later, I'm back as a returning fellow, a role I wish didn't exist.

In 2003, Amanda Davis, a thirty-two-year-old fiction writer and former
Bread Loaf waiter, staffer, and fellow, was killed in a plane crash. Amanda
loved the place as fiercely as I did, was beloved in return, and instigated
many of the conference traditions and jokes that got passed down to me,
and that I passed on to others. To honor her memory, Bread Loaf estab-

lished the Amanda Davis Returning Fellowship, which brings back a former fellow for a second and final time, an opportunity that would have made Amanda very happy.

Again, there was no application. I'm honored to have been chosen, but it saddens me that it's taken a tragedy to convince me I'm wanted here.

I dedicate my reading to Amanda and take a few minutes to tell the audience about her work. Though I never met her, I sense her presence in that hall of ghosts. For the rest of the conference, I am continually reminded how little time we all have to get our own work done, how it's always later than we think. For these few weeks, at least, I appreciate the luxury of my hours at the desk. To this day, nowhere do I feel that luxury more keenly than at Bread Loaf.

BARELY LEGAL

Yes, that's me in the corner of the Barn, hiding behind my laptop, writing this essay.

Yes, I was supposed to leave four days ago. But now I have this excellent excuse: where better to write about a place than the place itself?

It's 2008, my latest stint as Bread Loaf crasher. For the past three years, I've been asked back to teach one of the craft classes, which last a grand total of fifty-five minutes. In exchange, I'm given an honorarium and invited to stay a day or two on either side. Then I'm supposed to leave.

Each year, though, forces intervened. My best friend from my staff year was here as a fellow, and I needed at least two days to catch up with her, and catch her reading. My craft class over-enrolled, and I generously offered to teach another section. The weather was rainy, and how could I miss the chance to hike to Pleiad with the gang once it cleared? Couldn't I stick around till Thursday? Wednesday, at least?

They're patient with me, the Powers That Be. It's possible they actually like having me around, but I prefer to think I also add some value, that I'm useful as a poster child, an evangelist, a happy camper. They know I'm now the director of a writing center in Boston, and that Bread Loaf has always been its muse and inspiration. They know—or, at least, they do now—that there is not only flattery in that imitation, but deep love and appreciation for taking a chance on me.

Please Don't Write

Neil Gordon

I

Once when I was in college in the mid-seventies, a woman with black lipstick and a crew cut, a genuine Detroit Punk, pushed me onto her bed then climbed on top of me and, when I recovered from my surprise and put my arms around her, said, mouth against mine: *Please Don't Stop*.

She said it without any emphasis, leaving me to wonder, as she returned to the business at hand, where the punctuation went.

Was it *Please, don't stop!* Or was it *Please don't. Stop!*

She was a terribly smart person, and although that three-word phrase was about a particular sexual experience, I heard it, immediately and ever after, as a profound philosophic challenge, one that came to be associated intimately with the only motivation in my life as powerful as sex; and—no doubt because of that fact—in time a part of my imagination came to substitute the third word of her phrase with another, so that it came out: *Please Don't Write*.

The problematics of the ambition to write are, after all, inextricable from problematics of sex, or even love. Words came easily to me when I was young, as did love, but it seemed to me that only the hugely talented could possibly commit themselves to writing, and who can judge their own talent? I wrote and wrote, but without illusion that it was more than a child's work. I quit school, traveled for years, came back. I won a college literary prize, but was that enough? I worked—dishwashing, construction, cooking, tending bar; I graduated college, moved to Paris, struggled with a long short story that would never end, gave up, went to graduate school. New Haven, at the height of Deconstruction. During the day I saw myself as a tenure-track scholar, steeped in the arcana of semiotics and psychoanalysis, but at night I found myself an habitué of odd bars and lonely places up and down the dismal central Connecticut coastline, West Haven, Milford, and I never, ever declined any experience that gave access to emotion, just like that night in college on the wrong side of town with that brilliant and strange girl who pushed me onto her bed, wriggling out of her leather pants, and told me *Please Don't Stop*.

Please Don't Write. I wrote and wrote, and submitted stuff, and had stuff rejected. Publishing was an ambition so far from reality. Plus there was something wrong with the words. Too many were about myself; they were complex and too beautiful. In any case, I had nothing really to say.

But I could not imagine life without writing, could not imagine finishing my degree, going on the market, interviewing at MLA, becoming an assistant professor—publishing in order not to perish—and leaving this ambition behind. Writing fiction, see, was not tenurable work for a professor of literature. It was a sideshow, best indulged after the real work leading to tenure was done. But there was no profound experience of my life that was not informed by fictional reference, no place I had been or person I had loved not associated with written art. And there was nothing I could do that is not done in words. Become a professor? Please don't. Write.

Nights in New Haven I drank in the Anchor Bar with the little group of grad students: Rindala el-Khoury, Elissa Marder, Michael Syrotinsky, Mary Quaintance: deconstructionists; neo-Heideggerians; semioticians; psychoanalysts. Esin, a woman I had been chasing since college, came up from New York where, after years assigning photography at *Vanity Fair*, working for Tina Brown, she was now at the *Village Voice*. Watching what we were doing at the Anchor Bar through her wry gaze made me feel something like despair. Down there, real people were writing real things going into real print, while I was moving inevitably to a life in which I would never, ever, write. Esin said, *Look. Whatever you're doing isn't working. You'd better try something else.* She gave me a list of magazines to write to: *Harper's, The New York Times Book Review, The Nation*, and *The New York Review of Books*. Weeks passed, and in time came a call from an assistant at *The New York Review—can you hold for Mr. Silvers?* A gentle British-accented voice came on the line, inviting me for an interview.

That spring in New Haven, while the lilac and dogwood came out, waiting to meet him, I imagined the legendary Robert Silvers and his assistants housed in the first floor of a brownstone, likely in the West Village. I imagined my office there, perhaps looking out over a rambling back garden, the long days of writing and editing, the editorial meetings, the lunches and dinners. I pictured us in the offices, sending out for lunch, reading proofs, arguing politics.

Soon, naturally, I would be writing for the *Review*.

Soon I would be publishing novels.

Stay in graduate school? Please don't. Write.

Recently my work took me to the town where that lovely Detroit Punk had uttered her shamanic phrase to me, and wandering by what had been her apartment, I had the singular experience of understanding something dramatic. That young man on her bed, thirty years ago? Every single one of his ambitions, I had made true. It was a powerful realization to come to, on a gray winter day in the Midwest, and surprisingly, it did not make me proud but, rather, sad, almost frighteningly so. Is it that there is something disappointing about ambition realized? *How different they turned out to be*, said a character of mine recently, *even when they were exactly the same, the thing that you wanted and the thing you got.*

More precisely, I think, that thought made me sad because, in an inescapable way, the loss of illusions is the necessary predicate to the realization of ambition. And when I myself have this thought, the one I gave my fictional character, I feel enormous gratitude to Bob Silvers, for whom I indeed ended up working for those two years in the late 1980s, two years that were to allow me, at last, to begin to make real what that young man, boy really, had dreamed.

II

Of course, the genteel brownstone offices I imagined were nothing like what I found when I interviewed for and won the job of editorial assistant at the *Review*. The magazine inhabited a corner of the thirteenth floor of the Fisk Building, 250 West 57th Street, opposite the old Coliseum Books. I doubt that there is anyone who worked at the *Review* who does not think of those offices with a unique combination of high disgust and profound affection. You entered through a corridor of unimpeachable grime, turned left past a mailroom where a campy receptionist may or may not speak to you—he was usually to be found under a photo of Diana Ross, giving haircuts to staff—past the windowless little cubbyhole where the late Jonathan Lieberson sat in a pile of books, and the studio where a crew of artists laid out the magazine with scissors and tape and arcane instruments—photypositor, stat machines—that no longer exist. A handwritten sign next to a huge pile of issues read:

> *Do not throw out. These are current issues. Not garbage. Note the difference.*

Next to the assistant editors' office there was an unspeakably ratty couch, famous among book publicists, who spent many hours on it waiting for Bob to see them, a punitive experience made more miserable by the presence, right next to them, of a desk known as the "discard table." Here were deposited, every day, in an unruly pile of books destined for the Strand Bookstore, most of the hundreds of review copies received every week including, no doubt, many of the patient publicists' own offerings. Barbara Epstein sat in the facing office, her assistant just outside the door at an oak desk at which some privacy was improvised by whatever shelving could be scrounged up. And only by this means did you arrive in Bob's huge office where, on a table formed by a huge piece of wood on two file cabinets, he sat in a kind of cave constructed by a three-sided wall of books, piled perhaps four foot high on the edge of the desk.

Three other desks housed his three assistants, of which I was now the junior one, the disorder of each in inverse proportion to his seniority. Mine was, accordingly, perfectly tidy, whereas the desk belonging to the senior assistant was piled so high with papers and books that a typesetter observed one day, in awe, that "a dead elk could be buried under there and no one would know." High above the city, in an office continually occupied for some twenty-five years, the urban grime, complemented by decades of Bob's ever-burning Sherman cigarettes, could be wiped from any surface on a finger. Two imperfectly closing, single-paned windows, the one filthier than the other, gave a view downtown on Eighth Avenue and provided the only ventilation—that and a huge HEPA filter mounted on the ceiling which, like the industrial-sized ashtrays, provided at least a semblance of an effort to deal with Bob's two-pack-a-day cigarette habit. And books—on shelves, on tables, in piles on the floor, on all available surfaces—were everywhere.

Nor, I quickly learned, was there anything genteel about the workplace. Indeed, the editorial offices of *The New York Review* was the most complicated constellation of personalities I've ever encountered in my life, barring perhaps my own home. Bob Silvers and Barbara Epstein, co-editors since the founding of the magazine in 1963, seemed to coexist in a strained truce rather than a collaboration. Shortly before my arrival, they and the other owners had sold the magazine to a courtly Mississippian heir to a newspaper fortune, Rea Hederman, who had installed himself at the far other end of the offices, as if emphasizing the vast gulf—in intellect, ethnicity, and authority, as the editors retained complete authority despite their new boss—that existed between them, guarded by a secretary who seemed to view any evidence of the intellectual life with deep suspicion.

Directly below the editors on the editorial masthead, the Assistant Editors—as opposed to us, the Editorial Assistants, who lived on the masthead in a ghetto of tiny type—were housed in an office that resembled nothing so much as a crowded room in a British boarding school. Their duties were for the most part restricted to the mechanical acts of proofreading, fact checking, and overseeing production of the issue and, in the case of the late Bob Tashman, *aleva sholem,* a towering figure to me, mercilessly tormenting his coworkers and composing absurd jokes about Bob Silvers. (*What's the difference between Bob Silvers and Genghis Khan? Genghis Khan didn't send out marked-up galley proofs to his authors.* Etc.) This allowed Bob and Barbara, in an act of epic administrative legerdemain, to delegate virtually all the actual involvement with the magazine's intellectual content—suggesting assignments, researching writers, and an infinitesimal amount of hands-on editing that they might, from time to time, relinquish—to their own editorial assistants, that is, the entry-level clerical help such as myself. Thus, my duties ran from fetching coffee and placing phone calls—*can you hold for Mr. Silvers?*—to line-editing towering literary and academic luminaries. For the first few months of my tenure I could not figure this out. Then I got it: the structure meant that there was no possible promotional pathway up the masthead. No Editorial Assistant, such as myself, would ever become an Assistant Editor, because only the title was a step up—the work itself was a step down, and in order to move up—as many did, to high masthead positions—Assistant Editors had be move on. There was no threat from below. That the editors-in-chief of the most prestigious journal in the world would be so protective of their—it appeared to us, unlimited—power seemed to explain, at least to a degree, something profound not just about the office, but about the profession.

Our jobs were to run Bob's social life, financial life, work life; to traffic books to authors and collect articles from them; to stay abreast of publications and catalogs and authors and politics; to make coffee and fetch lunch; to decipher Bob's handwriting on articles and galley proofs; to type letters, answer and place phone calls; to research arcane subjects; to stay abreast of publishing and magazine gossip; to read every article that came in; to open mail; book restaurants; clean up spilled food and the detritus of Bob's addiction to Sherman cigarettes and his indulgence in a gooey diet supplement called Ultra Slimfast. Three strong young men working nearly round the clock were not enough to keep up with Bob, and a barely controlled chaos, exacerbated by his frequent frustration—usually with me—characterized our working life. I may not have been very good at my job, though if so, it is the only job I've ever been bad at. But I doubt I had been on payroll for more than a week before I first heard, emanating from Bob's office, the cry—*Where's Neil?*—that caused whoever I was with to freeze in embarrassment and which served as the prelude to what I believe is referred to somewhere by Kingsley Amis as "a stunning dressing-down."

I didn't mind. I loved everything about the *Review* from the moment I walked in. For one thing, copies of it had been on my parents' breakfast table my whole life, my parents charter subscribers on the legendary mailing list passed on to Bob Silvers by I. F. Stone. In that office, over two years, I met virtually every single member of the New York publishing firmament, from Jonathan Galassi to Bob Weil; from Alice Mayhew to Sonny Mehta and—although only by telephone—the legendary agent Swifty Lazar. As for writers, where to start? Susan Sontag, V. S. Naipaul, Isaiah Berlin, Murray Kempton, Irving Howe, Helen Vendler, Joseph Brodsky, and Izzy Stone, in the last years of his life. I worked so deeply with the heroic and maverick American historian Theodore Draper that the honor of a footnote was bestowed on me for a piece of detective work done over the telephone with an obscure archive in France (I convinced an archivist to read me a portion of a competing researcher's work while the researcher was out for lunch), and Esin and I were invited to Princeton to dine with Ted and his wife, an unforgettable experience.

Little by little, I peered into worlds I had never before imagined: the glamorous Page 6 functions that Bob attended with fashion designers and celebrities; the Council on Foreign Relations affairs and the Century Club dinners with Henry Kissinger and Felix Rohatyn; the European circuits of Bayreuth and the social season in London that he frequented with his titled girlfriend; Washington, where he maintained so many contacts; and last but not least, the byzantine world of New York publishing where ruled that little oligarchy of the *Review's* founders and editors.

Please. Don't write. In a way, I had traded one illusion for another. Whereas once I had tried, and failed, to see myself as an academic, now I was stress-testing a view of myself as an editor, an articulate, well-dressed, eager young man working his way up the publishing ladder, collecting a stable of authors, learning the trade. Night after night after night, I transcribed Bob's meticulous line editing onto clean manuscript. Why did he so hate italics? What is the difference between "presently" and "currently"? What in this sentence had made him throw a dictionary across the room? Is he deadening this language, as critics contend, or bringing forth clarity, as fans across the world claim? In issue after issue the mechanics of the *Review's* signature prose began to make more sense to me—and with it, although I did not know this yet, the mechanics of my own writing.

Please don't. Write. As insight into Bob's astounding line editing came to me, so did wider understanding of the patterns in which writers rose and fell: the name heard at a party; the recommendation through a friend; the advance knowledge of a new book; the tricks of placement and timing in which new writers are promoted and old ones sustained; the compromises with the market; the acts of idealism; and the implacable nature of the editorial judgment to which there is no possible appeal. To watch the fates of books and writers at the *Review* was to undergo a Balzacian loss of illusion. Again and again, I thought: so *this* is how it works. Strewn across Bob's desk (where, when I first started, I found unanswered correspondence from the mid-1960s) and in his closely guarded files I found countless tales, each one worthy of *Illusions Perdues*, of ambition and loss, hubris and inspiration. Countless? We filled five or six huge file cabinets with correspondence every year, which was hauled off to storage in an archive that will one day constitute a lifetime work for a lucky scholar.

Really, there was no height to which the brilliant writers of our day would not rise to work with the editor whom Sontag addressed, in her letters, as *Bob Dear*, nor was there any depth to which they would not sink. (Once I asked Bob if, as revenge for his annoying misaddress of a letter to Bob *Silbers*, I could write back to John *Ubdike*, but he wouldn't let me.) We learned to watch, with equal impassivity, the obedient submission to editing of the supplicants and the suicidal rejections of the proud, the one as pointless as the other. *Why won't he publish my piece?* asked a rejected writer once over the telephone, his voice filled with anguish. Sitting above Eighth Avenue, I tried to explain the calculus of influences and interests that governs the publication of a piece in any magazine, the nexus of prose, reputation, allegiances, commercial necessity, mailing rates, advertising, word count, and the imperious dictates of the *signature*, that is, the unalterable fact that the page count of anything printed on a web press can only increase or decrease by quanta of four, or eight, or sixteen.

Epic battles were to be read in Bob's files, along with shocking disappointments, glorious successes, and precipitous falls from grace. Bob's career and experience covered virtually every postwar literary circle in the world, from Doc Humes and George Plimpton in the Paris of *The Paris Review* to any of the current circles in contemporary New York. Once, a plaintive request for money arrived on the stationery of an inexpensive hotel in Athens, a destitute writer reminding Bob of a meeting in the fifties, at a party in the company of Alfred Chester. In the handwritten words, I felt the huge sweep of Bob's literary life.

But I also felt something else. In that letter, in his files, in the drama of the magazine, and the even larger drama of New York publishing, I felt just how small is the restricted world of literary success and how vast the possibility of disappointment, of failure, and how reckless one is to have the ambition to write.

Please. Don't write. Week after week I watched the books on the discard table piling up and being carted to the Strand. I learned everything there was to know about how books are published, and reviewed, and by whom. Week after week I became, under Bob's tutelage, more and more adept at rendering prose into the *Review*'s style.

Please don't. Write.

Esin and I were married. We began to hunt for a house. I turned thirty. We wanted a child.

Please don't write.

III

There are those reading this who are hoping for salacious details about *The New York Review of Books*, and certainly there are hundreds of people who have contemplated revealing them. Most, of course, are dissuaded by friends and editors, nervous of the power of the *Review*. But I like to think that others, like me, simply find the question too complex to gossip about. Just as the dynamics of literary success defy overly neat conclusions, the experience of working for a brilliant, driven boss like Bob is too complex for anything simple. Even as the nerve-fraying, confidence-shattering *Where's Neil?* thundered through the offices, I was also aware that I was working for a man with an abiding, lifetime commitment to liberal principle and motivated, at heart, by a profound decency. I witnessed throughout the office enormous acts of generosity as well as astounding instances of smallness. Cataloging either is a misrepresentation. One day I witnessed Bob overhearing Tashman's Genghis Khan joke, and I vividly remember the little, uncharacteristic smile on his lips as he walked away. Later, he helped Tashman effect a reassignment to *Granta* in London, work permit and all, so that he could live with the woman with whom he was in love, a huge and costly act of generosity. Probably there is nothing simple to say about any person. There certainly is not about Bob.

There was nothing he would not do for his writers, nothing. Every single article was the most important in the world, and within each article, every comma was a moral commitment. To edit a piece five, seven, nine times was normal, each round coming to us on 11x17-inch paper for retyping, the text on one half and the other filled with Bob's spidery editing. When the manuscript was sent back to the author, frequently there was no sentence untouched, often no sentence unrewritten. On particularly egregious pieces we were dispatched to read the books under review, research the often arcane subjects, and then entirely rewrite the articles for resubmission to Bob and, thence, the authors who were, usually, world-class experts on their subjects. An error

246

was an ethical outrage and could cause one to be summoned from far reaches of the office.

Where's Neil? I have never, not even during the years of torturing my parents during my adolescence, not even now, when I am tortured by my own adolescent children, been taken so much to task—never. And not until this very year when, at fifty, I became dean of a college, have I loved a job as much as I loved working for Bob. I vividly remember sitting in his office early one morning, working on the series of articles that would become Theodore Draper's towering book on Iran-Contra, looking out the window where Eighth Avenue stretched magically downtown, and realizing, as I have few times in my life, that I was totally, completely, thoroughly happy.

And then suddenly, I wasn't.

Suddenly, as happy as I had been, navigating through life at the *Review*, getting married, buying a house, having our first child, all the while writing my dissertation and spending endless hours in the enormous apprenticeship of Bob Silvers's office, suddenly, as immediately as it had started, it stopped.

Suddenly, the nexus between ambition and luck, artistic realization and public recognition, between the computer screen and the printing press, had entirely lost its mystery to me. I knew how people are published, how reputations are made, how singular the path to literary fame, and how much it depended on people like Bob, and how incredibly variegated the paths to failure. I knew the allure of literary success. Years before, while working at the Strand Bookstore, I had won a literary prize, and the novelist Paula Fox, a dear friend of my mother's, called to congratulate me. *Isn't it awful to win a prize? It's so important, so necessary, and yet it has nothing to do with writing.* Now, the huge importance of what she had just told me came clear.

It had nothing to do with writing. With the realization came, suddenly, the absolute inability to work for Bob anymore. Rea Hederman, the publisher, had been courting me for some time: now, when I told him of my wish to leave Bob's office, he offered me a job helping him in the business of publishing the other titles in his empire: *Granta, The Reader's Catalog. Are you really changing over from editorial to publishing?* Esin asked me. *You know you can never go back. They'll never take you seriously again.* I considered that, but only for a moment. I never wanted to go back.

Then something happened somewhere around there that put the question into profound relief.

One day I passed by to find that Barbara Epstein had a new assistant, none other than Mary Quaintance, with whom I had so often drunk in company of grad students at the Anchor Bar when we were both studying at Yale.

Only it wasn't the same Mary Quaintance.

That one had been a calm and brilliant young woman, famous for her acumen as a Demanian theorist, destined for a dazzling career.

This one was different and showed the effect of a great deal of difficulty since I had last seen her, and a great deal of booze. Slowly I came to understand that things had gone badly for her in the several years since I had left Yale, that she was heavily medicated, that things were not good. Janet Malcolm was a friend, I remembered, and had gotten her this job, and now, she had come to the *Review* to finish her dissertation and learn about publishing.

I had always liked Mary Quaintance, and I liked her now. We talked quite a bit. Her desk sat right outside my office. I learned of the medications she was taking, the writer's block, her wish to finish the dissertation. I suppose I tried to be helpful, though my relationship to her was one of an admirer, not a peer. I worried about her. But as I watched her trying to come to grips with the stall in her life, I turned to my own dissertation and my last language requirement, every morning before work, with renewed energy.

Somehow I knew I was in dangerous territory. Somehow, I knew that the *please* and the *don't*, as if in celestial choreography, were orbiting into a final, possibly fatal eclipse with *write*.

Writing fiction was not a mystery that could wait forever.

I worked for Rea for many years after I left Bob's office, still in the warren of offices in the Fisk Building, but it was a day job now. Working only eight hours a day speeded me to the end of my dissertation. The evening after it was granted, with our tiny daughter asleep in her crib, I began what was to be my first published novel. From the first sentence, I knew that I was writing something that I would publish. It was not about me, it was controlled, it was nuanced, it was paced. Was it good? Very possibly. My apprenticeship, it turned out, was over.

As smug young men and women moved in and took on my role, as the familiar folk with whom I had worked moved on and into their lives, as is often the case, the new people were never quite as vivid, never as real. In any case, I was soon persona non grata in the editorial offices. Little by little the circles in which Mary Quaintance and the other editorial assistants moved became closed to me, and slowly, the job became more and more of a dead end. But, perhaps in an uncoincidental inverse proportion, I grew in my writing and my novel grew in pages and slowly, steadily, in reviews and articles, my own words began to see print.

And then, in the winter of 1995, Mary Quaintance killed herself.

IV

I did not learn the details until I called one of the people from editorial who no longer spoke to me. It seemed that Mary had gone off her meds, and wandered out one night in a psychotic state. She was barefoot and delusional, ecstatic, apparently, and ended up on a train overpass uptown—from which she jumped. When I heard that, I knew with certainty that it had been on the Metro-North line to New Haven where, at the other end, lay her failed dissertation and all the promise of our nights in the Anchor Bar. I found her parents, somewhere out in the Midwest, and asked if I could help them in any way. Her brothers were apparently driving out to pick up her stuff, but there was nothing I could do. I believe, in time, that Janet Malcolm had a memorial service, but I wasn't invited.

My son was born and my daughter grew and I spent more time with them, ever more absorbed in the enormity of their upbringing. Esin went back to work full time, at *Vogue* this time, adding Anna Wintour to our collection of brilliant and demanding bosses. We bought a house. I had by then finished my first novel and, in an adventure nearly unbearably exciting, sold it in a two-book deal to Random House. *Boy*, Esin said to me when it hit the stores, rare praise. *You've done what every editorial assistant dreams of*. I wrote another book. And in time, I quit Hederman's employ altogether, launching myself again into the unknown, a reckless and stubborn young man, driven by the missing comma in a sentence heard decades before. And once again, I found purchase. In the ten years since my PhD, the discipline had radically shifted; universities were filled with writers, and fiction was as legitimate as scholarship. I encountered

Jonathan Veitch, a brilliant dean who opened the way to tenure and a full professorship, and a generous president—another Bob, oddly, Bob Kerrey—who encouraged me to move upward to a deanship. I published a ton of criticism. I finished and published my third book and, amazingly, sold it to yet another Bob for a movie, this one, Redford, as kind and generous as the first was harsh, and one after the other came all the good things of my adulthood.

Now, looking back, I'm not sure exactly when it was that I realized that the period of my life in which I worked for Bob was really over. In memory it was a night after Mary Quaintance died when Esin and I came home from a party, paid the babysitter, for all the world a pair of successful New Yorkers, publishing types. And yet already was inscribed in our lives a divergence from the stereotype to which we belonged, one that was going to grow and grow, and in retrospect, I see that it dated from the day I quit Bob's office.

I had been thinking all evening about Mary, her death on the New Haven line of Metro-North, my hurt that I had not been invited to the memorial. Esin went upstairs to check the kids, I saw the babysitter to a cab, and then for some reason, I found myself unwilling to go up and sat on the couch, still wearing my overcoat. To my huge surprise I put my head back, neck against my upturned collar, collar against the back of the couch, and cried in a way I have never cried before or since: enormously harsh tears, two, three hard paroxysms that stopped as suddenly as they started, more like orgasm than grief. I got up, wiped my face in the kitchen, and went upstairs. It was a singular experience, and for years I explained it to myself as my long repressed grief at the death of an old friend, a friend who had failed, the first suicide I had ever known in my life. But now, in retrospect, I think I was crying that night for the days in which I had thought the *Review* would be a nurturing office of like-minded people, united in a common interest and housed in a West Village brownstone; for the days before I quit Bob Silvers's office in a deep, barely understood tropism away from all that I had encountered there; the days before I realized so many of my ambitions and before I learned to write.

STORYING

Dinaw Mengestu

I learned a lot of slang from the high school students I worked with in Harlem; I used to make them give me impromptu lessons in the little back office of the after-school program I worked in. They were two- to three-minute lessons on the multiple uses and meanings of a phrase or word—"what's good" or better yet, "what's *really* good"—that I would turn around and use back at them. They came into our poorly outfitted center with their backpacks full of homework with which they desperately needed assistance, if the other teachers and I were lucky, or more often than not when we weren't, they came with nothing but a bored, indifferent attitude and a litany of complaints.

I was never particularly good at slang—something I think having to do with my foreign-accented parents, a few formative years spent at an all-white Southern Baptist church in Peoria, and later, even more years spent quietly imagining the sound of the voices in the novels I read. In junior high and high school my friends couldn't help but point out—particularly while drunk or high—that despite my best efforts and my near-flawless slang vocabulary, my words still came out sounding white. When they said, "Damn, why you gotta sound so white sometimes?" there was a slight hint of disappointment and sadness in their voices, akin to the tone parents must take toward a child who is always embarrassing them at parties by failing to make it to the bathroom on time: Son, couldn't you have just held it in a little bit longer?

By the time I had finished my MFA and was working at the after-school center, I had long since learned that it was better to stop trying to sound like anything or anyone in earnest. I spoke self-mockingly and self-consciously with my students and used what few phrases they taught me to elicit a grin or slightly bemused smile. Of all the slang I learned in my year and a half there, my favorite was "storyin'," a word that was thrown at me when I was halfway through a ridiculous, deliberately improbable narrative about my childhood. Storying was something I did on nearly an hourly basis with my students, who often came to the center, and to me by extension, frustrated and at times full of rage at injustices, real and imagined, that ranged from annoying teachers to the gang members who stalked the housing projects where many of them lived.

I had little to offer of real solace or comfort. I could no more solve their problems at school than their problems at home, and so I made up fanciful and sometimes completely implausible stories on a whim to get them to reluctantly smile or laugh with me. I'd invent individually tailored stories of my own childhood frustration to match theirs.

One of my students, Amanda, had little to no time for her own life since she was so busy taking care of her younger siblings, nieces, and nephews. She often came to the center late and left early with a toddler following close behind. John, the oldest and at six foot three the largest of my students, was constantly broke and in search of a job because, as he liked to remind me, "Women and clothes are expensive, and I gotta get paid." And so in these tales, which were always told in my office, often with me leaning against the door deliberately barring the exit, I was the oldest of sixteen children and was responsible for taking care of them all; I had my first factory job by the time I was eight; I didn't learn how to read or do math until I got to college; and of course every day I had to walk miles and miles in the snow. My attempts were feeble. The response was always the same. I was corny at best, a fool at worse. My jokes, much less my stories, were not funny, but sometimes you had to give it to me: I had heart.

I had begun working at the center shortly after completing a novel that I had spent nearly five years writing, and that no one wanted to publish. I did not come believing that I was going to make a substantive difference in anyone's life—I hated simple phrases such as "make a difference," or ones that echoed any sense of moral imperative. In part I came because I had failed at the one thing that I had constantly strived for, and having failed sought out the same type of after-school nonprofit programs that I had worked at in college. The programs were almost invariably the same and undoubtedly there was comfort to be had in returning to a line of work that I was already familiar with.

At the center in Harlem our task was to try and prepare roughly thirty-five high school students from poor and minority backgrounds for college by providing them with homework assistance and supplementary classes in math, science, and English. I was hired as an English teacher, and six months later, after the director and counselor had abruptly vanished from their jobs, I found myself loosely in charge of a program that by that time had only one other teacher and a handful of students who showed up sporadically to use the Internet in the computer lounge.

Left to my own, I decided to restructure the program. I hired a group of smart, young teachers still in graduate school and visited close to a dozen high schools in upper Manhattan and the Bronx in search of students who fit our program's demographics: African-American, potential first-generation college students who were living below or just slightly above the poverty line. The teachers created courses that we imagined the students would love and that I pitched in the high schools with a rare enthusiasm. "We'll teach you how to make Web sites, mix music, write poems, and chemistry," I said. And in case that wasn't enough I promised them field trips to college campuses, after-school snacks, and in exchange, I told them, all they had to do was show up.

For a few months we had our highs. Our enrollment numbers were up. We had a fresh supply of new books, ample computers, and on some afternoons it was possible to find fifteen to twenty students quietly working or studying in one of our mock classrooms. I began to set aside certain personal aspirations and stopped worrying about the fate of my ill-conceived novel. I read less and less, and then hardly at all, passing most of my mornings, nights, and the occasional weekend at the center rather than face beginning another project whose fate seemed irrevocably linked to the disappointment I had experienced with the first. The work I was doing now, I told myself, was real and important. I could trade in the imagined world of a novel for the daily challenges my students faced, from poverty to absentee parents, to a less tangibly defined sense that the future held little promise for them.

It didn't take long for things to begin to crumble—two, maybe three months at most. My students struggled and sometimes, on rare occasions, they earnestly strove. They wrote essays full of terrible grammar.

Many read years below their appropriate age. John was still broke and in need of money. Another student, Anthony, was arrested and placed on parole. Janet, who had stuck with the program throughout all of its various incarnations and often called herself "the queen" of the place, still had a near-complete failing average. When she showed me a few lines that she had written that were striking in their eloquence and grace, I found myself inadvertently welling up in tears as I tried to convince her that she had talent, and that we could help her do better if she would only let us. There were fights, or threats of fights, a few minor thefts, angry parents, and plenty of disappointed students. After six months, on some afternoons only four or five would be in the center, bored, and like myself, left with nothing to do.

There's not much you can do with disappointment and failure of that sort. I took mine and retreated in stages with it. I began to close the door to my office. One afternoon I decided to reopen the novel I had begun to write more than a year earlier. I listened to a quiet country ballad by Gillian Welsh with headphones on, and immediately a pattern was established. While some of my favorite students, including John, Amanda, and Janet, slowly walked out on me, I began to do the same with them. I would try and write some afternoons for fifteen or twenty minutes, always with the same song playing in the background, and for those fifteen or twenty minutes I would completely forget that I was working in a real world in which very little of what I had tried or intended to do had come to pass.

Perhaps this is where inspiration in the most conventional sense of the word is supposed to enter the story. I say, "I learned a lot from those students about writing, or wanting to be a writer." I say, "They taught me the power of words, or that words had power, or that I had nothing left to lose if I kept on writing." Of course it's the exact opposite that's true. What I learned and began increasingly to feel on nearly every occasion I saw my students was a frustration unlike anything I had experienced before, one that bordered on exhaustion and left me dreading the start of each day. I can see now that despite my best intentions and what I thought of as my cold, hard, pragmatic take on life, I had engaged in the worst type of fiction possible, the one in which the world is all too easily rendered into a version better suited to my own personal needs. Grades were supposed to improve, college applications were supposed to start piling up on my desk. My students were supposed to rise, and I was supposed to do so with them.

Lacking a better response, I hid from the program and my students, and in hiding found that there was solace and comfort in writing, in no small part because this was one sphere where I could marginally claim to be in control. The new novel I had begun just before starting my job began rapidly to take shape in the few stolen minutes I had each day in my office. The voice was replete with a newfound melancholy that had never been adequately expressed in anything I had written.

As the program I had imagined disintegrated and the novel grew, the clearer it became to me that the only adequate response I had ever had for my students, and myself, was part and parcel of the same storyin' that my students had accused me of. I tried to create an artificial world in order to soothe them. After more than a year, I was finally convinced that this was the best I could do, for them and myself, that storytelling may not be much, but it was the best I had.

When I finally quit, the program had passed into hands better suited than mine, a former high school teacher who had been born and raised in Harlem and had once attended a similar program. I immediately began to write full time on what little money I had saved, and while it would be too much to say that I thought of my former students constantly, I did and often still do remember them fondly. Some of the disappointment is still there. I know I wasn't able to make their lives better in any significant way. That would have required an imagination different from the one I possessed—a simple but not obvious fact I might have missed out on had I not been there.

Growing Pains

Caryl Phillips

Chapter One

He lives in Leeds, in the north of England. His is a strange school, for there is a broad white line in the middle of the playground. The boys and girls from the local housing estate have to play on one side of the line. His immigrant parents own their small house and so he is instructed to play on the other side of the line. He is the only black boy in the school. When the bell signals the end of playtime the two groups, one neatly dressed, the other group more discernibly scruffy, retreat into their separate buildings. The five-year-old boy is beginning to understand difference—in the form of class. The final lesson of the day is story time. The neatly dressed children sit cross-legged on the floor at the feet of their teacher, Miss Teale. She begins to read them a tale about Little Black Sambo. He can feel eyes upon him. He now wishes that he was on the other side of the line with the scruffy children. Either that, or would the teacher please read them a different story.

Chapter Two

He is a seven-year-old boy, and he has changed schools. At this new school there are no girls. His teacher asks him to stay behind after the lesson has finished. He is told that he must take his story and show it to the teacher in the next classroom. He isn't sure if he is being punished, but slowly he walks the short way up the corridor and shows the story to the other teacher, Miss Holmes. She sits on the edge of her desk and reads it. Then Miss Holmes looks down at him, but at first no words are exchanged. And then she speaks. "Well done. I'll hold on to this."

CHAPTER THREE

The eight-year-old boy seems to spend his whole day with his head stuck in books. His mother encourages him to get into the habit of going to the local library every Saturday, but he can only take out four books at a time and by Monday he has read them all. Two brothers up the street sometimes let him borrow their Enid Blyton paperbacks. The Famous Five adventure stories. Julian, Dick, Anne, George and Timmy the dog are the first literary lives that he intimately engages with. However, he tells his mother that he does not understand why the boys' mother warms the Enid Blyton paperbacks in the oven when he returns them. The two brothers have mentioned something to him about germs. His mother is furious. She forbids him to borrow any more books from these two boys. He begins to lose touch with Julian, Dick, Anne, George and Timmy the dog.

CHAPTER FOUR

His parents have recently divorced. He is nine and he is spending the weekend with his father, who seems to have little real interest in his son. He senses that his father is merely fulfilling a duty, but the son needs his father's attention and so he writes a story. The story includes the words "glistening" and "glittering" which have a glamour that the son finds alluring. When the son eventually hands the story to his father, the father seems somewhat baffled by this offering. His father is an immigrant, this much he already understands. But it is only later that he realizes that imaginative writing played no part in his father's colonial education as a subject of the British Empire. His father's rudimentary schooling never embraced poetic conceits such as those his son seems determined to indulge in. As the father hands back the story to his son, a gap begins to open up between the two of them.

CHAPTER FIVE

He is only ten years old when his father decides that it is fine to leave him all alone in his spartan flat while he goes to work the night shift at the local factory. There is no television. No radio. Nothing to seize his attention beyond the few comic books and soccer magazines that the son has brought with him from his mother's house. Then, late at night, alone in the huge double bed, he leans over and discovers a paperback in the drawer of the bedside table and he begins to read the book. It is a true story about a white American man who has made himself black in order that he might experience what it is like to be a colored man. The ten-year-old boy reads John Howard Griffin's *Black Like Me* and, alone in his father's double bed, he tries hard not to be afraid. That night he leaves the lights on, and in the morning he is still awake as his exhausted father slides into bed next to him.

CHAPTER SIX

At sixteen he has no girlfriend. The truth is, his brothers aside, he has few friends of any kind, and he seldom speaks with his father or stepmother. During the long summer holiday he locks himself away in his bedroom and he reads one large nineteenth-century novel after another. He learns how to lose himself in the world and lives of others, and in this way he does not have to think about the woeful state of his own life. At the moment he is reading *Anna Karenina*. Toward the end of one afternoon his heart leaps, and he has to catch his breath. He puts the book down and whispers to himself, "My God." His stepmother calls him downstairs for dinner. He sits at the table in silence but he cannot eat. He stares at his brothers, at his father, at his stepmother. Do they not understand? Anna has thrown herself in front of a train.

CHAPTER SEVEN

He is eighteen and he has completed his first term at university. He cannot go back to his father's house and so he travels 150 miles north to his mother's place. Mother and son have not, of late, spent much time in each other's company. His mother does not understand that her eighteen-year-old son is now, according to him, a man. They argue, and he gets in the car and drives off in a fit of frustration. He stops the car in the local park and opens his book. However, he cannot get past the sheer audacity of the first sentence of James Baldwin's *Blues for Mister Charlie*. "And may every nigger like this nigger end like this nigger—face down in the weeds!" This eighteen-year-old "man" is completely overwhelmed by Baldwin's brutal prose. He reads this one sentence over and over and over again. And then he closes the book and decides that he should go back and make up with his mother.

CHAPTER EIGHT

His tutor has asked to see him in his office. Dr. Rabbitt informs the student that he has passed the first part of his degree in psychology, neurophysiology, and statistics, but he reassures the student that at nineteen there is still time for him to reconsider his choice of a degree. Does he really wish to pursue psychology? The student patiently explains that he wishes to understand people, and that before university he was assiduously reading Jung and Freud for pleasure. His unmoved tutor takes some snuff, and then he rubs his beard. So you want to know about people, do you? He patiently explains to the student that William James was the first professor of psychology at Harvard, but it was his brother, Henry, who really knew about people. The student looks at Dr. Rabbitt, but he is unsure what to say. His tutor helps him to make the decision. "Literature. If you want to know about people study English literature, not psychology."

CHAPTER NINE

He is twenty, and for the first time since arriving in England as a four-month-old baby he has left the country. He has traveled to the United States, and crossed the huge exciting nation by Greyhound bus. After three weeks on the road, he knows that soon he will have to return to England and complete his final year of university. In California he goes into a bookstore. He buys a copy of a book that has on the cover a picture of a young man who looks somewhat like himself. He takes the book to the beach, and sits on a deck chair and begins to read. When he finishes Richard Wright's *Native Son* it is almost dark, and the beach is deserted. But he now knows what he wishes to do with his life. And then, some time later, he is grateful to discover that mere ambition is fading and is being replaced by something infinitely more powerful: purpose.

Chapter Ten

He sits with his great-grandmother in the small village at the far end of St. Kitts, the island on which he was born twenty-eight years earlier. He has now published two novels, and on each publication day he has asked his editor to send a copy of the book to his great-grandmother. But she has never mentioned the books and so gingerly he now asks her if she ever received them. Does she have them? When she moves it is like watching a statue come to life. She reaches beneath the chair and slowly pulls out two brown cardboard bundles. The books are still in their packaging. She has opened the bundles, looked at the books, and then neatly replaced them. Again she opens the packaging. She fingers the books in the same way that he has seen her finger her Bible. Then she looks at her great-grandson and smiles. "I was the teacher's favorite," she says. She was born in 1898 and so he realizes that she is talking to him about life at the dawn of the twentieth century. "And," she continues, "I missed a lot of school for I had to do all the errands." Suddenly he understands what she means. She cannot read. He swallows deeply and lowers his eyes. How could he be clumsy enough to cause her this embarrassment? She carefully puts the books back in their cardboard packaging and tucks them back under the chair. She looks at her great-grandson. She doted on this boy for the first four months of his life. The great-grandson who disappeared to England. The great-grandson who all these years later now sends her stories from England.

Iowa City, 1974

Jane Smiley

When I was in the Iowa Writers' Workshop, in the mid-seventies, there was a story going around that one of the instructors had taken a particular shine to the work of one of our fellow students. He expressed his admiration for her potential by devoting himself to trashing her work. He would have her into his office, and then subject her to brutal line-by-line criticism, making her defend every word, every phrase. He "held her to a very high standard" and only praised her when she met it. He challenged her.

Thank God, I thought, that I was not this teacher's pet. That I was seen to have much smaller potential. That my work was of so little interest that it could safely be ignored by the powers that be (or were).

The seventies were the years of swaggering male writers, editors, and F. Scott Fitzgerald (the "sensitive" alternative to Norman Mailer—both drunks and as such entirely familiar to me and of no interest). Every so often, a tall, big-shouldered editorial power would swoop into Iowa City and survey us. He would have been shown some of our work, somehow. He would court one or two, then return to New York. Sometimes a story by that student would subsequently appear in his magazine. I saw the entire system as continuous with all the educational systems I had known: teachers had pets. In this they were not at all mysterious. It was the pets who were mysterious.

As always, the pets in the Workshop were precocious. As a rule, they were stylishly dressed. By this, I don't mean that their oufits were up-to-the-minute, expensive, or straight out of *Vogue*. What I mean is that they were distinct and chosen with an eye toward standing out from the crowd. Those of us who wandered to the closet in the morning and rummaged around among the items on the floor didn't approach our wardrobe in this way; we approached it as children do—we had play clothes and party clothes. The play clothes were casual and more or less the same as everyone else's clothes, whether that was jeans and sweaters or peasant dresses (remember, this was the seventies) and Birkenstocks. The party clothes were more exotic—I had a lace-covered vintage satin nightgown from the twenties or thirties that was substantial enough to wear to a dinner party. But our party clothes were few and saved for special occasions. The pets dressed as if every day was a special occasion. One of the pets wore an elaborate brocade dressing gown when he was alone at home. The rest of us wore any old thing.

The pets had manners, usually, but more importantly, they had a manner. They knew how to look an adult in the eye—not dutifully, as those of us who were still ma'aming and sirring as our elders made ourselves do, but forthrightly, and even, I thought, speculatively. They understood that the teachers and editors were looking for something and they wondered what that might be. They were able to contemplate using the teachers and the editors in a way that reciprocated the use that the teachers and the editors thought of putting them to. They knew that being a pet was not a one-way street, that the teachers and the editors needed a little flattery. They didn't wait until the day the teachers and the editors introduced themselves to bone up on the work of that person. The pets were knowing. Of course there were other knowing ones who were not petted—this was where the style and the manner came in. The pets were able to distinguish themselves in an attractive way. There were others—you might call them mavens or nerds—who sensed what was at stake but couldn't act on their knowledge. They tended to be frustrated and to resent the pets.

I don't know how I was seen by either teachers or editors. I don't know how I was seen by my fellow students, either. I did not feel like a pet, I did not feel like a nerd. I felt like one of the ones who occasionally gets a passing pat on the head, and is grateful, simultaneously, for the praise and the inattention. I felt free and happy and more or less out to lunch. I cared hardly a thing for most of the teachers or the editors, but I adored my fellow students.

Iowa City was still reverberating from the late sixties—the plate glass windows of the university bookstore had been broken so many times in antiwar riots that they had been replaced by cubbyholes. But the revolution had passed, having no political effect, only a social effect—students lived together in loose, communelike groups, did what they wanted for much of the day (everyone had a roommate who devoted himself to smoking and/or growing marijuana), and slept around as a token of solidarity. By the time I was admitted to the Workshop, I had already lived in Iowa City for two years, and had been studying medieval literature in the English Department for a year and a half. I was a long-termer; I had a TA teaching a freshman lit course and an office on the fifth floor that I shared with a Shakespearean. To all appearances, I knew my way around, but when, on my first day at the Workshop, I was introduced to Allan Gurganus, who was starting his second year and was a Teaching-Writing Fellow, and he suggested that we walk up the street and have a sandwich at a local sub shop, I felt he was leading me into an unexplored domain.

Allan may not have actually been wearing a white suit that afternoon, but he was wearing something archaic, elegant, and pale. He gave me his characteristic smile—simultaneously merry, welcoming, rueful, and irreverent. But much to my regret, on the way out of the building, he asked a short person to join us. We walked up the hill, chatting. I was on Allan's right, the short person was not very visible on his left. The day was pleasant for August, not hot and a little breezy. Conversation died for a moment, and as I was wondering what I could come up with to *impress* His Elegance, the short person leaned forward, then stepped a little ahead, and said, to me, "Want to be friends?"

I looked at her, startled and yes, flattered. I didn't say anything just then, but moments later, standing in line at the sub shop, I said, "Yes." Her name was Barbara Grossman. She, too, was a Teaching–Writing Fellow. Why she wanted to be friends with me I could not imagine—here I thought we were vying for the attention of Allan.

We constituted a broad geographic sampling. Allan Gurganus was from North Carolina, Richard Bausch was from Virginia, Barbara Grossman was from Philadelphia, Meredith Steinbach and Mary Swander were (actually!) from Iowa. Douglas Unger was from the distant reaches of the upper Missouri. Bob Chibka was from Connecticut. John Givens seemed to have been to Asia, as had Richard Wiley. Joanne Meschery came from the West, and also the world of married life; her husband,

Tom, a poet, somehow managed to come from basketball, Japan, and Russia. And then there was T. C. Boyle, who arrived directly from a cooler, hipper realm.

Our teachers seemed blander to me. Jack Leggett was like someone who would have shown up at a party given by my parents—prosperous, well mannered and educated, always kind, frequently ironic and even rueful, but not vivid enough to capture my attention. Vance Bourjaily seemed even paler. Stanley Elkin was tainted, in my mind, by his connection to St. Louis, where he taught and where I had grown up. There could not be, for me, an interesting person from University City, Stanley Elkin and William Gass notwithstanding. That left Jane Howard, *Life* magazine writer. Though she had never written fiction, the Workshop hired her to teach for my first semester. She was a character, and we became friends instantly.

Jane Howard was all New York City, even though she had grown up in Illinois. The sign that she was all New York City was that she would say anything and then laugh. She had an apartment on the Upper West Side and tossed around names like "Zabar's" and "H & H Bagel" and the New Yorker movie theater. She was single and friendly, an emissary not from the New York male literary scene but from the New York female social scene. She took to Barbara and then she took to me. It was clear, though, and a relief, that she neither knew what she was talking about, fictionwise, nor had any plans to lever us into fancy literary journals. She was rarer than that—she was fun. And she wasn't old—fourteen years older than I was—a sister rather than a parent, that sister who had broken away, gotten herself a wilder, happier life, and was now returning to tell us about it.

I wrote nothing of interest in Jane's class. When I uncover stories I wrote in the Workshop now, I can't believe they are mine. They are, for the most part, enigmatic seventies stories, vaguely threatening and fragmentary. I am sure that when they were critiqued in class, the suggestions of my fellow students went in one ear and out the other, because I didn't have an actual aesthetic that might have understood or retained those comments. I am sure I latched on to whatever positive judgments went sailing past—"I like this" or "This is pretty good"—and ignored the rest. What lodged in my brain at the time, and what I retain now, are sharp images from the stories of my fellow students. Barbara wrote a story about a girl who cannibalizes her boyfriend on a canoe trip. Allan mentioned in a story that a child's mother drives him twenty-five miles to a particular barber who can "cut with the curl." Tom Boyle wrote about the seven members of a commune who always wear white clothes and sleep through a series of plagues, including a rain of blood that drenches their white clothes. Bob Chibka wrote a story in which all the nouns were capitalized. Dick Bausch wrote about a family that takes in the children of a sister and brother-in-law who have died in a car crash. Joanne Meschery wrote about a woman whose mother sends her a nightgown sewn shut across the bottom so she won't have any more children.

It didn't matter to me what the teachers had to say, or how they liked or didn't like these works. It only mattered that these images and ideas were flying around, generated in the Iowa City air, somewhere between the bookstore and the Mill Restaurant, Barbara's house at the top of Dodge Street, Dick's place in married student housing, our farm on the west side, and the English Philosophy Building where, one day, I stretched out on the floor of Barbara's office and lamented that I wasn't a genius, would never be a genius, the years of genius were long past (I was twenty-seven). Barbara (twenty-four) kept reading our workshop stories for the day. She knew I would get over it.

Because of the parties. We had parties for everything—birthdays, Christmas, Thanksgiving, visiting authors, Passover, extra workshop sessions, just to try out new foods or meet new people. Many of the parties were at our farmhouse, where the kitchen was big and the dining room could be set up to accommodate lots of eaters. Personally, I never minded roasting a turkey and I was willing to consult my two-volume set of the *Gourmet Cookbook* any time. To the east of the house, my boyfriend and his brother had planted a huge garden with long rows of potatoes, tomatoes, green peppers, beans, cabbage, carrots. They were always harvesting something. The party I remember best was for E. L. Doctorow. He read from *Ragtime,* then unpublished. I sat in the back of the auditorium, aghast and agape at the daring of his imagination—he had Freud and Jung at Concy Island, in the Tunnel of Love. He had Houdini in an airplane, watching a wheel spin slowly in the wind. For me, such things were wrenchingly daring. And later, in our very own living room, he seemed to enjoy himself.

Spring succeeded autumn. Jane Howard went back to New York. John Irving was around. He had published a novel called *The 158-Pound Marriage,* which seemed to be about wrestling, so when Henry Bromell showed up, I signed on with him instead. Henry Bromell, though our teacher, was just the same age as every boyfriend I had ever had. I could have met him at a mixer in college, or roomed with his girlfriend, if I had gone to Mount Holyoke instead of Vassar. In other words, he expanded our group instead of floating above it. And he had an exotic background, since he had spent much of his childhood in the Middle East before ending up at Amherst. Henry was just publishing his first book. He seemed bemused, or befuddled, by teaching, publication, the Midwest. He did his best with us. But he was new in town, and we were veterans. We showed him around.

For us, he did that essential thing—he embodied the bridge between aspiration and realization. His book was real, was published by a name publisher, Houghton Mifflin, had a pleasing dry weight so different from and more respectable than typed pages. To buy it and then talk to him about it, to read the stories and then have dinner with him, shortened the distance between the impulse that had brought us to Iowa City and the potential realization of that impulse. I no longer lamented that I wasn't a genius. It was not that Henry was not a genius, it was that you couldn't tell whether he was a genius or not. He was so close to us and so similar to us that he had nothing to bestow upon us except the tangible evidence that what you really had to do was write that book and that was way more valuable than genius.

In the spring, I gave a party. I cooked out of the *Gourmet Cookbook*. I set out candles rather than using the overhead light. I wore my pink 1930s nightgown as a dress. I used the good china from my abandoned marriage. I invited Allan and Barbara and two or three others. I put the dog and cats outside. My boyfriend told his brothers to stay away. We put Maria Muldaur on the turntable, but at a low volume. Possibly Allan wore his white suit. It was very elegant.

It took another month to generate "Jeffrey, Believe Me," a short story in which a woman about my age invites her gay friend to dinner, gets him drunk and stoned, and then seduces him. It was all fiction, something of a daring joke, and I kept it to myself for a few days. But I liked it. The woman's voice was consistent from beginning to end; the dinner seemed detailed and plausible. I had done something that I hadn't imagined myself doing, or foreseen—I had gotten inside the mind of a woman who had done something I would never have done. Here was the lesson

I learned: desire sparks imagination, imagination generates detail, details take you from the beginning to the end. I typed up a neat copy.

Someone came to read, some older male. He sat at a table in the front of the seminar room. He read earnestly, staring at the papers he was holding with two hands. His forearms were resting on the table. The story was a somber one, and we, the audience, listened respectfully. Except that after about five minutes, I slipped "Jeffrey, Believe Me" to Barbara, who was sitting to my right. She placed it quietly on her desk and began to read it, surreptitiously removing each page when she was done with it. The reader never looked up. And then she laughed out loud, a disruptive and wholly inappropriate bark. Everyone looked at us. We smiled deflectively. Nevertheless, I had just received the best compliment ever and, as it turned out, I was on my way.

The school year ended. Allan and the other second-year students left. Henry went away for the summer. At our house, we went back to gardening. One morning, my boyfriend's brother stood up from the breakfast table, went out through the back porch, picking up a twenty-two. He circumnavigated the house, and as we watched him, he took down a rabbit in the pea patch. Then we went for a month's trip to the West, and came home to find that the cats had had it out all over the house, including on top of the refrigerator. By the end of that year, Barbara had gone to New York to find a job in publishing, my boyfriend had left for California, Jane Howard had published a book that included a chapter about us, her friends in Iowa City, officially putting us in the past tense. I nearly fell into the well in our front yard. I moved to an apartment. I placed "Jeffrey, Believe Me" with *Triquarterly*, my first publication. I went to Iceland, where there were no parties, no other writers, few English speakers, and lots of books. It was there, as an antidote to seasonal affect disorder, that I began to write a novel. In other words, life went on. When I came home, I was grown up. And eventually, I sold my first novel to Barbara Grossman, an assistant editor at Harper & Row. But what I took from the Iowa Writers' Workshop was a lesson about the inspirational effect of pleasure and friendship. It turned out that Fitzgerald and Mailer weren't the last word—the words are different in every generation.

ACKNOWLEDGMENTS

My deepest gratitude goes to the writers who contributed their work to this collection. Several have written books that were muses and mentors to me early on. Many have been colleagues, and a good number have been role models and advisers of such long standing it's painful to imagine what might have become of me had it not been for their counsel, example, and generosity. Maybe it takes a village to raise a writer. I reserve another sort of appreciation and affection for three contributors who were students of mine, Christopher Castellani, Alexander Chee, and Jonathan Safran Foer. I thank all the writers for bringing to my attention — and yours — the names of favorite books and the writers who have meant so much to them, making the collection something of an annotated booklist.

I am indebted, as always, to Gail Hochman, Marianne Merola, and Joanne Brownstein, for insights and intelligence of every variety. I feel privileged to work with Wylie O'Sullivan, whose enthusiasm and sharp-eyed editing have made this project a pleasure from beginning to end.

I owe special thanks to Rob Spillman, the unwitting father of the anthology, for having invited me to write about Elizabeth Hardwick for *Tin House*, which led directly to the conception of this book. And I'm grateful to Harriet Lowell, for her support and understanding.

AUTHOR BIOGRAPHIES

Elizabeth Benedict is a graduate of Barnard College and the author of five novels, including the bestseller *Almost* and the National Book Award finalist, *Slow Dancing*, as well as *The Joy of Writing Sex: A Guide for Fiction Writers*, which is widely used in U.S. and UK writing programs. Her new anthology on mothers and daughters is forthcoming from Algonquin. Her fiction and nonfiction have appeared in *The New York Times, Boston Globe, Esquire, Tin House, Salmagundi, Narrative Magazine, Daedalus, Harper's Bazaar, Huffington Post*, and *The Rumpus*. She is on the fiction faculty of the New York State Summer Writers Institute. Please visit: www. elizabethbenedict.com.

Robert Boyers is editor of the quarterly *Salmagundi*, which he founded in 1965, director of The New York State Summer Writers Institute, and Professor of English at Skidmore College. He is a frequent contributor to *Harper's*, where he has written on Susan Sontag, John Updike, Ingeborg Bachmann, Witold Gombrowicz, Nadine Gordimer, and other writers. Among his nine books, the most recent are *Excitable Women, Damaged Men* (short stories) and *The Dictator's Dictation* (essays on the politics of novels and novelists). In 2009, New Directions brought out *George Steiner at The New Yorker*, edited and with an introduction by Robert Boyers. His contribution to this collection, "Imagining Influence," appeared in *The Yale Review*.

Jay Cantor is author of the novels *Krazy Kat, Great Neck*, and *The Death of Che Guevara*, and of a collection of essays, *On Giving Birth to One's Own Mother and Other Essays* (Knopf). A winner of a MacArthur Prize Fellowship, he is the director of Creative Writing at Tufts University.

John Casey is the author of *Spartina* (National Book Award, 1989), *Room for Improvement, Compass Rose, An American Romance, Testimony and Demeanor, Supper at the Black Pearl, and The Half-Life of Happiness*, as well as two translations from Italian. He is currently the Henry Hoyns Professor of Creative Writing at the University of Virginia and a frequent teacher at the Sewanee Writers' Conference. Please visit: www.johnd-casey.com.

Maud Casey is the author of two novels, *The Shape of Things to Come*, a *New York Times* Notable Book of the Year, and *Genealogy*, a *New York Times* Editor's Choice Book, and a collection of stories, *Drastic*. She lives in Washington, D.C., and teaches in the MFA Program at the University of Maryland and the low-residency Warren Wilson MFA program. The essay, "A Life in Books," appeared in *The Oxford American* and was listed as a "Notable Essay" in *Best American Essays 2010*, edited by Christopher Hitchens.

Christopher Castellani is the author of two novels, *A Kiss from Maddalena* (2003) and *The Saint of Lost Things* (2005), both published by Algonquin Books of Chapel Hill. He has taught at Swarthmore College, the Fine Arts Work Center in Provincetown, and in the Warren Wilson MFA program. He is the executive director of Grub Street Writers in Boston.

Alexander Chee is the author of *Edinburgh* (Picador, 2002), and *The Queen of the Night*, forthcoming from Houghton Mifflin Harcourt. He has received a Whiting Writers' Award, a NEA Fellowship in Fiction, and fellowships from the MacDowell Colony, the VCCA, Leidig House, and Civitella Ranieri. His essays and stories have appeared in *The Morning News, Out, Bookforum, The LA Review of Books, Granta, The Paris Review Daily*, and many other publications and anthologies. He has taught at Amherst College, Wesleyan University, the Iowa Writers' Workshop, and the Columbia University MFA in Writing. He writes the popular blog Koreanish.com and is a contributing writer to *The Morning New*, where his essay for this collection first appeared. The essay also brought him a Massachusetts Cultural Council for the Arts fellowship in prose.

Michael Cunningham is the author of the novels *A Home at the End of* *the World, Flesh and Blood, The Hours,* and *Specimen Days. The Hours* won the 1999 PEN Faulkner Award and the Pulitzer Prize.

Jonathan Safran Foer is the author of the novels *Extremely Loud and Incredibly Close* and *Everything Is Illuminated,* which won a National Jewish Book Award and a *Guardian* First Book Award. He is the editor of A *Convergence of Birds: Original Fiction and Poetry Inspired by the Work of Joseph Cornell* (2001), and co-editor of *The Future Dictionary of America* (2004) with Dave Eggers, Nicole Krauss, and Eli Horowitz. His short fiction has appeared in *The New Yorker, The Guardian,* and *Granta.*

Julia Glass is the author of the novels *Three Junes,* winner of the 2002 National Book Award for Fiction, *The Whole World Over,* and *The Widower's Tale. I See You Everywhere,* a collection of linked stories, won the 2009 Binghamton University John Gardner Book Award. She has received fellowships from the National Endowment for the Arts, the New York Foundation for the Arts, and the Radcliffe Institute for Advanced Study. Other honors include the Sense of Place Award from Writers & Books, the Pirate's Alley Faulkner Society Medal for Best Novella, the Tobias Wolff Award, and the Ames Memorial Essay Award. She lives in Massachusetts with her family.

Mary Gordon is a lifelong New Yorker; she was educated in Catholic schools for twelve years, then attended Barnard College and received a master's degree from Syracuse University. Her memoir *Circling My Mother* was published in 2007. Her latest novel, *Pearl,* was published in January 2005 by Pantheon Books. Her previous novels—*Final Payments, The Company of Women, Men and Angels, The Other Side,* and *Spending*—have been bestsellers. She has also written another critically acclaimed memoir, *The Shadow Man.* In addition, she has published a book of novellas, *The Rest of Life;* a collection of stories, *Temporary Shelter;* two books of essays, *Good Boys and Dead Girls* and *Seeing Through Places;* and has written a biography of Joan of Arc. Mary has received the Lila Acheson Wallace Reader's Digest Award and a Guggenheim Fellowship. For three years (1983, 1997, and 2000), she was the recipient of the O. Henry Award for best short story. In 2008 she was named New York State Author and was awarded the Edith Wharton Medal by Governor Eliot Spitzer. She is the

McIntosh Professor of English at Barnard College.

Neil Gordon worked for many years at *The New York Review of Books* and as Chair of Writing and Literature at Eugene Lang College of The New School. Currently he is literary editor at the *Boston Review* as well as dean of Eugene Lang College. He is the author of three novels: *Sacrifice of Isaac*; *The Gunrunner's Daughter*; and *The Company You Keep*, a *New York Times* Notable Book of the Year, currently under development by Robert Redford; and of a screenplay under development by Jesse Dylan. He reviews regularly for *The New York Times Book Review* and elsewhere, and has written for many other publications, including *Salon* and *Tin House*.

Arnon Grunberg was born in Amsterdam in 1971. After being kicked out of high school at age seventeen he started his own publishing company, specialized in non-Aryan German literature. Grunberg's latest novel is *Tooth and Nail*. His most recent novel in English translation is *The Jewish Messiah*. Other novels are *Phantom Pain* and *The Asylum Seeker*. Grunberg has published many literary reports, columns, essays, reviews, and short stories in various Dutch and international newspapers and magazines, including *NRC Handelsblad, Süddeutsche Zeitung, Die Zeit, Times of London, New York Times, L'espresso, Courrier International*, and *Libération*. He is the recipient of various literary prizes, including the NRW Literature Prize in Germany. Grunberg's work has been translated in twenty-four languages. He lives in New York City. Blog: www.arnongrunberg.com.

Samantha Hunt's second novel *The Invention of Everything Else* was a finalist for the Orange Prize and winner of the Bard Fiction Prize. Her first novel, *The Seas*, won a National Book Foundation award for writers under thirty-five. Hunt's fiction has been published in *The New Yorker, McSweeney's, A Public Space, Tin House, Cabinet, Blind Spot*, and a number of other fine publications. She teaches at the Pratt Institute in Brooklyn. Her essay about Breece Pancake from *Mentors, Muses & Monsters* appeared in *Poets & Writers*.

Denis Johnson is the author of several novels, plays, and books of verse, as well as the short story collection *Jesus' Son*. He is the recipient of Guggenheim, Lannan and Whiting awards. His novel *Tree of Smoke* received the 2007 National Book Award.

Margot Livesey was born and grew up on the edge of the Scottish Highlands. She has taught in numerous writing programs including the Iowa Writers' Workshop, Boston University, and the Warren Wilson MFA program, and is the author of a collection of stories and six novels, including *Eve Moves the Furniture* and, most recently, *The Flight of Gemma Hardy* and *The House on Fortune Street*, which won the L.L.Winship/PEN New England award. She lives in Cambridge, Massachusetts, and is a distinguished writer-in-residence at Emerson College in Boston. "Only Plump The Pillows" appeared in *The Normal School*.

Dinaw Mengestu is the author of the novel *The Beautiful Things That Heaven Bears*, a 2007 *New York Times* Notable Book. He is the recipient of a *Guardian* First Book Award, a *Los Angeles Times* Book Prize, France's Prix du premier meilleur roman étranger, and a Lannan Fiction Fellowship. His work has appeared in numerous publications, including *Rolling Stone* and *The Wall Street Journal*. He lives in Paris.

Sigrid Nunez has published six novels. She is also the author of *Sempre Susan: A Memoir of Susan Sontag* (Atlas and Co., 2011), a book that grew out of her essay "Sontag's Rules," which was commissioned for this anthology. Please visit her at: www.sigridnunez.com.

Joyce Carol Oates, the Roger S. Berlind Professor of Humanities at Princeton University, is the author most recently of the novel *Little Bird of Heaven* and the story collection *Dear Husband*. She is a recipient of the National Book Award, the Prix Femina, and the PEN/Malamud Award for Short Fiction, and she has been a member since 1978 of the American Academy of Arts and Letters.

ZZ Packer is the author of the short story collection *Drinking Coffee Elsewhere*, a PEN/Faulkner finalist and a *New York Times* Notable Book. Her stories have appeared in *The New Yorker, Harper's, Story, Ploughshares, Zoetrope*, and *Best American Short Stories 2000* and *2004*, and they have been read on NPR's *Selected Shorts*. Her nonfiction has been featured in *The New York*

Times Magazine, The Washington Post Magazine, The American Prospect, Essence, O, The Believer, and *Salon.* She was named one of America's Young Innovators by *Smithsonian* magazine and one of America's Best Young Novelists by *Granta.* She is the recent recipient of a Guggenheim Fellowship.

Caryl Phillips is the author of several novels, including *Crossing the River,* which was shortlisted for the 1993 Booker Prize, and *A Distant Shore,* which won the 2004 Commonwealth Writers Prize. He has received fellowships from the Guggenheim and Lannan foundations. His nonfiction includes *The European Tribe, The Atlantic Sound,* and *A New World Order.* His novel *In the Falling Snow* will be published in the fall of 2009.

Carolyn See is the author of five novels, including *The Handyman* and *Golden Days.* She is a book reviewer for *The Washington Post* and is on the board of PEN Center USA West. She has a PhD in American literature from UCLA. Her awards include the prestigious Robert Kirsch Body of Work Award (1993) and a Guggenheim Fellowship in fiction. She lives in Southern California, and has recently found, to her considerable surprise, that she is a direct descendant of Pocahontas.

Jim Shepard is the author of six novels, including most recently *Project X,* and four story collections, including most recently *Like You'd Understand, Anyway,* which was a finalist for the National Book Award and won The Story Prize, and *You Think That's Bad,* released in 2011. His stories have been included in the *Best American, PEN/O.Henry,* and Pushcart Prize anthologies. He teaches at Williams College.

Anita Shreve is the bestselling author of twelve novels, including *Body Surfing, Sea Glass, All He Ever Wanted, The Pilot's Wife, Fortune's Rocks, The Weight of Water, Eden Close, Strange Fits of Passion, Where or When,* and *Resistance.*

Jane Smiley is the author of thirteen novels for adults, including the Pulitzer Prize winning *A Thousand Acres, Private Life, Horse Heaven,* the novella *The Age of Grief,* a series of horse books for young adults, and five works of nonfiction, including *Thirteen Ways of Looking at the Novel* and *The Man Who Invented the Computer.* She has written essays on politics, child rearing, farming, horse training, literature, impulse buying, getting dressed, Barbie, marriage, divorce, and many other topics for publications that include *The Guardian, Self, Vogue, The Huffington Post, The New Yorker, Practical Horseman, Harper's,* the *New York Times Magazine,* and the *New York Times* travel section, *Victoria, Mirabella, Allure,* and *The Nation.* She is a member of the American Academy of Arts and Letters and has received a Lifetime Achievement Award from PEN.

Martha Southgate is the author of three novels, most recently *Third Girl from the Left* (Houghton Mifflin). It won the Best Novel of the Year Award from the Black Caucus of the American Library Association. She has received a New York Foundation for the Arts grant as well as fellowships from the MacDowell Colony, the Virginia Center for the Creative Arts, and the Bread Loaf Writers' Conference. Her *New York Times Book Review* essay, "Writers Like Me," appeared in *Best African-American Essays 2009.* Her nonfiction has appeared in *The New York Times Magazine, O, Premiere,* and *Essence.* She is working on her next novel, to be published by Algonquin Books. Visit her Web site at www.marthasouthgate.com.

Cheryl Strayed is the author of the memoir *Wild* (Knopf) and the novel *Torch* (Houghton Mifflin). Her writing has appeared in *The Best American Essays,* the *New York Times Magazine,* the *Washington Post Magazine, Allure, Self, Brain, Child, The Rumpus, The Sun,* and elsewhere. Her essay in this anthology—"Munro Country"—was also published in *The Missouri Review* and won a Pushcart Prize. Strayed lives in Portland, Oregon.

Evelyn Toynton, an American living in England, is the author of the novels *Modern Art,* a *New York Times* Notable Book of the Year, and *The Oriental Wife,* recently published by Other Press. Her essays and reviews have appeared in *Harper's,* the *Atlantic,* the *Times Literary Supplement,* the *New York Times Book Review,* and *The American Scholar,* where the essay commissioned for this volume first appeared. Her book on Jackson Pollock was published by Yale University Press earlier this year, as part of its Icons of America series.

Lily Tuck was born in France and is the author of the novels *Interviewing Matisse or The Woman Who Died Standing Up, The Woman Who Walked* on *Water, Siam*, a PEN/Faulkner Award finalist, *The News from Paraguay*, winner of the 2004 National Book Award, a collection of stories, *Limbo and Other Places I Have Lived*, a biography, *Woman of Rome, A Life of Elsa Morante*, and, most recently, the novel *I Married You for Happiness*.

Edmund White has written twenty-five books—novels, three collections of essays, two memoirs, travel books, and so on. His most recent titles are *Jack Holmes and His Friend* (a novel) and *Sacred Monsters* (essays). He teaches writing at Princeton.

PERMISSIONS

"'Why Not Say What Happened?': Remembering Miss Hardwick" by Elizabeth Benedict. Copyright © 2008 by Elizabeth Benedict. "Why Not Say What Happened?" first appeared in *Tin House*.

"Imagining Influence" by Robert Boyers. Copyright © 2009 by Robert Boyers. "Imagining Influence" appeared in *The Yale Review*, October 2009.

"Fathers" by Jay Cantor. Copyright © 2009 by Jay Cantor.

"Mentors in General, Peter Taylor in Particular" by John Casey. Copyright © 2009 by John Casey.

"A Life in Books" by Maud Casey. Copyright © 2009 by Maud Casey. "A Life in Books" appeared in *The Oxford American*, Fall 2009.

"Coming of Age at Bread Loaf" by Christopher Castellani. Copyright © 2009 by Christopher Castellani.

"Annie Dillard and the Writing Life" by Alexander Chee. Copyright © 2009 by Alexander Chee. "Annie Dillard and the Writing Life" appeared in the online magazine, *The Morning News*, October, 2009.

"Company" by Michael Cunningham. Copyright © 2009 by Mare Vaporum Corp.

"The Snow Globe" by Jonathan Safran Foer. Copyright © 2009 by Jonathan Safran Foer.